SCALE

SCALE

A Successful Agent's Guide to Leveling Up Their Real Estate Business

BY DAVID GREENE

BiggerPockets®
PUBLISHING
Denver, Colorado

Praise for the series

"As the person who brought David into real estate sales, I've watched his growth in this area from zero to hero. David's explanations and systems for how to become a top-producing agent are unquestionably effective. I can't think of a better person to write a book this needed in the industry."

—David Osborn, *New York Times* best-selling author of *Wealth Can't Wait* and *Bidding to Buy*

"David opens up his entire playbook here and doesn't leave anything out. A must-have for any agent who takes their business seriously."

—Aaron Amuchastegui, host of *Real Estate Rockstars* podcast and author of *Bidding to Buy*

"I wish this book had existed when I was selling real estate! David has done a fantastic job of breaking down what it takes to be successful into simple, easy-to-follow steps that help agents master their craft and become top producers. I love this book!"

—Pat Hiban, former No. 1 agent for both Keller Williams and RE/MAX, *New York Times* best-selling author of *6 Steps to 7 Figures*

SCALE: A Successful Agent's Guide to Leveling Up Their Real Estate Business
David Greene

Published by BiggerPockets Publishing LLC, Denver, CO
Copyright © 2023 by David Greene
All Rights Reserved.

Publisher's Cataloging-in-Publication Data

Names: Greene, David, author.
Title: SCALE: a successful agent's guide to leveling up their real estate business / by David Greene.
Series: Top-Producing Real Estate Agent
Description: Includes bibliographical references. | Denver, CO: BiggerPockets Publishing, 2023.
Identifiers: LCCN: 2022947435 | ISBN: 9781947200869 (paperback) | 9781947200876 (ebook)
Subjects: LCSH Real estate agents. | Real estate business. | Success in business. | BISAC BUSINESS & ECONOMICS / Real Estate / Buying & Selling Homes | BUSINESS & ECONOMICS / Sales & Selling / General | BUSINESS & ECONOMICS / Sales & Selling / Management | BUSINESS & ECONOMICS / Development / Business Development
Classification: LCC HD1382 .G74 2023 | DDC 333.33068--dc23

Printed on recycled paper in Canada
MBP 10 9 8 7 6 5 4 3 2 1

TABLE OF CONTENTS

CHAPTER THREE

GENERATE LEADS LIKE A ROCKSTAR

CHAPTER FOUR

YOUR TARGET CLIENTELE

CHAPTER FIVE

HOW TO EXCEL WITH BUYERS

CHAPTER SIX

EXCELLING WITH SELLERS

CHAPTER SEVEN

SUCCEEDING IN DIFFERENT MARKETS

CHAPTER ONE

TRANSITIONING TO ROCKSTAR AGENT STATUS

"Always dream and shoot higher than you know you can do. Do not bother just to be better than your contemporaries or predecessors. Try to be better than yourself."

—WILLIAM FAULKNER

In *SOLD*, the first book in this top-producing real estate agent series, I provided a blueprint to help agents become top-producing agents. As that book pointed out, the most difficult part of any real estate sales career is the beginning. Every inch of progress comes with massive effort and a lot of mistakes. The return on effort is low and so are the conversion rates. Conversely, top-producing agents have the momentum, confidence, experience, and skill using the tools of the Sales Funnel. It takes time and repetition to build these abilities, which is why getting started is the toughest part.

When an agent first enters the business, they are advised to talk to everyone they know until they get a lead. Every day in the office is the same thing. Lead generation, ask for business, be persistent, and get told no. This is the most exhausting and least fun part of the journey. Many new agents want to quit, and many do.

The Transition Process

Think of a real estate career as pushing a boulder up a steep hill. Every step is agonizingly slow. Your muscles burn, you're breathing hard, and you're sweating profusely. Your fingers are rubbed raw. It takes everything within you not to quit, and you sometimes fantasize about letting go of the boulder. But to quit the real estate business before closing a single deal means you will lose money, you will lose time, and you will lose effort. You might even lose face. But you keep pushing. You attend meetings, hand out business cards, make phone calls, and ask for referrals. After several months, you garner a couple leads—but don't get them into contract. Several months later, you finally get one into contract—but it doesn't close. Nine months later, you have your first closing. It's a close friend. And now it's back to pushing the boulder uphill.

After enough time and experience, the boulder gets easier to push. You find your rhythm. You close enough deals to make a living, and you no longer hate the job. Then, in one month you have three houses in escrow. You realize that you're not half bad at this! You get recognition and respect from others in the office. You've crested the mountain top, and you can roll the boulder faster because the land has flattened out.

Top-producing agent status feels great. Ironically, though, it's at this point when most successful agents take it easy. Why? Because they are no longer in danger of the boulder rolling backward and over them. The fear factor is gone, and they don't have a Big Why for being in this business. If that Big Why isn't big enough, they put in less effort, have less focus, and spend less time creating their business. These top-producing agents make a good living but stall in their career.

However, I believe any agent can become a rockstar agent. The key is to keep your focus on pushing that boulder further and further. If you do this, you make it to the other side of the mountain where business is doing well almost without you. Being on this side means leads flow to you, clients get into contract more easily, and more deals close with less effort.

You recognize problems before they occur, so your deals are smoother. This is when the business becomes fun. Your boulder's momentum is taken over by gravity as it starts down the other side. You jog next to the boulder while the money rolls in. Once you can no longer keep up with the boulder, you hire a team so as not to lose momentum. This is the life of a rockstar agent.

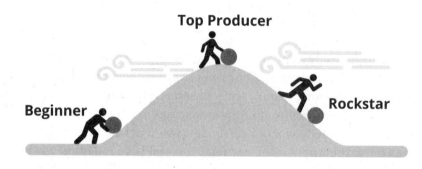

This book covers your next transition: from being a top-producing agent to becoming a rockstar agent. Rockstar agents have distinguished themselves from their competition. They are well respected in their sphere of influence and their community, earn a higher living, and have built a team that makes them look good (like a rockstar with a great band of musicians). Rockstar agents have an exceptional staff and clients who love them. If this is what you pictured when you were studying to get your license, this book can help you reach your real estate dream.

Is it tough to get there? Of course. Is it a pipe dream? Definitely not. Not only is rockstar status possible, but it is also the natural progression for agents who follow the advice and models laid out in this book. Those who master the Sales Funnel and convert leads at an elevated level generate so much business that they cannot keep up without a team. Many top-producing agents are closer to this point than they believe.

The key to unlocking your rockstar potential is leverage, which is covered in Chapter Two of this book. Once you control what is keeping your mind occupied and your eyes off the prize, you'll notice all the opportunities you're missing. Most agents who crest the hill and become top-producing agents then do very little lead generation. Truthfully, you don't have to. If you're making a good living and want to stop at top-producing agent level, of course you can. If you want to be a rockstar agent, though, you'll want to keep reading this book.

The Sales Funnel Recap

The Sales Funnel I describe in my book *SKILL* helps agents track where they are in the sales process with a prospect or a task that crosses their desk. It allows agents to make quick decisions regarding next steps in order to move that prospect or task forward and to use the correct tool to help them do so. In the figure, the right side is the tools to move the Lead to Client and then to Closing.

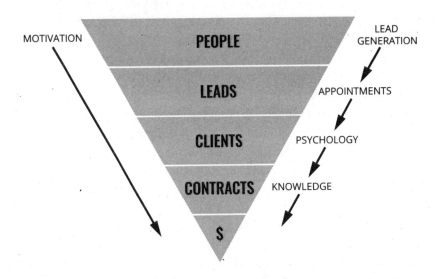

CLASSIFICATION	DEFINITION
People	Anyone (though typically those in your database)
Lead	A person who knows who you are and wants to buy or sell a house
Client	Someone who has signed a listing agreement or a buyer representation agreement
Contract	A purchase agreement fully executed by both the buyer and seller
Closing ($)	The event when a title is transferred from seller to buyer and the funds are transferred from buyer to seller

When you get a phone call from one person asking about the current state of the market and a text message from another person asking about the disclosure packet you sent them for a listing, how do you prioritize your work and figure out where these two people are on the motivation scale? By using the Sales Funnel. With a quick call to the person asking about the state of the market, you quickly determine they do not want to buy a house right now but want to know if a "crash is imminent." This would classify them as People, and you would use lead generation to move them down your funnel. They are clearly not as motivated as the texter, who qualifies as a Client, and you'd use psychology to move them further along the funnel. By helping them feel less worried about the disclosure packet, you are one step closer to putting them in the Contract category.

This method of classifying information and referring to the appropriate tool to progress prospects through the funnel should begin at the start of an agent's career because it offers direction in a new and confusing world. This method remains critical for top-producing agents who are juggling incoming leads, client questions, and issues with escrow while continuing to grow a lead database. A system that keeps Leads flowing along the Sales Funnel could mean hundreds of thousands of dollars in commissions. The Sales Funnel creates the structure and direction to be efficient in getting to Contracts.

As a rockstar agent, people will look to you for your knowledge, your time, and your advice. The Sales Funnel will keep you productive with revenue-creating tasks made with fewer mistakes. Rockstar agents, much like rockstar musicians, do whatever is necessary to give the performance their audience expects.

The Role of the Rockstar Agent in Their Business

As a solo agent on the way to becoming a top-producing agent, you were the salesperson, accountant, administrator, listing agent, buyer's agent, showing agent, database manager, counselor, and more. Even if you didn't want to, you had no choice. As a top-producing agent on your way to rockstar status, you go from viewing real estate as a job to viewing it as owning a business. You need a team to perform the various tasks you used to do. This mental shift is the first thing you must accept on the path to becoming a rockstar agent. You cannot do it alone anymore; more importantly, you *should not* do it alone.

The job of the rockstar agent isn't to close the deals, complete the files, and post to social media platforms—it's to draw in the crowds and make them love the selling or buying experience. Just like rockstar musicians showcase less-famous bands as opening acts, you showcase your agents and administrative assistants as they develop their skills working for you. Rockstar shows create revenue for the food and beverage companies supplying the refreshments at the venues. You do the same by creating business for lenders, title companies, home warranty representatives, and others. Rockstar agents have contracts in which they get a cut of all these sales. While the Real Estate Settlement Procedures Act makes it illegal for agents to receive referral fees and kickbacks, you can still receive leads or marketing dollars. These are major perks to the rockstar agent's business.

The crucial point to understand is that rockstar agents draw in the buying and selling crowd; they don't do the actual servicing. People are attracted to your knowledge, expertise, experience, and the way they feel supported throughout the process. The more tasks a rockstar agent takes on—or worse yet, refuses to give up—the less focus there is on growing the agency. Wouldn't you rather hear Adele on stage singing, not serving you at a concession stand? Deliver your stellar performance as the rockstar agent. Create opportunities for others. Train your team to be the best at their jobs.

As a rockstar agent, you'll split your time between performing high-dollar activities and training your team to grow your business—and their careers. There is a vast difference between delivering information to clients (you) and collecting it (your team), skill work (you) and busy work (your team), and setting your business up for success (you) and running everything (your team). Your mindset must change. You must teach your team how to do the things you used to do because your job is to keep up with the speeding boulder. I go into the mindset shift in great detail in Chapter Thirteen.

Rockstar agents recruit not only clients but also talent. This book will teach you how to interview, how to hire the right people, and how to train them properly. You'll learn the incredible difference the right team member can make to your business compared to the drain of an employee with the wrong energy. You'll also learn a lot about yourself, including how difficult it can be to accept change, embrace growth, and adapt your thinking so you can hit your highest potential.

The business's most important tasks are summed up with the acronym PLAN:

- **Prospect** (lead-generate)
- **Lead Follow-Up** (set appointments)
- **Appointments** (secure clients)
- **Negotiate** (put properties in escrow, and keep them there)

Even your PLAN work is supplemented by your team. When you embrace the power of leverage (Chapter Two), you get so much done in an abbreviated timeframe (see Chapter Eight on efficiency). In order to shift from being a solo agent to a top-producing agent to a rockstar agent, your goals must evolve. You will no longer handhold a client the entire way through a process; your team does that. You therefore need a team to accomplish your top two priorities: convert Leads into Clients and move Clients into Contracts.

The following table describes some of the ways the PLAN makes your office more efficient. This is the PLAN for an administrative assistant:

Prospect	• Film you in a meeting; upload the video to your social media
	• Schedule you for real estate podcasts; blast the link across your social media and to leads in your database
	• Call past clients on your behalf and ask them if there is anything you can do to help them
	• Print out lists of For Sale by Owner, expired listings, and contact info of members of your database; upload these printouts into an auto dialer
	• Schedule meetings or events; prepare slide presentations; send out Eventbrite links; enter all attendees into your database
Lead Follow-Up	• Track new leads that come in via email; enter them in a spreadsheet
	• Enter new leads into database; attach a follow-up plan to them
	• Call leads to schedule a time for you to talk with them; offer to connect buyer with your preferred lender
	• Enter notes into your calendar or database re: what the lead said they want
	• Fill out a Lead Sheet to save you time

Appointments	• Call leads to schedule appointments; prepare prelisting packet for you to bring on listing appointments
	• Put appointments on your calendar; prepare buyer-broker agreements or listing agreements
	• Set up space to receive leads (with marketing info, branded pens, flyers, bottles of water, etc.)
	• Create customized cover page with clients' names; insert photos on the first slide
	• Become licensed; conduct presentations on your behalf
Negotiate	• Prepare a spreadsheet summary of offers received on your listings; make relevant data easy to find
	• Review inspection reports with your clients before you speak with them
	• Weed out the lowest offers on your listings by speaking with the listing agents
	• Call lenders of those looking to buy your listings to see who is the most qualified
	• Speak to listing agents to find out how many offers they have and what price the seller is hoping to receive

The Purpose of Leverage

Rockstar musicians are the magnets that draw the best people to them. They work with the best producers and promoters and perform in the best venues. Rockstar musicians surround themselves with talented teams and limit themselves to writing and performing. To be a rockstar agent, you must accept that you too cannot achieve your potential without a team. Of course, not everyone you hire will turn out to be the right choice. You must learn the skills to hire good people, train them, and manage them. You will experience frustration and failure in this process. I sure did. That's why I explain hiring in its own chapter.

Seth Mosley, the Grammy-winning music producer of twenty-eight No. 1 songs, told me, "I've seen a hit song turn a career from crawling to crushing. It can literally change overnight for an artist that feels like they have been struggling for a decade or more to succeed. As we say in the music biz, a hit can cover a multitude of other sins. Meaning, even if they fail at most everything else, having a hit can make up the difference." Many musicians struggle in the competitive world of music and don't earn much income. The process of trial and error is exhausting, and not everyone makes progress at the same pace. Musicians experiment with different sounds, instruments, styles, and writing genres. It's a messy process to produce a hit. But if, like Adele, you keep working at it, it *will* happen. And when it does, you will feel like you went from zero to hero.

With any "overnight" success, people simply don't see the arduous work you put in to get to the other side of the mountain. It took ten long years for my team to look like an "overnight" success. Hiring, structuring, restructuring, rehiring—it was a confusing and frustrating journey while I was also selling and buying houses. Most agents want a fast and easy journey. But if you commit to the process and don't quit, you will find talented people who take you to the next level. The key is being dedicated to the process, because a solid team takes time to build. The following vignettes highlight what responsibilities to pass on to others and guide you in that decision-making.

Catching Fish Versus Cleaning Fish

Every business must generate revenue and then service that revenue. Moving to a new analogy away from boulders, I believe there are things you do that make money (catching fish) and things you do to keep the money you've already made (cleaning fish). As a rockstar agent, I keep my focus on the former and rely on my team to do the latter.

Salespeople create the revenue, and this is typically more difficult, requires higher skills, and offers less financial security than servicing revenue. This is why the task of cleaning fish is easier to delegate. Provided that enough fish are caught, the fish cleaners stay busy and earn their wages. If that's not the case, however, the fish cleaners are still paid but have nothing to do.

This doesn't mean you can't teach your team to help you catch fish. Assistants can create comparative market analyses (CMAs) for you, set up for listing appointments, help nervous clients feel good about meeting you, and so on. Lead generation is like the number of casts you make to put your worm in the water. Meanwhile, putting clients in contract is like the number of hooks you set that reel fish toward the boat.

Consider the fisherman who must clean the entire catch before they can go back out on the water. They cannot be effective in hitting high numbers when their focus is on both catching the fish and cleaning the fish. Focusing on catching more fish means focusing on dollar-producing activities.

Skill Work Versus Busy Work

Figuring out what you pass on to your team and what you must keep as your responsibilities can be done by breaking all tasks into two categories. Skill work obviously requires skill. Choosing the right lure, knowing where the fish are likely to be, working the bait, and setting the hook are all developed skills. Conversely, busy work can be done by anyone. Putting gas in the boat and carrying the day's catch does not require much skill, and there are fewer consequences if the work is not done well. Thus, the first thing a rockstar agent should do is to give this type of work to someone else.

Practical examples of busy work are entering listing information into the Multiple Listing Services (MLS), scheduling appointments for vendors, setting appointments for showing agents, and filling out paperwork that does not require any negotiation. Many agents do not accurately estimate how much time these activities take and how much production time they steal. Busy work is not unimportant work, and it would be a mistake to consider it as such. Rather, it is something that is easier to learn, and any mistakes have lower-level consequences for your business. Skilled work, on the other hand, includes negotiating deals, helping clients choose the right home, determining the offer price, going on listing appointments, following up with leads, solving problems with escrows, and hiring additional staff. These duties should be delegated after the right people are hired.

Sales Versus Organization

The last distinction to make is between sales and organization. I say this because these two skill sets are rarely found in the same person. Sales skills require persuasion, emotional intelligence, charisma, and the ability to influence others. Organizational skills involve controlling chaos, recognizing problems before they occur, creating systems, cleaning up messes, and instructing others on what to do. People with these skills juggle multiple tasks, understand how to prioritize their work, and know how to plan effectively.

The sales mindset can be like the Tasmanian Devil from the Looney Tunes. It whirls around creating a huge mess—but with that mess comes opportunities. The organization mindset looks at that mess, recognizes the opportunities it presents, then cleans up the rest. It focuses on efficiency.

When deciding what to leverage, start by understanding your and your team's strong suits. If you have strong sales skills, which most rockstar agents do, hire a person with strong organizational skills to keep you on track and aware of your tasks. If you are better with organizational skills, look for a salesperson who can generate leads, create interest, and get in front of clients. Then you close the deals by creating efficient systems.

Adjustments

The last point I'll make is about the required adjustments in your thinking that are needed to thrive at a rockstar agent level. Let's look at thinking in one degree, two degrees, and three degrees. Thinking in one degree means going in only two directions: forward and backward. This easy concept is found in a simple diagram.

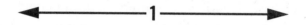

SOLD described the two-dimensional journey to becoming a top-producing agent. There is a set of specific things you must do to be successful. If you do them, you will be. If you don't, you won't. Not only must you do well in your own role, but you must also be successful in your hiring skills and ensuring your team does well in their roles. To understand this two-dimensional journey, consider Mario in the popular Nintendo game Mario Brothers. When Mario runs forward or backward, he is traveling on a one-dimensional plane. The moment he jumps, however, he introduces a second plane: up and down.

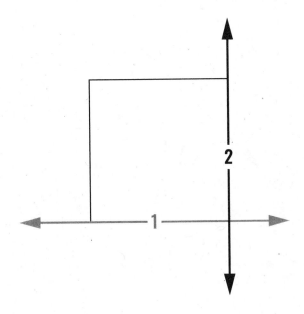

This creates a slightly more complicated scenario that makes success more difficult to achieve, but it also explains why there is so much opportunity for those who can do it well. Learning this second dimension requires an adjustment period. When you adjust your thinking, business becomes very sweet.

The adjustment to the third dimension is covered in this book. I will explain how you become more successful by hiring others to use your funnel and allowing others to succeed while removing yourself from that system. This third dimension is how you create an exceptionally profitable business and how you run your business with little to none of your own time or influence. The third dimension is complicated—and because of that, much more lucrative than the first two dimensions.

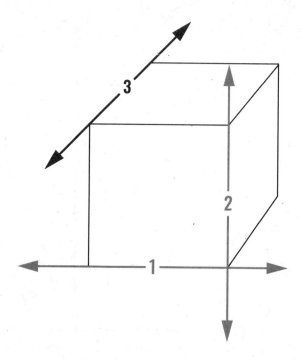

Top-producing agents run into trouble when they lack systems and support. This prevents them from running at top speed alongside that boulder. They excel at finding leads but lose focus on everything else. Rockstar agents run fast by creating systems, hiring employees, and transitioning their business from a solo show to a bigger business. They make more money, take more vacations, and work fewer days.

Rockstar agents stop focusing only on themselves and become leaders. These skills aren't easy to learn, but the effort is worth it. Rockstar agents embrace continual growth. They know how to overcome obstacles and understand their team and their business. They meet whatever challenges arise.

Becoming a top-producing agent also requires a shift in thinking. The lesson here is that when you reach the top of the mountain, the journey isn't over. Reaching the top is an incredible accomplishment. The worst is behind you! Now you must focus on keeping that boulder rolling as fast as possible, this time without gravity working against you. As you build your team as a top-producing agent, you are no longer a sole proprietor, but you also do not own a passive business. You are still involved with your team and function as one cohesive unit.

Your final adjustment from top-producing to rockstar agent is in your responsibilities. If you lose focus, lose motivation, or get burned out, the consequences to your clients and your team members are very real. At this stage, your influence impacts people. Everything you do or don't do affects others.

The best advice I can give is to be aware that many people only worry about what they want and what is best for them. When you are a member of a team—even more so if you are the leader—your feelings and desires take a back seat to the good of the firm. When the team is doing well, you are all doing well. When one team member doesn't care enough, no one is doing well.

I'll explain how to build the right work culture, how to limit negative impacts, how to master being a rockstar agent, and how to develop your success. I'll also describe how to work efficiently at an elevated level with buyers and sellers, how to add a branch to your business to service investors, how to buy real estate for yourself, and how to thrive in any market. By the time you're done reading this, you will have the collective knowledge of every mentor I've had, the agent training I received, and my own experiences moving from a top-producing to a rockstar agent.

If you're worried you don't have what it takes to become a rockstar agent or aren't sure you want to be one, I'll posit that there is a strong chance you're more worried than necessary. All agents became licensed for the same reason: to make money while helping people with the biggest and most expensive decision they'll ever make. Rockstar agents make more money, help more people, and teach bigger teams their craft.

You may not feel like a rockstar agent now—at one point I did not either. The reality is that if you keep pushing that boulder, you'll get stronger and reach the top of that mountain. The path to becoming a real estate rockstar can happen naturally through your excellent service to your clients. Eventually, being an agent becomes a lot more lucrative and fun, especially after you hire staff so that you can focus on all the responsibilities that energize you.

In short, rockstar agents do the parts of the job they love, avoid the parts they don't, and make a fantastic living doing so. Who doesn't want that? Therefore, let's start by learning how to master the work and process until we are all running alongside that boulder down the mountain.

➡ KEY POINTS

- In the beginning of your career, every inch of progress comes with massive effort and a lot of mistakes.
- Conversely, top-producing agents have built their momentum, confidence, experience, and skill using the tools of the Sales Funnel.
- The key to becoming a top-producing agent is to keep your focus on pushing the boulder further and further, even when the fear of it falling on you is gone.
- Once you have crested the mountain and can no longer keep up with the boulder, you hire a team so as not to lose momentum.
- Every business must generate revenue and then service that revenue.
- Focusing on catching more fish means focusing on dollar-producing activities.
- The third dimension (leadership) is how you create an exceptionally profitable business and how you run your business with little to none of your own time or influence.
- Rockstar agents run fast by creating systems, hiring employees, and transitioning their business from a solo show to a bigger business.
- PLAN:
  - **Prospect** (lead-generate)
  - **Lead Follow-Up** (set appointments)
  - **Appointments** (secure clients)
  - **Negotiate** (put properties in escrow, and keep them there)

CHAPTER ▶ TWO

LEVERAGE AND SUPPORT

"If you want to go fast, go alone. If you want to go far, go together."

AFRICAN PROVERB—MARTHA GOEDERT

To use a new analogy, achieving your maximum potential without help from others is like Tony Stark taking on a supervillain without his suit of armor. Even if he figures out a way, the effort and luck required would make it unsustainable. His real superpower is his brain, which allows him to take advantage of his suit. Tony's suit, like your team members, is an extension of his creative ideas and talent for design. He needs it to achieve his goals.

Your team should become an extension of you. They incorporate your experiences and knowledge and manifest them into positive impacts on your business. They reduce your own weak areas and double down on your strengths. The right team amplifies your business.

Conversely, the wrong team—or more specifically, the wrong team member—does the opposite. An uncaring assistant can erase the client goodwill you built up in your previous interactions. Team members who pick up on others' negativity, resentment, or corner-cutting can easily create a work culture in which everyone does that too. If this happens, they wreak havoc on your business.

Like most things in life, what can help you can also hurt you. That's why it's so important for you to get the leverage component right. The best team is an extension of you, and you must build it with that in mind. Every agent has different skills and as such will need different skills in the people they hire. The order of your hires and the way your team is structured should precisely follow the model I provide. However, don't hire members who are simply carbon-copy molds of another agent's team.

Consider a sports franchise, which is the best model for how to build a team. No two sports teams are the same, yet every team wants the same talented players. If it were as simple as hiring talent to overpower the opposition, the team with the most talent (and highest payroll) would always win. Yet, this isn't the case. Time and time again, it is the team with the best chemistry that keeps winning.

For example, the New England Patriots dominated the National Football League for twenty years. They did so with roster changes every year. While nearly every player on the team cycled in and out, two stalwarts remained throughout the dynasty: their quarterback, Tom Brady, and their head coach, Bill Belichick. Brady and Belichick created an environment of success unlike any other sports franchise. The system worked no matter which other players were on the team. Do you think the Patriots actively hired mediocre talent? Absolutely not. They looked for the best they could find—as did every other team in the NFL. What made the Patriots different? Their culture.

Belichick and Brady have incredibly talented football minds. They wanted players who could amplify Brady's strengths (e.g., he was a pocket passer) and cover for his weaknesses (e.g., he didn't move well in the pocket). He was an easy target to sack if he held onto the ball too long, so the Patriots stacked wide receivers around Brady to help him get rid of the ball quickly. Brady ran drills with these wide receivers off-season to ensure they were where he wanted them and when he wanted them there. That means the Patriots needed players who played well together, not simply talented individuals. The Patriots actively hired the players that Brady needed around him, not just the fastest or strongest guys available from the draft or with free agent status.

We all know the combination of chemistry, communication, and the time spent getting on the same page beats raw talent any day. Real estate agents can learn a lot from this football dynasty. Your team must function the same way. As a rockstar agent, you must remain focused, be committed to excellence, and want the best players around you. Are you charismatic and influential but incredibly unorganized? Do you see leads slipping away? This problem costs agents a lot of money. Don't make the mistake of hiring someone like you. Hire people who can highlight your strengths and downplay your weaknesses. Are you bold and direct but bad with numbers and contractual minutiae? Then hire the person who excels in those areas. You need people who round out your abilities and can help you grow your business.

Rockstars Don't Do It Alone

Let me start by saying you cannot be a rockstar agent by yourself. It's not sustainable, it's not enjoyable, and it's definitely not efficient.

- Time-consuming tasks, of which there are many, don't generate income and should be done by someone else. For example, attending listing appointments can earn you thousands of dollars an hour, while other jobs like filling out paperwork can only save you $15 an hour.
- Closing deals requires a lot of time communicating with clients, and much of that does not have to be done by you. You can be working the funnel instead.
- Solving problems and making decisions should be done by you while executing solutions should be delegated.
- Working the parts of the job that drain you can cause you to lose the drive needed to run your business. Hand those off to someone else so your level of customer service remains high. Focusing on the parts that energize you increases your business's volume.
- Working alone means you can efficiently handle five or six buyers at a time. Working with an admin who schedules appointments, reviews paperwork, and arranges assistants to show houses frees you up to work with up to fifty buyers at a time.

In my experience, top-producing agents cap out at fifty closed deals in a year. Most work conducted by an agent does not generate income. If you're closing fifty deals in a year, you're probably working with up to 150 solid leads, and that is a lot of work with no payoff. As with everything else, there is a point of diminishing returns in real estate where the work you are putting in no longer results in the same amount of success. When you're spread so thin that you lose focus on putting clients in contract or following up with leads, you're working hard but not winning.

In every real estate transaction, there are more than one hundred small steps to get to a close. If you do all but one step flawlessly, you make zero money. When an agent has too many clients and not enough help, they hit the point of diminishing returns. Adding more leads at this point only contributes to less sales. The key to avoiding this problem is not to work less but to work smarter.

Italian economist Vilfredo Pareto is credited for creating the 80/20 principle. Pareto observed that 20 percent of effort is often responsible for 80 percent of results. While this is clearly not a hard and fast rule, it helps us to understand the importance of sticking to what is most meaningful, most beneficial, and what we're best at. Working only in our 20 percent is a battle that never ends, but it is a battle worth fighting.

Rockstar agents understand their business depends on their ability to generate leads and to convert escrows to close. A rockstar agent's ability to set appointments with leads and put those new clients into contract are the two most important activities for a thriving business. This means these two activities are the 20 percent that rockstar agents should focus on. If you can't do these two things well, nobody on your team will have much to do. You'll still have payroll costs, and you won't be generating revenue. If you can do these things well, your team will have plenty to do to help you grow your agency.

These two skills are difficult to master, but once you can do them well, they don't take nearly as much time to continue to do them well. The table below will help you understand the tasks you should do and the tasks you should leverage. Use this simple list for every decision on tasks.

TASKS YOU DO:	TASKS YOU LEVERAGE:
Generate revenue	Service revenue
Are skill-based	Are time-based
Are sales-based	Are organization-based
Require leadership	Support your work
Cast vision	Execute your vision

The following are examples of tasks that fall into these categories:

ACTIONS YOU TAKE:	ACTIONS YOU LEVERAGE:
Follow up with leads	Schedule phone calls with leads
Go on listing appointments	Prepare your listing appointments: CMA, prelisting packets, ask client questions, etc.
Negotiate contracts	Do research for successful negotiations
Work with scared, difficult, or unhappy clients	Prepare clients for phone calls; soften them up first
Create systems	Implement/improve systems
Negotiate credits with listing agents	Research cost of repairs on property

It's impossible to list every job a rockstar agent does, but it's useful to understand the types of jobs you should do and the types you should leverage. This may be confusing at first, but it gets easier the more you do it. You will develop an instinct for this division of labor. The empire builder doesn't ask, "How can I build this?" They ask, "Who can help me build it?"

Hybrid Theory

I should clarify the difference between the top-producing agent who is crushing it in sales and the truly hands-off rockstar agent you are working to become. To make this illustration easier to understand, the following are the three phases to structure real estate sales.

Phase 1 (explained in *SOLD*) is when you're a solo agent doing everything yourself. There is limited help from other agents in the office. Using the above analogy, this is like Tony Stark operating without a suit of armor. He is smart and creative and gets things done, but he's limited in what he can do.

Phase 2 (*SKILL*) is when you don the armor and learn how it can amplify all your best parts while limiting your weaknesses. Tony's creativity is in his design abilities and working around conventional thinking. Tony's armor makes him more powerful, more creative, and more effective. You are more powerful when you become a top-producing agent.

Phase 3 (*SCALE*) is when you shift from being Iron Man to creating other Avenger-types to work for you. I should point out that some agents create this group from the ground up while others find a team someone else has already created. You don't have to be the one to build it, but once your skills and experience have reached a certain level, you'll find yourself with so much more to offer than presentations and negotiating deals. The younger generation of agents will always need guidance and support from those with experience, and finding a role to provide this on a team is an emotionally gratifying and financially rewarding way to achieve this.

The key concept to understand here is you are not replacing yourself. Rather, you are hiring others to take over many of the tasks so you can grow your business. Start with the activities that are the least important in generating revenue, then add the activities that drain you the most. From there, leverage the tasks that are important but you are not good at or don't like doing. It's important to have team members who can do things better than you. Always.

You are the rockstar agent. Your clients want to work with you. The challenge is to prevent yourself from being spread too thin. Your ability to provide high-level service at the most important junctures in a transaction is infinitely more important to your success than trying to do everything yourself. I'll provide more specifics throughout this book, but the following examples are tasks to leverage.

For example, your showing agents should show houses to your clients so you can have more time to negotiate the best deals. And your inside sales agents can follow up with leads and put them into a system so you can focus on generating more leads for them.

Meanwhile, one or two administrative staff can handle the schedules of showings for your showing agents so they can show more houses in a day. Admins can run the comparative market analyses and follow up with pending listings so you are more prepared for your listing appointments. They can review inspection reports with the clients so you can solve the problems found. They can send the contractual paperwork so you can move on to making the next important step. They can summarize the information in the offers you receive on listings so you can review them more quickly. They can call the agents who showed your listings to receive any feedback, which you present to the seller. They can input new prospects or leads into your database and assign them following a plan you created. And they can read your email and correspond appropriately so you can spend your day on appointments, networking, and generating leads. Imagine how much income-generating work you can do when you're not doing this lower-skill work.

In these examples, you are still doing the revenue-generating work. You haven't replaced yourself, but you have enabled yourself to work better, faster, and at a higher volume. This will place more pressure on you, and some people don't work well under this pressure. Again, there's nothing wrong with being a top-producing agent if that is what fulfills you, but if you think you want more, remember that if you use your funnel and have a team that supports you, you will become so skilled and confident that you'll crave the pressure of being a rockstar agent, not avoid it.

To construct your support team in the way that benefits your strengths and weaknesses, avoid the temptation to follow another rockstar agent's lead. They are different than you. Being human, we find comfort in blueprints. For obvious reasons pointed out so far in this book, this becomes a problem. Were you to build a team exactly like mine, you would likely fail because we need different team members.

As I found my style and landed more clients, I noticed that some of my responsibilities gave me an uh-oh feeling in the pit of my stomach. My subconscious was trying to tell me I had done or was about to do something poorly—but I didn't understand that at the time. I would get that feeling when telling a client, "I'll look that up and get back to you tomorrow"; or when a client would admit they were nervous about the process and wanted to review the inspection report with me; or when I drove clients around in my car; or when I had a listing presentation and had to remember what to bring. This feeling happened with other tasks too.

I know now these feelings were guides pointing me in the direction of who I should hire. Every uh-oh feeling was my body's way of helping me, but pride told me to ignore it or that it was acceptable to struggle with these tasks. It wasn't until I learned how to hire a team that I began to thrive. The following are my strengths and weaknesses and are what I used to hire my team. Remember, your accounting of your strengths and weaknesses create a different list and, therefore, a different team.

MY STRENGTHS	MY WEAKNESSES
See the big picture	Handle the details
Create a work plan that is efficient, synergistic, and likely to succeed	Manage the moving components to execute that plan
Articulate the value in my perspective, plan, or idea	Remember the meeting materials
Know the right move to make in any given situation	Remembering the details of what the right move will require
Create materials to explain difficult concepts	Stay motivated to repeatedly deliver that material to multiple clients
Maintain focus on difficult tasks	Handle several tasks at one time

It wasn't easy for me to accept that there are certain components I am remarkably terrible at—not only in business but also in my life. On several occasions, I have left for listing appointments without the folders containing the listing agreements and all the other materials. I frequently have conversations with clients and remind myself to run a CMA for their property (fully intending to do so), only to forget to do so until days later. I learned I was often anticipating conversations with the clients or solutions to problems during the time I should have been collecting the materials needed for the appointment. It became obvious that organizational tasks were my weak spot when I was better at preparing for the larger, more complex decisions ahead of me.

I also realized that even ten-minute phone calls to explain simple steps in the process (such as when the home inspection was scheduled or when the house would go live on the MLS) were incredibly draining to me. I felt guilty about this for a long time and tried to improve my work in these areas. I failed. Things that were simple for others to do were difficult for me, and I was embarrassed to admit it.

My first admin hire, Krista, heard me on the phone having a difficult conversation with a stubborn seller who was yelling at me and expressing his displeasure in a disrespectful way, even though my office hadn't done anything wrong. When I hung up the phone, she said, "That's why you're the top agent in this office. I could never have pulled that off." My initial response was to tell her it wasn't a big deal, but before the words were out of my mouth, I was hit with the realization that to her, it *was* a big deal. The things I could do well appeared impossibly difficult to Krista. She was grateful I did them, so she wouldn't have to. Krista had zero problem accepting there were aspects of the business she would have struggled with.

Once I realized it was okay for me to admit I struggled with some areas, I did. In fact, Krista was shocked when I told her I had been insecure about these aspects of the business. She told me it made her feel useful to hear I was struggling in those areas and that for the first time she realized what a crucial part she played in my success. That conversation was an epiphany for me. Everything changed from that day forward.

Give Yourself Permission to Admit Your Strengths and Weaknesses

I realized that my 20 percent was a skill set most people in my office wanted to avoid. This included: handling confrontational conversations; making tough decisions with limited information; risking upsetting clients when they didn't see the greater good in my advice or respectfully telling them they were wrong about something; anything to do with price, numbers, or saving money; sharing a perspective different from that of the clients; confidently explaining why I was the best agent option among the several that clients were considering hiring; deciding to fire clients; having difficult negotiations with other agents or clients; creating office policies and procedures; finding creative, outside-the-box solutions; being the face of my company; generating healthy leads; risking the rejection of a lead telling me no; and asking direct questions that could lead to emotionally painful responses.

When I looked at my strengths, I realized few Realtors were willing to excel in these areas. These are hard skills, but I am good at them. My conversations with Krista opened a powerful way to think about myself, and that forever changed the way I approached my business.

My 20 percent tasks have an 80 percent impact on my business and how successful we are.

When I wrote the list of tasks that drained me, caused me unreasonable anxiety, or I was flat-out bad at accomplishing, I found that I'm not good at scheduling anything. I am also bad at remembering what I have to do in the future, like meetings; ordering supplies for the business or anticipating those needs; wiring money, inputting credit card information, or paying vendors for services I ordered; tracking expenses or revenue; waiting on hold for any type of customer service representative; completing a thorough check of paperwork; finding the correct document and filling it out quickly; sharing in the emotions of my clients, both highs and lows; remembering to remove signs from sold listings and mark the MLS as sold; deciding on the order of the pictures in the MLS; calling the clients to ask them about the features of their home; being able to walk through a listing and see it as a buyer would; choosing gifts for our clients when they close; designing social media advertising or anything to do with aesthetics; following up once a deal is in escrow; printing and collating documents; scheduling the showing of homes or showing them; looking up information in the MLS; or talking to the other agent. And a whole lot more!

My epiphany made me realize how many aspects of being an agent I should leave to other people. It was nothing to be embarrassed about; in fact, my weaknesses created jobs and opportunities for others. The more areas I admitted I needed help with, the more people I could bring into my world to help me and the more jobs I could create. This realization was the catalyst that jump-started the creation of the David Greene Team from David Greene the Realtor.

I shared this story in the hopes that you too will give yourself permission to admit there are things you are not good at. That admission is the first step to creating a thriving business. It will allow you to figure out the best people to hire for success in your business. When you clearly understand which jobs are most important to keep and to leverage within your business, your productivity will soar. Your list will create job opportunities for other people. It's a win-win cycle.

Going back to an analogy in Chapter One, rockstar musicians make opportunities for everyone around them. The stadium sells tickets, vendors sell clothing and food, technicians build sets. This is the definition of a rainmaker.

As a rockstar agent, your ability to influence, be persuasive, and solve problems improves the lives of your team members, your clients, and everyone you do business with. This is why pushing that boulder to the top of the mountain is so important. Your business becomes more than just a revenue stream for you. It becomes a group endeavor, a source of wealth for many, and the pinpoint of purpose in your life.

You are hiring people to help you do what you do best so your business can operate more efficiently. Remember, no two agents have the same strengths and weaknesses, so no two teams will look the same. You hire around *your* skills, *your* weaknesses, and *your* needs. This is a necessary component to *your* success.

Creating chemistry in the hybrid business model of no longer being a solo agent but not yet being a hands-off business owner centers on the positions you hire for and who you hire. Therefore, let's discuss how you can structure your hiring process to create the best possible chemistry.

Your First Hire

Your first hire will be the toughest to complete, with subsequent hires becoming progressively easier. The first position to fill is the most difficult because that person represents the biggest split in the duties of running a real estate business. Each hire after that will be for more specific jobs, but your first hire will assume as many of the administrative duties as possible so you can focus primarily on sales. This is the first division between fish catching and fish cleaning. As a top-producing agent, you did everything yourself. As a rockstar agent, you can't.

In my case, my first administrative assistant was hired to schedule my appointments, remind me to follow up with leads, create my list of daily duties, enter information into my database, manage my transactions, order office supplies, pay bills, and keep me in compliance with the MLS. It was going to be a complex job that would encompass the duties that were keeping me from growing my business.

Your first hire will start on the ground floor with you. They will have the opportunity to grow with you. This growth will afford them first right of refusal for any future positions your company will need as it grows. Many top salespeople started off as administrative assistants. The knowledge they gleaned allowed them to move up the ladder.

The Sales Funnel: People to Leads

The tool to turn People into Leads is lead generation. Your first hire (in my case, Krista) will help organize your high-touch campaign, gather content and post on your social media, reach out to past clients to let them know what their house is worth, and follow up with buyer leads to warm them up for you. Most agents severely underestimate how staying in touch with people in their database impacts their business. Giving your admin assistant these duties will increase your sales results.

The Sales Funnel: Leads to Clients

The tools to move Leads into Clients are: setting appointments, delivering presentations, and following up with Leads (this is where most agents blow it). Getting help in this area will impact how many appointments are set and thus how many Leads are converted to Clients.

Your admin assistant can schedule these appointments, follow up with Leads to see if they are ready to meet with you or have any questions, and, more importantly, they can track Leads to prevent them from falling through the cracks. My team now uses a spreadsheet to do this.

Finally, your admin assistant can prepare the paperwork you'll need for presentations and update you with information to help you seal the deal. Once Leads are signed up as Clients, your assistant can then set them up for MLS searches and do check-ins with them.

The Sales Funnel: Clients to Contracts

Your assistant can also help with the Client portion of the funnel. When it comes to listings, a good assistant can handle 90 to 95 percent of the work required to sell a home. While you are the one negotiating on the seller's behalf, your assistant can save you time by:

- Preparing you for listing presentations.
- Providing you with a CMA and calling other agents to determine the price of pending listings.
- Entering everything in the MLS.
- Scheduling photos, inspections, cleaning, and other related activities.
- Keeping the seller informed on where they are in the process.
- Ordering the yard sign, preparing marketing materials, and advertising the listing on social media.
- Scheduling calls for you with the seller and preparing you with information to deliver on those calls.

- Answering emails from buyers' agents.
- Preparing and uploading disclosure packets and inspection reports.
- Summarizing offers received.

For buyers, your assistant can, among other things:
- Schedule showings.
- Schedule appraisals, inspections, etc.
- Ask listing agents questions your buyers want to know.
- Touch base with your buyers to see if they have any questions.
- Look up information in the MLS, tax records, title records, or other databases.
- Receive listings from the MLS.
- Fill out counteroffers and addendums, and help write offers (if licensed).
- Communicate with lenders and title and escrow agents.
- Look up comparable sales.
- Get quotes from contractors and repair people.
- Communicate with local associations of Realtors.
- Pay your bills.
- Help you stay in compliance.
- Post your sales on social media.

An assistant saves you time when working with your clients. And the best part? Clients rarely know you are not doing all the work. As long as you're the one communicating the information, it doesn't matter to them who's collecting the information so long as it's accurate and timely.

Your Second Hire

Your second hire will be a transaction coordinator. Their primary responsibility is to handle everything in escrow, or the last two stages of the funnel: Contracts and Closings. This removes two steps of the Sales Funnel and allows you to focus on People, Leads, and Clients. This reduces your level of focus from five stages to three, or a 40 percent reduction in workload. With your transaction coordinator focusing on the last two stages, your admin assistant can help you with the first three stages, which are on the sales side.

Your Third Hire

Your third hire will be on the sales side. Some rockstar agents first hire a buyer's agent while others hire a showing agent. Either way, you remain the primary agent for both sellers and buyers, but you give the showings of the homes to your recent hire. Regardless of which route is best for you, the point of your third hire is to leverage the duties that take up most of your time: working with buyers.

Buyers require the most time for several reasons. They need more handholding because the process tends to be more emotional for them than for sellers. The job is also more tedious because the work to get into escrow is done on behalf of buyers. Inspections, appraisals, loan approvals, and title reports are all steps that buyers do to protect themselves. The seller doesn't have to do much after the house is ready for the market. In addition to all the escrow requirements, the other factor that takes up the most time in real estate sales is showing houses to buyers.

This is the most laborious part of the process as it demands the most attention. It's hard to do anything else while showing homes because your clients expect, and deserve, your full attention. This is why having an admin assistant and a transaction coordinator to field your calls and organize what you need is so important. It's a huge relief to know nothing is falling through the cracks while you're showing homes. This is also why many rockstar agents (myself included) use showing assistants and showing agents. In my opinion, these support roles for your sales agents are vital to your business. Having someone who can show homes allows you to focus on moving Clients to the Contract part of the funnel and to negotiate the best deal possible for them.

With this third hire taking over the work with buyers, you can focus on listings, which are the lifeblood of your business. They directly determine your financial success. Listings help generate buyer leads, which feed opportunities to your buyer's agents or showing assistants.

This is a great entry-level position for a person to learn the sales ropes while you focus on listings. Having more listings allows your business to grow faster because one listing often leads to two and to several buyer leads as well.

People and Systems

Another big part of building your business is systems. That word is often used to describe a repeatable and scalable series of tasks. A good system can also easily be performed by a team member. It is the combination of people and systems that will allow you to pass responsibilities onto others and to scale your business.

Systems help in the following ways:

- They reduce errors of omission (forgetting to do something).
- They reduce errors of commission (doing something incorrectly).
- They make it easier for a new person to understand their responsibilities.
- They streamline processes and add efficiency.
- They reduce "lead bleed" (when you lose a Lead because you forget to contact them or don't respond to inquiries).
- They create a blueprint that allows oversight.

Creating a system means creating a checklist of tasks that need to occur at specific points. This links to a second checklist of tasks that will pick up where the first ended. These checklists will eventually morph into a single streamlined process so you can assign certain tasks to specific team members. The next step is to have the system automatically assign tasks to team members. At that point, you have an efficient, autonomous, and self-sustaining process of moving Leads through the funnel to Closings.

Let's discuss the many benefits of systems.

They Reduce Errors of Omission

When you have a series of checklists for everything that needs to be done, it becomes difficult to forget to do something. Most errors of omission occur because our brain is a terrible source for short-term memory (like RAM in a computer). We are not designed to remember multiple small steps, which is why important things "slip our mind." Creating a checklist is the remedy.

The following are the checklists I use to sell a house. I started by writing out every step involved in selling a listing and arrived at five lists. These five checklists combine to form my system for selling houses. As one checklist ends, the next begins. Someone reviews these checklists daily so we don't forget a step. On the rare occasions when something goes wrong, we add a step to ensure it doesn't happen again. The checklists for selling a house are spelled out more fully under *The Birth and Development of a System with Checklists* in this chapter. For now, they are:

1. Prelisting appointment checklist
2. Prelisting checklist
3. Active listing checklist
4. Pending listing checklist
5. Sold listing checklist

They Reduce Errors of Commission

Most errors of commission are made from inexperience. When a team member forgets to do something, it is usually because there were no established rules or procedures to guide them. Systems allow your team members to focus on the specific parts of their job, which increases their experience level and decreases the number of mistakes they make. This, in turn, results in fewer lost deals, fewer "fires" in the funnel, and more time for you to focus on lead generation.

They Make It Easier for a New Person to Understand Their Responsibilities

When you hire a new team member, they will likely have a "W-2" mindset; that is, an employee mindset. This comes from their previous experience of working for a company and having set job responsibilities. You can help them adapt to your checklist workflow more quickly by having a set of tasks for them to perform.

This avoids telling them that "it's your job to close the escrow," when they don't know what that means. By providing a specific series of tasks, you make their transition smoother. This allows you to train them by showing them each step, offering direction, and setting boundaries. It focuses them and protects them from the chaos and overwhelm of real estate sales.

They Streamline Processes and Add Efficiency

Once a series of tasks is created, it becomes easier to see where work is being duplicated. As a team member performs their tasks, they learn where their time is being wasted. For example, most new agents are so excited to work with a new-buyer lead that they immediately show them homes. When their lead finds a home they like, they have a lot of questions about what to do next. The new agent then looks up the price, what comps are in the area, what the monthly payments would be, how many offers there are, what the school scores are, and more. This is highly intensive work.

Then, the new agent realizes the buyer needs to be preapproved. This process usually takes several days, and the agent may very well find out the buyer is not approved at the price the home is listed for—or even worse, does not qualify for a loan at all. The agent will have wasted all the time they spent showing the buyer homes and researching this property. A checklist to work with buyers reveals getting a preapproval letter comes before showing leads any homes. This example shows how one checklist in a system saves you time and effort. When your boulder is on the other side of the mountain, systems become even more important.

They Reduce "Lead Bleed"

Losing contact with leads is a huge factor in lost revenue. If you don't have a system to assist with lead follow-up, I guarantee that you're losing leads and, therefore, revenue every month. The following is the New-Buyer Lead checklist that my team uses:

1. Enter all new leads into your customer relationship management (CRM) system and use its automatically assigned checklist option (to automatically complete steps).
2. An automatic text is sent that reads: "Hey! Thanks for reaching out. I see you're interested in buying a home. When is a good time to talk more?"
3. An automatic email is sent with a similar message.
4. An inside sales agent/admin is assigned an automatic task to follow up after a lead's reply or to reach out again if lead does not reply.
5. An inside sales agent/admin fills out a Lead Sheet, which poses questions about a buyer's intention (e.g., where do they want to buy, are they preapproved with a bank, what are their goals, etc.).
6. An agent is assigned for follow-up.
7. An automatic reminder is sent to the agent to do follow-up.
8. If the agent has not made contact, the inside sales agent/admin schedules a phone call between the agent and lead.
9. Start the lead's preapproval process (if not yet preapproved).
10. Add the lead to Buyer's Lead Board spreadsheet for tracking. (I discuss Lead Boards and additional methods to prevent lead bleed in Chapter Three.)

These ten steps have eliminated nearly all the lead bleed I used to experience and significantly increased my conversion rate of Leads to Clients.

They Create a Blueprint that Allows Oversight

At this point in my business, I no longer perform the work that moves a Client down the Sales Funnel; my transaction coordinator does this with the aid of checklists. My goal is to have systems that allow me to step away from the funnel altogether. At that point I will have created the blueprint for a closed sale and can delegate the work to others to replicate it. The attraction to move to oversight includes:

1. I can do this from any geographic location.
2. I can attend trainings or further my education to improve my systems and expand my reach.
3. I can retire from the sales part of the business and earn passive income.
4. I can choose other business opportunities (e.g., house flipping, buying rentals, creating apartment syndications, opening a title company, etc.).
5. I can offer jobs and opportunities to more people.

Doesn't every American dream of retiring and doing what they love? Real estate sales make this very possible, but you can't do that without systems. I understand that systems take time to create and the need to overcome the mentality of "it's easier to just do it myself." But this is short-term thinking. It may be faster *now* to do things this way, but you are trapping yourself into a "job" you can never retire from, and you can't scale.

If you love growth, love excellence, and love to reach your potential in this business, you must hire the right people and create the right systems.

The Birth and Development of a System with Checklists

When I first heard about systems, I was intrigued but incredibly frustrated. I knew what I wanted to do, but I didn't know the platform to use or how it should work. Therefore, I called my friend and future team member Kyle Renke (who has a fabulous technical mind) and explained my problem. Kyle solved it in thirty seconds, and from there I created my systems. I will now share these with you to spare you the time I wasted and the frustration I felt in creating them.

The Five Steps of the Birth Stage

1. Create a real estate sales folder in Google Drive.
2. Create subfolders for the checklists you need to create (e.g., checklists for sellers, buyers, hiring, etc.).
3. Create a Google Doc for each checklist and place in the appropriate subfolders.
4. On each Google Doc checklist, include every step involved for that procedure.
5. Break the checklist into subsections and sub-subsections.

These are the checklists for selling a house, which a team member would find in a Google Drive subfolder.

a. **Prelisting appointment checklist:** the steps to prepare for an appointment with a seller Lead. All the tasks should be listed in the order they are to be performed.

b. **Prelisting checklist:** the steps to take after the listing agreement is signed and the house is ready to be listed on the MLS. All the tasks should be listed in the order they are to be performed.

c. **Active listing checklist:** the steps to communicate with the seller and help sell the home once the MLS is active. All the tasks should be listed in the order they are to be performed.

d. **Pending listing checklist:** the steps to ensure the buyer's agent is doing what they need to do to close on time and we are in compliance with pending status regulations. All the tasks should be listed in the order they are to be performed.

e. **Sold listing checklist:** the steps required when a house sells, the seller moves, and we market our sold property. All the tasks should be listed in the order they are to be performed.

Anyone on my team can access these checklists. After you create your own checklists, you can start to refine them as you find missing elements until they are as clear as possible for all team members.

The Five Steps of the Growth Stage

1. Color-code the steps of the checklists and assign those colors to different team members.
2. Train your team on how to accomplish their tasks (let new members practice a few steps).
3. Anything not color-coded is your responsibility.
4. As your team members grow in their jobs, assign them additional steps from the checklists.
5. Create weekly training sessions on how team members can improve their workflow.

The Five Steps of the Development Stage

1. Purchase a CRM system that includes automatically assigned checklists, or auto plans. (I use the Brivity Platform for our CRM, which I discuss at length in Chapter Twelve.)
2. Create auto plans for a fluid stream of reminders throughout the Sales Funnel.
3. Make the final step of each auto checklist "assign [name of next] auto plan."
4. Set the auto plan to assign tasks to appropriate team members.
5. Hire a manager to oversee task completion.

Voila, this is how agents get houses sold without missing a step. As a rockstar agent, your only tasks are finding new listing leads, getting listing agreements signed, and putting your listings into contract. With this system, you are now freed up to focus on higher-dollar activities.

Creating Cohesiveness

Your team members can even create their own checklists if they find a situation that needs one. Not every team member will do this, but those who do usually become leaders in your office and are ready for management roles. Notice those who create useful systems; mentor them to help them grow personally and help your business grow.

Establishing the right work culture that builds your business is vital. Clients come to your agency often because they are drawn to *you*. This includes your work ethic, your attitude, and—most important—the way you make them feel. Many of your leads may not continue down the Sales

Funnel if your team members have a wildly different style from yours. If the contrast is too much, your agency will lose leads, revenue, and the time put into acquiring them. The attitudes and styles of your team members must complement your buyers' and sellers' expectations.

I hired my first showing assistant in 2017. She was a hard worker, smart, and fearless. I wasn't planning on hiring a showing assistant, but she talked me into it with her enthusiasm and confidence. I spent hours training her, showing her what to do, and coaching her through various scenarios. After she started showing houses, I noticed a significant decrease in the number of properties put into contract. Buyers just didn't seem as motivated to write offers. When I called them to see how things were going, their answers were often vague and generalized.

I eventually received feedback that while she was driven and smart, her approach was too different from mine. The clients complained she did not clearly explain the steps of the transaction, and she didn't listen to them when they told her what they would like to do differently. Her style was efficient, fast, and to-the-point—which was ineffective because it made the clients uncomfortable. I realized that her style would work in some agencies, but it was a bad match for my agency because I specifically attracted leads who wanted to be educated in real estate during the process of buying a house.

It was my knowledge and ability to convey that knowledge that drew people to my agency. When she took over showing duties, many Leads fell out of the Sales Funnel. That lesson helped me hire the right person as a showing assistant. Skill, experience, and talent are important, but the right chemistry and style can't be taught.

Another situation to avoid is hiring staff that look out for themselves first. This creates chaos, inefficiency, and distrust in the office as well as bad experiences for the clients. To create a cohesive team, everyone has to work from the premise that the business comes first, not any particular individual. Your team members must believe that building the agency means building their careers within the agency. To create a team that works together, you (as the rockstar agent) must convey this clearly. The two factors of (1) having everyone work smoothly as a team and (2) following your lead in style play significant roles in moving Leads to Closings.

Your team will experience more opportunities this way. Happy Leads become happy Clients, and these Clients move down the funnel to more Closings. We have a rule in our office that anytime a decision is made at any point, a team member internally asks: "What is best for the firm?"

It's best if you can keep each team member in their 20 percent space. When people operate within their area of expertise, they are more confident, more satisfied, and more efficient. Working too long in their 80 percent space will affect their attitudes and increase the number of mistakes made. This has the double-whammy of slowing down your business and creating dysfunction within the team.

The fewer team members you have to do the work or the more team members you have in the wrong roles, the slower the process, the more energy required to get there, and the more Clients quit before getting to Closing.

When you have team members operating in their respective zones, your real estate Sales Funnel is smooth. It takes work to get here, but the result is worth it. That's why building the right team is so important. As noted above, those members with the right attitude, the right belief systems, and the right approach to problem solving will thrive. Those who don't will struggle and eventually quit or be fired.

The following table hangs in my office.

The Value of Talent in a Role

NON-TALENT	TALENT
Brings you problems	Finds solutions
Doesn't fulfill your needs and ends up giving you back your job	Shares your goals and fulfills your needs as a natural by-product of fulfilling their own
Doesn't know what they want and isn't searching	Knows what they want or is actively searching to know
Requires pushing	Pushes you
May not know where the existing bar is set or even what bar you're talking about	Is continually raising the bar
Doesn't care who they spend time with and repels talent from them	Demands to be associated with talent and attracts talent to them
When they try to talk action and results, they can't back it up	Talks the language of action and results

When someone on the team responds in a way inconsistent with the talent side of the table, I ask them if they are acting like talent or like non-talent. It nudges that person to accept this concept. In our world, talent is an attitude, an approach, and a value system. It has nothing to do with intelligence, resources, or natural aptitude.

⮕ KEY POINTS

- Chemistry, communication, and the time spent getting on the same page beats raw talent any day.
- You hire around *your* skills, *your* weaknesses, and *your* needs. This is a necessary component to *your* success.
- Your first hire will be the toughest to complete, with subsequent hires becoming progressively easier.
- Systems allow your team members to focus on the specific parts of their job, which increases their experience level and decreases the number of mistakes they make.
- If you love growth, love excellence, and love to reach your potential in this business, you must hire the right people and create the right systems.
- Systems help reduce errors of omission, errors of commission, make new employees' roles clearer, streamline processes, reduce lead bleed, and create a blueprint that allows for future oversight.
- In our world, talent is an attitude, an approach, and a value system. It has nothing to do with intelligence, resources, or natural aptitude.

CHAPTER THREE

GENERATE LEADS LIKE A ROCKSTAR

"You are out of business if you don't have a prospect!"

—ZIG ZIGLER

Every successful agency has strong lead generation. Your team members will look to you, as the rockstar agent, for one main purpose: bringing in leads.

How Rockstars Generate Leads

As detailed in the previous chapters, the point of being a rockstar agent is to no longer do everything yourself. What rockstar agents do well is (1) generate new leads and (2) move clients into contract. I would argue that nearly every sales job revolves around these two points of contact with a client.

By having a team to handle the other sections of the Sales Funnel, you can be more productive at those two priorities. Remember the PLAN in Chapter One? This is what allows you to do what you do best.

How successfully these two points of contact are executed will determine how profitable your business will be and how long you retain your staff. These are the two most important tasks. Hiring skilled staff and training them are the next tasks.

In short, the rockstar generates leads. Your admin assistant follows up with that lead and sets an appointment. One of your agents meets with the lead to deliver a presentation. Your showing agent takes the new client to see homes. Your contract manager writes the offers on the homes the client likes. From there, your transaction manager takes over and begins the escrow process. Showing agents arrange to meet inspectors and appraisers. Admin assistants communicate with lenders. But none of this can happen if you don't get Leads into the Sales Funnel.

The two most important metrics of lead generation are (1) appointments to deliver presentations and (2) houses put into contract. To hit your target number of appointments, you must have enough leads and follow up with them. To get clients into contract, you must find houses your clients like and make them feel comfortable writing strong offers to buy those houses. Your sales skills and psychology skills as a rockstar agent are crucial to putting clients in contract. This is why lead generation is the rockstar agent's job.

Team Lead Generation

This is not to say that members of your team won't also generate leads. This is where you can embrace your team's strengths.

In Chapter One, I described the difference between busy work and skill work. Skill work is obviously work not anyone can do, as it requires experience. Your job as a rockstar agent thus includes training your team to do skill work.

While your team supports your lead generation, they also learn from you. They hear how you handle objections on the phone, see how you read leads, and watch you put new clients at ease. They slowly build their confidence to do the same when the time is right. This is a powerful way to teach your team members.

Part of the training is also teaching team members to do MLS searches, contact listing agents to schedule showings, and answer questions the client asks. My team members go on showing tours with me. After they learn what I do, they can take over those responsibilities. Imagine having a team of people who can build your business while they build up their careers. This is how my team is structured.

This works for selling clients too. I bring promising team members to my showing appointments. I ask them for staging notes and design recommendations. I ask them to get spare keys made. I have them schedule the inspections or repairs we order.

When they sit with me during listing presentations, they hear how I deliver information, see the way the leads receive it, and watch as I conduct a delicate dance with the lead. They learn how to get the listing agreement signed. This not only makes my job easier as the listing agent, but it also helps them learn how to land their own leads and convert them to clients. I firmly believe this teaching approach is the future of real estate sales.

Most leads will come from your sphere of influence, your open houses, your online sources, your social media, and your past clients. But your buyer's agents can hold open houses on your listings and find their own leads that way. Your assistants can call past clients to ask if they know of anyone who is looking to buy or sell a home. They can manage your social media and send newsletters to your email list. When you have a team of people working on lead generation, you obviously find more leads than on your own. When you show your team the value of creating leads, they take more ownership in the success of the agency. More leads create job security and more opportunities to make more money. Offering bonuses for Leads that reach Closing in the Sales Funnel creates a natural incentive for your team to increase their efforts in lead generation and lead follow-up.

Lead Follow-Up Systems and Support

It is at this point that the CRM system and checklists discussed in Chapter Two become a necessary component of your business. In our office, leads are entered into our CRM. The CRM automatically sends out introductory messages to the leads and reminders to the appropriate team members to follow up with the leads. An auto plan via the CRM reminds the team members of the next task in the series. As one auto plan is completed, the next one is assigned.

The following describes how my team assists in the Sales Funnel, moving buyer Leads to client Closings. It highlights the job duties of the inside sales agent, showing assistant/agent, and transaction coordinator. This example uses three auto plans: the Buyer Lead Auto Plan, the New-Buyer Auto Plan, and the Buyer Pending Auto Plan.

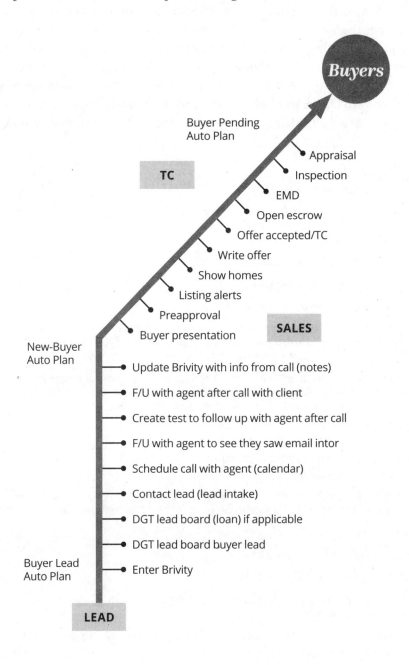

The Buyer Lead Auto Plan

The inside-sales agent prepares the buyer leads before I speak to them. Before this happens, though, the agent is notified about a new lead by our CRM system, or I advise them of a lead that came directly to me. The agent tags the lead in the CRM with the Buyer Lead Auto Plan. This process automatically notifies and reminds the agent of the steps listed in the diagram above. The agent follows up with the lead to gather information I need to secure the lead during the presentation. This information is collected via a Lead Sheet (see the figure below), which is a list of questions the agent asks the lead. It is then stored in the CRM for future reference.

Date:
Buyer's Name:
Agent Assigned:

1. Can you give me a brief description on what you were looking to do (GOALS) and what's important to you? Is this a house to sell, live in, a rental property, are you looking to house hack, etc.?

2. Have you ever purchased real estate before?

3. Where do you live currently? (if renting)

4. Have you been preapproved for a loan yet?

YES: We like to get a second opinion from lenders as David wants to help you save money on your loan as well as the house. Can I have David send you a link to a 15-minute application that will help him get a feel for how you can save on your loan?

NO: Great! I can set up a call with David but he's going to need to know what price range you're comfortable with before he can give you advice. Can I connect you with someone to get started on that while working on your consultation?

5. Who else is going to be involved in the process? — We ask this so we can make sure each decision maker is valued an included in the process
- what kind of down payment do you have?
- where is it coming from?
- is anyone else going to be on the mortgage?
- is there a family member or gf/bf that is going to be involved with your decision?

Now for the fun stuff!

What are you most excited about?

What are you most nervous bout?

What do you think we should know about you to make sure you have a great experience and love this?

6. Anything else you think we should be aware of before taking the next step?

The New-Buyer Auto Plan

After I conduct a successful lead presentation, my showing agent assigns the New-Buyer Auto Plan. My showing assistant handles the steps between a client's preapproval and showing homes. The showing assistant calls the client daily for check-ins, looks for homes, shows homes, and lands on a property the buyer likes. At this point, I step back in to put the buyer in contract, and I notify my transaction coordinator.

The Buyer Pending Auto Plan

Once in contract, my transaction coordinator assigns the Buyer Pending Auto Plan and begins the escrow process. The transaction coordinator schedules the inspections, appraisals, and other necessary elements of an escrow. They also notify the showing assistant of the times and locations of these events so the agent can be on site. The transaction coordinator completes the paperwork required to stay in compliance, monitors contractual timelines, and notifies me in the event something goes wrong (e.g., a bad inspection report, low appraisal, loan approval problems). They then gather the information I need to solve these problems.

To review, I generate leads. My inside sales agent brings the Lead to the point where I can secure them. The showing assistant then finds the home our new Client wants to buy. I step back in to put the Client in Contract where it continues down the funnel until it becomes a Closing. As long as I generate leads, I create opportunities for everyone else.

The other responsibility I have is putting Clients in Contract. If I do these two components well, I keep my team busy and happy, increase their skills, and grow the agency.

Lead Generation Evolution

Top-producing agents already know how to generate leads, but the process evolves when you reach rockstar agent status. Consider the agent who makes their living by calling For Sale by Owners (FSBOs) and expired listings. This person starts the arduous process of dialing sellers one by one to try to land a listing appointment. If an appointment is made, the agent goes to the home to meet with the sellers, does whatever it takes to secure the listing, and then begins the process of selling the house.

While this method works, it is both time-consuming and intensive. Only a skilled salesperson can use expired listings and convince a seller to meet with them. It then takes an elevated level of skill to convince them to sign a listing agreement at a meeting. Once signed, these sellers might need an inordinate amount of time and psychology skills to stay happy as they likely had an unpleasant experience with their previous agent. Otherwise, why do they have an expired listing? This model produces results, but those results are dependent on the agent's skill and time.

Knocking on doors in neighborhoods, holding open houses, and converting Zillow or Realtor leads to prospects also requires strong sales skills and market knowledge. As a rockstar agent, you must generate leads that are easier to convert and easier to leverage. You'll want to capitalize on your personality, relationships, and reputation to draw leads that are loyal to your brand. These people will be happier with your service, be open to the idea of speaking with your assistants, and appreciative of when a team member reaches out to schedule the next step. Ask yourself how you'd feel in the following situations when dealing with a team member versus a rockstar.

Car Dealership Analogy

You are shopping at a car dealership but don't want to make a decision yet. You're greeted by the salesperson who was recommended to you by a friend. This person is not pushy and listens to your concerns. The salesperson offers their advice, waits for you to suggest cars you prefer, then shows you only those that match what you want. When you have questions, the salesperson has answers; plus, you are given answers to questions you didn't even realize you should be asking. You feel so comfortable that you decide to buy a car that day. You go into their office, you sign the contract, you are told about the rest of the sales process, and you are thanked for your business.

The finance manager then walks in to help you sign the loan paperwork. This is followed by sessions with the service department representative, the warranty provider, and the customer service manager. You deal with each person. At the end, you drive off the lot with your new car.

Were you upset when you had to talk to the finance manager or the warranty provider? Did you walk out when the service department representative explained how to make appointments to service your vehicle? Odds are, once trust was established and you were prepared for the process, you had no problem submitting to the established system and sticking with it to the end.

Now, consider this alternative.

You are looking at cars online. You find an advertisement for a Honda Civic priced 20 percent below all other online Civics. You go to the dealership and ask about the car in the ad. Then you're left alone for thirty minutes in the showroom until a salesperson asks if they can show you around the lot while another person investigates the specific Honda. An hour later, you've seen every car in the lot and have been pressured to buy most of them. Then you're told that the Civic at that price is no longer available.

The salesperson introduces you to the finance manager to discuss what you're eligible to borrow and the warranty representative to learn about how the program works. The salesperson walks out, leaving you with two strangers. They don't have the car you came in to see, and you have no trust in this dealership. Do you continue the process to buy a car or walk out?

While both dealerships likely make money, only one sales model allows a trusted team approach. In the same way, rockstar agents generate leads in a way that gives their team members responsibilities and creates a cohesive experience for the client.

The following are more ways you can generate leads for your team members.

Sphere of Influence

Your personal sphere of influence (SOI) is your best resource for leads. People want to work with a Realtor they know, like, and trust. Who better than those in your daily life? I'm continually amazed at the amount of time and money agents spend on online leads, trying to convert people they don't know to work with them while routinely ignoring the people who would love to work with them.

Members of your SOI are also more likely to be willing to work with your team. When you hire your first assistant and transaction coordinator, you will see just how powerful your SOI can be. It becomes simpler to identify clients when you have your assistant or transaction coordinator call your friends, family, and former clients to see if they know of anyone looking to buy or sell a house. Your staff's connection to you will put easy referrals in your pipeline.

When a member of your team calls anyone in your database, they should start their conversation with: "[Rockstar name] asked me to call and... ." This opening line creates an immediate connection between the person in the SOI and your team member because they have a mutual bond with you. It gives credibility and makes the conversation easier to have. The following are scripts your team can use when calling people in your database on your behalf.

The Past Client

Agent: Hey there, it's [Name] with the David Greene Team. David asked me to call and see how things were going with the house! It looks like it's been over a year since you bought and we just wanted to ask if you needed anything. Is the AC still working correctly? Any issues with the sprinkler system we can help find someone for?

[Answer.]

Agent: Glad to hear it's all going well. Prices are rising and we are trying to find new homes for more buyers before they get any higher. Do you know anyone looking to buy or sell we can contact and see if we can help?

The Possible Listing

Agent: Hey! It's [Name] with the David Greene Team. David asked me to give you a call to ask a few questions to see if we could save you any money. Do you have a minute?

[Answer.]

Agent: Great. First, what's your current interest rate?

[Answer.]

Agent: Thank you. I've written that down. If you could refinance and save on your monthly payment, would you want us to investigate that for you?

[Answer.]

Agent: Second, do you know what your house is worth right now? [If no:] That's not a problem; most people don't check it very often. I ask because home values have been increasing and David likes us to help our clients track their net worth. Do you mind if I investigate this for you and send you an email telling you what it's worth and how it stacks up to other homes in the neighborhood?

[Answer.]

Agent: I'd be happy to!

The Client Appreciation Party

Agent: Hello, this is [Name] with the David Greene Team. David asked me to call because he hasn't spoken to you in a while. He wanted to make sure we invited you to our next client appreciation party. I know you aren't technically a client of the team, but David said you're basically family, so he wanted to see you at the party. Do you mind if I text you the details and the address and you can let me know if you can RSVP?

[Answer.]

Agent: Sweet! Can you do me one other favor? David's going to ask if you know anyone looking to buy or sell at the event. Can you keep an eye and ear out for others who may be looking to get into the market, so we can invite them as well? It's a fantastic way for everyone to get comfortable with each other. Please invite anyone you think would be interested, and just let me know. Thanks!

The Family Member

Agent: Hey there, this is [Name] with David's real estate team. David asked me to reach out and say he's sorry he's been busy lately, but he wanted me to call everyone who is most important to him and see if there's anything you need. Can you think of anything I can tell David you need right now?

[Answer.]

Agent: Our goal is to sell one hundred homes this year, and I know it would mean the world to David if you were able to help us get there. Have you heard of anyone looking to buy or sell that I could call and introduce myself to? [If no:] Would you do me a favor? Can you keep an ear out and let me know if you do hear about someone? I'll call back in a month or two to check in. Anything you'd like me to tell David?

[Answer.]

Agent: Okay, that's great. Good talking to you!

Your team can have conversations like this with your former coworkers, circle of friends, parents of your children's friends, etc. The opportunities are limitless when it comes to your SOI. Those people will be talking with a salesperson who works for someone already known to them, who they like, and who they trust. This supports the ideal that a team needs to have cohesiveness, chemistry, and share your style. The more your staff looks and sounds like you, the easier your SOI will accept communicating with them.

Past Clients

The other area where top-producing agents blow it, besides not following up with leads, is not staying in touch with past clients. The temptation is to always look toward converting new leads, so many agents forget to look "backward" at their past clients. This is a big mistake. Meeting new clients requires building trust and rapport from scratch and performing the delicate dance of getting to know one another. This takes time and effort. It's natural to lose some prospects in your funnel because of personality conflicts. Why not focus your efforts on people who have already shown they like working with you?

Another advantage to prospecting past clients is that they have most likely already worked with your team members too. There's no awkward introductory phase. This is such a powerful lead generation tool that I recently hired new assistants so I could promote my first assistant, Krista. She has become so familiar to my previous clients that her ability to generate leads from my database has outpaced the impact she had as a transaction coordinator and my personal assistant.

My team has campaigns to send Baskin-Robbins gift cards to clients' children on their birthdays, to send congratulations to clients on their home and wedding anniversaries, to send invitations to events I'm throwing, and more. This effort to stay in touch with past clients pays off with referrals.

Social Media

According to Oberlo.com, in 2021 approximately 45 percent of the world's population used social media.[1] As social media gains in popularity, more eyeballs are looking at it more frequently. If you want your business to thrive into the future, learn how to harness the power of social media. Oberlo.com shares the following additional statistics:

Facebook remains the most widely used social media platform with 68 percent of U.S. adults claiming they have a profile[2]; additionally, 90.4 percent of Millennials, 77.5 percent of Gen X, and 48.2 percent of Baby Boomers are active social media users[3]. People spend more than two hours a day on social media, on average[4], and 54 percent of social media users search for products online[5]. Seventy-one percent of those who had a positive experience with a company they found on social media would recommend it to a friend or family member, and 80 percent of all social media interactions occur through mobile means[6]. Finally, almost 50

1   Maryam Mohsin, "10 Social Media Statistics You Need to Know in 2021," Oberlo, September 6, 2022, https://www.oberlo.com/blog/social-media-marketing-statistics.

2   Aaron Smith and Monica Anderson, "Social Media Use in 2018," Pew Research Center, March 1, 2018, https://www.pewresearch.org/internet/2018/03/01/social-media-use-in-2018/.

3   "US Social Media Users, by Generation, 2019," eMarketer, August 2018, https://www.emarketer.com/chart/226029/US-Social-Media-Users-by-Generation-2019-of-population.

4   Simon Kemp, "Digital 2021: Global Overview Report," DataReportal, January 27, 2021, https://datareportal.com/reports/digital-2021-global-overview-report.

5   Chris Beer, "Chart of the Day: Social Browsers Engage with Brands," GWI, June 13, 2018, https://blog.gwi.com/chart-of-the-day/social-browsers-brand/.

6   "32 Social Media Marketing Statistics That Will Change The Way You Think About Social Media," Lyfe Marketing, June 13, 2022, https://www.lyfemarketing.com/blog/social-media-marketing-statistics/.

percent of social media users depend on "influencers" for recommendations[7], and 73 percent of social media marketers believe social media advertising has been effective for their business[8].

It's safe to say that future usage numbers for social media will be even higher. If people are going to social media and are shopping while they're there, it's important that you give them something to look at. If almost half of social media users admit to following influencers, it's important that you become an influencer to your own audience. When it comes to real estate, be the person they listen to. Your team can help you do this.

Creating content will keep you top of mind in your SOI. This can be professionally made videos, infographics, pictures of happy clients, or you simply documenting your day and posting about it. Choose the social media you feel most comfortable using, and have your team help you stay consistent in scheduling posts.

A creative team member can film you conducting a mock presentation, for example, then edit the video and post it on your social media. If you don't have time to reply to comments in the posts, have your team members respond. Creating engagement on your behalf is great for lead generation. When a team member finds a serious lead, it'll be easy for them to update you on the conversation up to that point so you can take it from there. This allows inside sales agents to have conversations with dozens of potential leads and then bring you into the conversation only when a lead is serious enough to warrant your time and attention.

Social media also makes it easy to market your past sales. My team posts every listing. We use different pictures of the same properties to showcase the listings, which prevents us from looking like we posted the same content several times. When your business is in a lull, you can post the same listing five separate times to make it appear as though you have more business than you do. This will create engagement on your social media. Here are ways to post about the same home:

1. **Coming Soon!** (feature a picture of the front of the house with a second picture of the home's best feature)
2. **Just Listed!** (feature a picture of the front of the house)
3. **Pending!** (feature pictures of the interior or backyard)
4. **Just Sold!** (feature the same pictures as above)

7   Olivia Osborne, "To #ad or not to #ad – insights on influencer marketing," Four Communications, February 18, 2019, https://fourcommunications.com/insights-on-influencer-marketing/.

8   "State of Social 2019," Buffer, January 2020, https://buffer.com/state-of-social-2019.

5. **Congrats to our clients!** (feature a picture of the smiling clients standing in front of the house while holding some form of your marketing; you can also tag your clients)

Posts like these remind your followers that you sell homes. They also keep you top of mind and make it easier for them to engage with you. People love commenting on attractive houses or congratulating your clients on their accomplishments. This also makes it easier to contact you when people are thinking about selling their own home or buying a new one.

Making yourself approachable, available, and easy to contact are important factors in your lead generation. It's possible for people to think you're too busy for them, but when your followers see you interacting in the comments section (or your team commenting on your behalf), you appear open to communication. When you make videos commenting on the state of the market, on your personal thoughts, or on things that are important to you, your followers feel they can reach out and connect with you.

Social media allows you access to a large database without having to communicate with everyone individually. Much like Iron Man's armor, it is a tool that allows you to take your strengths (i.e., your personality, knowledge, and experience) and amplify them to reach more people than you could without it. This principle is true for a rockstar agent's team too. When your office is generating leads, you must think about how to have the largest reach with the biggest influence in the smallest amount of time. There isn't a much more effective tool for this than social media.

I note here that you should post about more than just work. Your sphere follows you, and it was your relationship with them that made them want to work with you. It's completely appropriate to post quotes that affect you, images that move you, and pictures of your friends and family (with their permission). Posts like these offer a window into your life and your heart. For those who know and love you, they appreciate being a part of your life, even when your more demanding work schedule makes that tough.

IDX Website

An Internet Data Exchange (IDX) allows those visiting a real estate site to search for homes on the MLS. IDX is used on popular websites like Zillow, Redfin, and Realtor.com; it's also available for personal agent sites.

I use IDX on my website (www.DavidGreene24.com) to show my clients houses that fit their criteria, and I encourage them to search for homes there as well. While it's true they can use any home site, having them use my site offers advantages to my business, such as lead generation, closing more deals, and staying in better touch with my clients. Other advantages include:

The Ability to Follow What Your Client Sees

When your clients look at houses on different websites, you don't know what they're looking at. When they look on your site, you know exactly what they're viewing. With IDX on my site, I can see which houses clients have viewed, how many times they viewed them, and which they marked as favorites.

Clients can also request to view specific homes and request information such as disclosures and inspection reports. Using IDX on my website allows my team to understand a client's preferences. We notice when a client who originally wanted to look at homes in one area starts searching for homes in another area. This is a clear indication we need to talk about possibly adjusting criteria, which is made possible by IDX.

Notifications When Your Client Is Looking at Properties Again

We have all been in the situation where a buyer takes a pause in their search. We often lose touch with this client, and they don't always tell us when they start looking again. This results in us losing the client to another Realtor without us even knowing it.

A solution to lost revenue is receiving notifications from IDX that this client is back online looking at houses. Once you receive this notification, you can reach out, reestablish the connection, and pick up the process in the Sales Funnel where you left off.

Forced Registration/Lead Capture

This is definitely my favorite IDX feature. Before someone new can enter my site and view homes, they must register information. (My website collects a name, phone number, and email.) This information is then automatically uploaded into my CRM, which sends an automatic notification that there is a lead interested in buying homes. The CRM also creates a profile for the prospect with their contact information and assigns a New-Buyer Auto Plan (discussed earlier).

Once you have a system like this set up, you can look for ways to capture more leads from your site. For example, you can share your website URL (with the handy IDX) on social media, email the URL to your database, or text it to friends. You can also publish it on materials handed out at open houses or on business cards for whenever you meet someone who expresses interest in buying or selling a home. I even put my website link on my Instagram and Facebook pages. Anyone who clicks on the link goes to the site and must register to look at the MLS listed homes. The CRM does its automatic work, and these leads are captured. I am collecting leads from everyone who connects to my website. This process means I don't ever lose leads.

Open Houses

Open houses are a staple of every successful real estate agent's lead generation, and they become even more important when you have a team helping you take advantage of them. In *SOLD*, I discussed in detail how to succeed at open houses. As your business grows, though, it becomes increasingly difficult to justify the return on investment on open houses in generating leads. They are a great tool and a huge revenue source, but if you're doing your job well, you should outgrow them as you reach rockstar agent status.

This doesn't mean you stop doing them or that they lose their value. It just means you need your team to do them instead. With a team of buyer's agents and salespeople, you can hold several open houses over a weekend. By sharing your knowledge and skills, you equip the agents on your team to generate leads for themselves.

I recommend having an open house system to help keep your salespeople accountable. My system consists of the following:

1. Provide all the materials the agents will need at the open house.
2. Provide open houses for them to hold; ask other agents to let your agents hold their listings open.
3. Have them knock on doors in the neighborhoods beforehand.
4. Have them collect contact information from every attendee.
5. Provide training on how to convert leads into appointments and then into clients.
6. Have them insert every lead into your database and have them assign an Open House Lead Auto Plan for each lead.

7. Have them follow up in three ways over the next twenty-four hours (e.g., phone call, personalized video, mailed notecard, email, etc.)
8. Put all attendees into a database or MLS drip campaign that will alert them to new listings and check in weekly after that until an appointment can be set.

Open houses allow your agents to improve their sales and interaction skills, convert leads into clients, and post their activity on their social media for their own SOI to see. By having your agents do this work, you amplify their opportunity to gain new Leads and to put them into your agency's Sales Funnel. Open houses aren't agent specific. Leads who walk in the door often don't have an agent or aren't happy with the one they hired. Therefore, providing this opportunity for your agents increases how Leads are generated and makes it inclusive for your entire team.

Outside Agents

Rockstar agents produce a lot of business and, as a natural consequence, know a lot of other agents. You will both remember interactions if they are pleasant and agreeable. This provides an opportunity for outside agents to generate leads for you when you prove to them that your system is airtight and your results are positive.

The first way to capitalize on outside agents is to ask them if you can be their referral partner for areas they don't service. I use this method often. Not every agent is willing to travel to or service the same areas that I do. I make it clear that I'd be happy to become their go-to agent for that area. I also let them know if they ever experience personal difficulty, need time away, or become overworked, I am willing to help them out. Many deals come my way from these relationships.

In addition to securing deals for your business, you can also secure agents and employees. By changing your mindset from finding leads to finding talent, you can bring in proven, successful, experienced, and hardworking agents to service your pipeline of clientele. These agents will help you by both closing the deals you bring in and bringing in deals from their own spheres. It's a win-win for everyone!

As your business grows, you will need help servicing your leads. It's best to start planning now for how you will find talented people to do that. Keep this in mind when speaking with other agents you like or whose work you respected on the other side of the transaction.

Lenders

As a rockstar agent, you generate a large number of buyer leads, as do your teams of buyer's agents and showing assistants. This will create a large number of buyer referrals who need to be preapproved. Most agents have a preferred lender to service these clients and make sure the deals close on time.

Rockstar agents make it clear to their lender partners that they expect value in return for all this business. One way for lenders to do this is to send leads your way. There are laws and regulations that prohibit how lenders and agents compensate one another, so check with your lawyer about Real Estate Settlement Procedures Act (RESPA) requirements. This just means developing a two-way relationship with your lender that is aboveboard. You are simply supporting their business and they are doing the same for yours.

Lenders are an often overlooked part of a lead generation strategy, but they can be an incredible resource for the top of your Sales Funnel.

New Agents in the Office

Do you remember how you felt as a new agent in the office? I sure do. I had a million questions, a massive amount of anxiety, and a strong need for direction that I didn't get. New agents have untapped databases and SOIs that are ready to be marketed to, but they don't know what to do. These agents often start hard on lead generation, get a fish on the hook, and have no idea how to reel it in. When that happens, they need someone who does know what to do. That person can be you.

Forming relationships with the new agents in your office can be fruitful for you and for them, but you must hire the right people with the right attitude. I start promising agents in my office as showing assistants, which allows me to see who will and won't be a good mix in my office. I watch them work with experienced agents and see who is willing to give up a chunk of their commission in exchange for learning how to secure and close deals. If you put strong systems in place and have the right instinct for hiring, new agents will generate leads and become talented members of your team.

Meetup Events

You can create a real estate Meetup event for those interested in learning more about real estate. Attendees can be leads, new investors, and other agents. This is a fantastic way to add new leads into your database, and you get invaluable in-person time with them or those already in your database. A Meetup event allows you to become more than just a branded logo to those attending. They get to see a personal side of you they often miss out on.

The topics you choose for your Meetup can range from learning how to do first-time homebuyer presentations and how to sell a home for top dollar to how to invest in real estate and how to partner with a lender and handle real estate financing. Keep the topic interesting, and people will show up to learn about it.

My team uses Eventbrite for reservations to my Meetups. Eventbrite captures attendees' info (name, number, and email) on a registration page, and attendees must input this information before they can receive details on where and when the event will take place. This list is then manually uploaded to my database and the CRM automatically assigns a Buyer Lead Auto Plan to each registrant. Meetups grow my database and connect me with those who follow me without requiring any action on my part. This is exactly why Meetup events are such powerful tools for rockstar agents with teams. You are the reason why anyone attends, but your team does the follow-up work of making connections, asking for referrals, and growing the relationship.

I also use Meetup events to help grow the databases of individual team members located in other regions. For instance, I held an event in the Sacramento, California, area for my Sacramento-based agent, Kyle Renke. Kyle organized the event using my database, and my team advertised it and ran the process. I introduced Kyle at the top of the Meetup, and he was responsible for all follow-up with attendees. He has developed ongoing relationships in the area as a trusted member of my team (and as a teacher of the curriculum I created).

This format allowed Kyle to meet attendees in an inviting environment and vice versa. It also gave Kyle the opportunity to become comfortable speaking in front of groups, developing a presence, finding his voice, and representing me as I wanted to be represented. As of this writing, Kyle has worked full-time in real estate for only three months and currently has ten deals in escrow. Meetups work.

Lead Capture Strategies

You will be generating most of your team's business opportunities. A system with checklists, as described in Chapter Two, keeps everything under control, and these leads provide your team members with the experience to learn your business. This is a huge perk you can offer when interviewing new staff.

Lead bleed, as you now know, causes the highest revenue loss. This lesson was no different for me. I had to learn the hard way how much money I was losing.

In 2017, I promoted Krista and hired a new assistant who had previously worked for a major airline assisting C-suite executives. While she had exceptional problem-solving skills, I failed to recognize how important it was to teach her the value of a lead. At one Meetup, an attendee told me that he was thrilled to finally meet me and had recently put his East Bay Area home under contract. I jokingly asked why he did not use me as his listing agent and let him know I could have gotten him more money for the property. He told me that he had emailed me to take the listing, but no one replied.

I looked on my computer after the fact, and I found his email. That's when I realized my assistant had read it but not notified me. When I spoke to her about it, she told me she didn't know what to do when someone asked that question, so she ignored his email and focused on the tasks I had given her. Suffice it to say, I wasn't very happy. That was an easy $20,000 commission the team lost out on.

I took time away from work from November 2018 through January 2019. When I returned in February and looked at the books, I saw that the team had lost money during those months despite selling homes. A quick investigation revealed that no one had been following up with leads that came into my email. If leads were not calling the office number, they were not being pursued. This was also a significant loss.

When I stepped back in and responded to leads, our revenue quadrupled. That's how I learned that my biggest enemy is lead bleed. From that point forward, I developed the systems and checklists to eliminate it as much as humanly possible.

Lead Boards

Our Lead Board is one tab in a Google Sheet where we track leads and the steps that move a Lead into a Client, which is another tab. The Lead Board tab looks like this:

NAME	LEAD SOURCE	INTRO CALL	NOTES ENTERED	PRESENTATION SCHEDULED	PRESENTATION PREPPED	PRESENTATION DELIVERED	BUYER REP SIGNED
Tom Smith	SOI	yes	no	yes	yes	yes	yes
Susan Tran	SEO	yes	yes	yes	no	no	no
Mary Barnes	Referral	no	yes	yes	yes	yes	yes

Provided your inside sales agents enter the leads into the sheet immediately and your team checks the Lead Board every day, the odds of dropping a lead become very low. Because of this manual friction point, I harp that the first thing to do when an inside sales agent is notified of a lead is to enter that info into the board even before an agent calls the lead. I tell my team to leave this Lead Board up on a separate computer monitor and check it every day to move Leads to the next step in the funnel.

Once Leads progress to the last column (Buyer Rep Signed), we move them to Active Buyers, which is the next tab in the spreadsheet. They are then tracked until they reach escrow and enter the next step in the Sales Funnel: Contracts. When a client goes into escrow, they are moved off the "lead sheet" and are entered into a separate sheet managed by our transaction coordinator.

Inside Sales Agent

Inside sales agents (ISAs) enter the leads in the Lead Board and into our CRM, and they then assign a buyer or listing agent. ISAs also assist with generating leads, but their primary responsibility is to eliminate lead bleed.

You may wonder if a position like this is necessary or if your buyer's agents or showing assistants can do this. They can, but I urge you to remember how expensive lead bleed is. I've found that ISAs offer the best overall return on investment in my business. In addition to making sure leads are quickly connected with an agent, ISAs:

- Check my personal email and my business email as well as the general team email daily for leads.
- Answer the office phone when leads call.
- Monitor my text service for leads.
- Check my YouTube, Facebook, and Instagram (IG) accounts for comments that could be leads.
- Check my IG direct messages for leads.
- Contact IG followers in my area to ask if they are in need of real estate services.

Multiple Points of Overlap

Every time a lead is passed from one person to another, there is a chance it will get lost. The same is true when a client is passed from a buyer's agent to a showing assistant and from a buyer's agent to a transaction coordinator. A system with multiple points of overlap lowers these risks. Your ISA (or an administrative assistant) needs to ensure that your buyer and listing agents are contacting their assigned leads and setting up appointments. This can be done most effectively by having the ISA monitor the Lead Board daily.

Here's how the overlap works: Your buyer's agent receives a call about a lead while at a showing. The agent logs the intro call into the Lead Board. However, the agent forgets to follow up with the lead for a new-buyer presentation. Enter your ISA. By monitoring the Lead Board, your ISA notices that a presentation has not yet been scheduled. The ISA then contacts the lead directly to schedule the presentation or reminds the agent to do it.

This prevents big money from being lost. It becomes especially important when you consider the multifaceted impact a single client can have on your team's growth. One buyer can work with several administrative assistants, a showing assistant, and a buyer's agent. When your team debriefs after each closing, the rest of the team benefits from the knowledge of this sale. It's not possible to measure the exponential benefits of keeping leads, turning them into clients, and bringing them to closings in a team atmosphere.

Weekly Check-Ins

I hold weekly check-ins with the agents who are the sales leaders in my team structure. A sales leader is an agent who manages other team members and is responsible for helping them. In the figure below (which I also shared in *SKILL*), you see that the check-ins flow from me to the buyer's agents (B/As) and from the buyer's agents to the showing assistants (S/As).

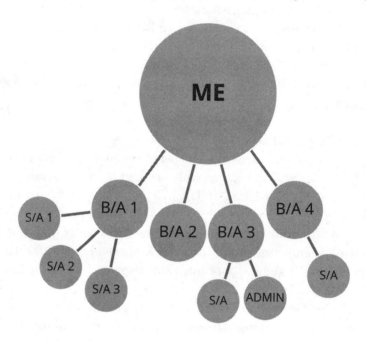

The check-in structure is simple. You meet in-person or virtually. In my meetings with buyer's agents, we pull up the Lead Board to discuss each person they have been assigned. These weekly check-ins accomplish several things:

1. **Staff are held accountable for their work goals.** Knowing they will be meeting with their manager (and you could choose to not share leads with buyer's agents in the future) helps everyone to do their best work.

2. **Staff are guided through problems.** This is obvious for buyer's agents and showing assistants. For buyer's agents, each lead is a different puzzle to solve because they require different psychological approaches. As the agent with the most experience, your insight and advice on moving people through the Sales Funnel will

bring experience to the agents and put money in both of your bank accounts.

3. **Staff see things through your eyes.** What your team members truly want is advice and guidance. For the buyer's agents, you share your perspective as a rockstar agent. They joined your team because they want to be like you. The advice you share with the buyer's agents can then be shared with the staff that they supervise.

4. **You learn who's effective (and who's not).** As a rockstar agent, you are responsible for multiple components of your business, and it's easy to lose track of how staff are performing. Weekly check-ins with buyer's agents make it clear how many leads they have, how many clients they have put in contract, and how many properties have closed. Weekly check-ins of buyer's agents with their staff also stop problems in their tracks. You need this level of insight and accountability the bigger your business grows.

The Road Map

What I've explained here and in Chapter Two is the step-by-step road map that moves Leads through the Sales Funnel to Closing. The road map includes the Lead Board, multiple points of overlap, and weekly check-ins. Finally, remember that lead generation is the most important step in your business. The sources you market to and how you market yourself will evolve as your business grows.

➡ KEY POINTS

- What rockstar agents do well is (1) generate new leads and (2) move clients into contract.
- Your sales skills and psychology skills as a rockstar agent are crucial to putting clients in contract. This is why lead generation is the rockstar agent's job.
- Your personal sphere of influence (SOI) is your best resource for leads.
- As social media gains popularity, more eyeballs are looking at it more frequently. If you want your business to thrive into the future, learn how to harness the power of social media.

- Making yourself approachable, available, and easy to contact are important factors in your lead generation.
- Open houses allow your agents to improve their sales and interaction skills, convert leads into clients, and post their activity on their social media for their own SOI to see.
- Forming relationships with the new agents in your office can be fruitful for you and for them but you must hire the right people with the right attitude.
- Provided your inside sales agents enter the leads into the sheet immediately and your team checks the Lead Board every day, the odds of dropping a lead become very low.
- A system with multiple points of overlap lowers risks.
- The sources you market to and how you market yourself will evolve as your business grows.

CHAPTER FOUR

YOUR TARGET CLIENTELE

"The way you position yourself at the beginning of a relationship has a profound impact on where you end up."

—RON KARR

Inexperienced people tend to err on the side of FOMO, or fear of missing out. I see this with new financial investors all the time. The fear of missing out on the "great" deal is stronger than the discipline to focus on a specific set of criteria. This FOMO causes investors to cast too wide a net, which leads to too many investments that they can't seriously analyze in a meaningful way.

The same is true of real estate agents. Those who make themselves available to all types of clients in all types of markets spread themselves too thin, which means they can't satisfy anyone. This results in a lot of work and no closings. To first scale your business, you had to niche down to the types of clients you wanted to work with. Now, as a rockstar agent, you'll need an even tighter filter. Targeting the wrong clientele for your business will prevent you from closing with the right ones.

The first step is knowing who you want to work with and, more importantly, who wants to work with you. Who will most appreciate your rockstar services, skills, and knowledge? Who will have expectations you are not likely to meet? The right clientele will energize you. Plus, maintaining the right level of work will keep you in love with your job and grow your business.

As new agents, we all had to take what we could get. As a top-producing agent, you could be pickier. As a rockstar agent, you must be even more selective.

Clientele Who Know You, Like You, and Trust You

People want to do business with those they know, like, and trust. You probably already learned this as a top-producing agent, and it is doubly true when choosing your clientele as a rockstar agent. Use "know you, like you, trust you" as a blueprint for your rockstar agent business.

Know You

This is the first step because this is where we have the most control. Put everyone you meet into your database. This marks them as leads and creates an opportunity to develop a stronger relationship with them. Through this stronger relationship, you become more liked and more trusted. Rockstar agents are always looking to meet new people and to be known by as many people as possible. You can't be liked or trusted by someone who doesn't know you, which is why the Meetup events mentioned in the previous chapter are also important.

Like You

This may be the least influential of the three factors, but it is still important. People want to work with people they like. This especially helps when you reach rockstar agent status. The double-edged sword of being a rockstar agent is that more people will be interested in working with you, but they may also be hesitant to reach out because of your status. If leads are hesitant, that hurts your business.

Being likable makes it easier to set appointments, to get calls returned, and to build trust faster. Developing an agreeable personality is within everyone's control. Many agents I've met are unapproachable, boring, or unengaging. Top-producing agents, on the other hand, tend to be friendly, fun, and fast to engage. The process of buying a property is stressful, so being an agent with a convivial personality can lower a client's anxiety. This is true even for those clients who are subconsciously nervous.

Most clients decide on which agent to hire based on a gut feeling. This feeling is frequently affected by factors like likability. People often confuse likability with having a trustworthy character. While you need both, many believe they are the same. Use this to your advantage!

Trust You

Being likable makes it easier for people to trust you, but so is being forthright. Clients are asked to blindly trust us with the biggest purchase or sale of their lifetimes. Because our work is based 100 percent on commission, there will always be a concern about conflicting interests. This is a unique situation and a bit of a contradiction in terms: an agent's fiduciary position requires them to work in the best interest of the client but not be paid for it.

This complicated relationship is the root cause of much of the mistrust in our profession. Our clients know we want a commission. We know we want a commission. This commission is a powerful motivating factor, so you must make it easy for your clients to trust you.

Agents must hold themselves above reproach. We will share unwelcome news about a sale, purchase, preapproval, or something else along the Sales Funnel. While many agents worry this will turn their clients off, it often has the opposite effect: It builds powerful trust between you and your clients. Telling a client you don't think they should buy a certain house or letting them know their house is not worth what they expected can give you credibility. This actually makes it easier for them to work with you.

When someone trusts you, they will follow your advice even when they are scared or nervous. They will let you lead them even when their fear tells them to stop. They will listen to you and see things from your perspective more than their own.

In *SKILL*, I introduced a concept called "frame control," which I learned from the book *Pitch Anything* by Oren Klaff. Frame control involves getting others to understand things from your perspective. The point is to improve your skill at being heard. This skill, ultimately, affects your success. Controlling the frame means controlling the direction of the conversation and getting the other side to see the virtue in your opinion or perspective. If your clients' fears get out of whack, controlling the frame allows you to lower the impact of their emotions. If you can see the benefit of your clients buying a certain home through your twenty-year agent perspective, but they can't see past the dry rot in the inspection report, it's very important that you get them to see things from your side, for both your sake and theirs.

Trust will move things forward and, when necessary, help you pivot to a new direction when that is best.

For example, when your clients are attracted to the low price point of a condo, but you know a detached home would be best for their lifestyle, the clients are not realizing that an interest rate below 4 percent makes the price difference of $50,000 between the condo and the single-family home only about $225 a month. The clients aren't considering the condo's homeowner association fees of $200 a month or the limited ways they are allowed to improve the property's value. For these clients, the condo is a far inferior investment. As you try to persuade them to see the bigger picture—that in the long run, the more expensive home is better for them than the less expensive condo—all they see is you angling for a higher commission. The harder you advise them, the greedier you look, and the more influence you lose. Like a fly in a spider's web, the more you struggle to show them your side, the more constricted you become.

If there is no trust in this relationship, you're in trouble. If there is, they will eventually see that you are looking out for their best interests. When your clients trust you, they relate to you more easily, and then it's easier for them to see your perspective. As seen in the previous scenario, this is important because you have far more experience in real estate than your clients do. Unless they're agents themselves, they can't know what you know. Frame control works when you know something the other person doesn't, and that knowledge would benefit them.

People You Relate To

With frame control being such an important component in the client-agent relationship, you'll want to target those with whom you can build a strong relationship; that is, those who are more apt to like, know, and trust you. One way to do this is to talk to people within your sphere of influence. The more you can start a relationship having something in common, the stronger the connection you can build, and the stronger your frame control will be. The following are ways to network with leads.

Children

Children are the centerpiece of family life. After an adult becomes a parent, their entire perspective on life changes. Goals shift to center on their children. For clients with children, they must see how a relationship with you also benefits their children, either directly or indirectly.

The good news for you is helping them create wealth through real estate will allow them to create generational wealth, not just short-term wealth. Generational wealth affects their children and their children's children, and this is a significant selling point. You can talk about your own children's desires when discussing a house. Your kids love pools, nearby parks, and having their own room. These are all selling points in a conversation about why buying or moving could be the right option for their family.

Your kids can be the bond that attracts a family-oriented clientele to you. Your children may play the same sports as theirs, attend similar schools, be of a similar age, or have the same hobbies. Those with kids have lives that revolve around them. Therefore, talking about kids can create a trusting bond.

Look to generate leads where parents are likely to be, such as school sporting events, PTA meetings, parades, birthday parties, etc. When you meet other parents, start a relationship that could eventually lead to you being their agent.

Religion

While religion can stir up dissension, it can also bond people together. You can look to build relationships at your house of worship and thus with people who share similar morals, values, and character. Many religious communities have social events for members of their congregation. These can be excellent opportunities to find new leads and market your brand to people. Most religions place a premium on honesty and trustworthiness. If you can show you already have these traits, you can more easily secure these leads as clients and build a clientele in this community.

Politics

Politics too can stir up dissension. While discussing religion or politics is wise to avoid when around others who may disagree with you, it can be smart when you're with people who feel the same way as you. These subjects are emotionally charged because people's views are often a reflection of the deepest, most personal parts of themselves. This means when you find people who share your views, it's easier to start building a bond. And that bond may translate to working in real estate together and building a clientele with like-minded people.

Recreational Activities

Who doesn't want to talk about what they do for fun? If you find common ground with leads based on things you both enjoy doing, you are one step closer to mastering the "always working, never working" concept I covered in *SOLD*. That's a win-win in my book!

Agents can dominate an area related to a particular recreational choice or activity. For example, in my town of Discovery Bay, in California, the handful of agents who water-ski and boat on the local delta river command the real estate market because they know everyone out on the water. When you play together, you bond together—and that bond translates into sales.

Activities to find leads include hunting or fishing groups, running or hiking clubs, bowling leagues, CrossFit classes, and auto clubs. Whatever you like to do, do more of it. You can become known as the real estate agent of choice for everyone in that group, and they'll tell people in their SOI. You'll get to work with the people you play with, have fun while making money, and your business will keep growing.

Occupation

People who work a common job or in a common industry also often find it easy to bond. While real estate is your industry now, there likely was a time when you worked somewhere else. (This will be especially true for the newer agents as you build your agency.)

I often see this bond in the airline industry. Flight attendants, pilots, and ground crews share a common vernacular, belong to unions, and deal with similar frustrations. The same is true of those in the medical industry, those who are first responders, those in education, and so on. As you build your clientele, remember that these former coworkers could hire you as their agent.

Background

We can all relate to those who grew up with backgrounds like ours. There are people who grew up in rural areas, on farms, in suburbia, or in cities.

The same is true for geographic areas, which generation you belong to, and even what cartoons you watched as a child. Did you attend a certain college and belong to a fraternity or sorority? Your background deeply affects the person you are today.

Sharing a common background makes it more likely that your lead will understand you and your communication style. It can be a delicate balance when you're first getting to know someone and the things you say can be misinterpreted. Speaking with someone whose perspective was shaped by forces similar to yours decreases the likelihood of unintentionally offending them or not conveying what you're saying in a way the lead can hear it.

Sports

Some people couldn't care less about sports. For others, they are near-religious experiences. If you are interested in sports, you know exactly what I mean. Talking with someone who follows the same team as you can create an instant connection. In some cases, it is close to a brotherhood or sisterhood. The opposite effect can happen between two people who support rival teams, but that doesn't mean that rivalry will prevent building a relationship.

If you follow a particular team and notice someone wearing their gear, comment on that. If you are about the same age, even better. You probably remember the same players and maybe looked up to them in the same way. This is an effortless way to build rapport with someone and add them to your database. Some of the most successful Realtors I know are avid golfers. They developed solid relationships with club members who became clients. Of course, these club members then share the agent's info with their spheres of influence.

Whether you played football in high school, now play softball on the weekends, or coach your child's Little League or soccer team, there are endless opportunities to connect and relate to sports fans and turn them into leads.

Hobbies

With the growth of the internet over the last twenty years, it is easy to find others who share a common hobby. Whether you're into magic, building computers, or bird watching, you can rest assured that there are others who are too. Join groups for both the fun of it and the work aspect.

The more unusual the hobby, like stamp collecting, the stronger the bond will be among those who share it. This is another win-win: bonding with others over hobbies while picking up leads who trust you.

Playing to Your Strengths

As I noted earlier, rockstar agents know both their strengths and weaknesses. The good news is there are many ways for rockstar agents to bring value to their clients. For example, all agents have unique styles and skill sets, and your style and skill set belong to you alone. Knowing your core strengths and where you shine the brightest will attract the type of clientele that will help build your business.

As you continue reading, consider which rockstar description feels natural to you. Keep in mind not every agent has only one strength. The key is to determine which of the following feels right for you.

The Numbers-Oriented Agent

The rockstar numbers-oriented agent is most comfortable working with all the numbers that make up a real estate transaction. They have an innate ability to understand how finances impact the decision to buy a property and are excellent at analyzing all the options and converting them into the common denominator of a dollar amount. This rockstar agent does best with clients who are nervous about the financial implications of the decision they are making, and they help them feel comfortable carrying the weight of the commitment.

This type of agent tends to focus on the numbers part of the transaction and assumes their clients will too. They can get in trouble if they miss the emotional concerns of the client, which may lead to the client feeling that the agent doesn't understand them—or worse, that their feelings aren't validated. A numbers-oriented agent must remember that many clients are emotional in their decision-making process. The numbers only matter as they impact the client's feelings.

Easily drawn to the financial side of the transaction, a rockstar numbers-oriented agent has a natural ability to understand the numbers behind what makes a sound investment and can quickly calculate the payment on a mortgage. They will frequently rely on the price of comparable sales in the neighborhood to determine if the house is the right fit for the client, and they will use these numbers well. The numbers-oriented agent is strong when it comes to explaining the closing costs of the deal and negotiating them into being paid by the other side of the transaction. They look at everything in terms of costs and usually make recommendations by weighing costs versus benefits, often without realizing this is what they are doing.

These agents can often advise on the mortgage side as well and can walk clients through the credits and debits on a mortgage statement. They can help clients interpret inspection reports because they know how much the work will cost, and they often deal with the appraisers and confirm the property appraises at value.

They can quickly read a CMA and explain important metrics like list versus sale price, declining and increasing days on market numbers, and overall market data. They help their clients feel comfortable with the decision to purchase a house using the numbers to frame the benefits of home ownership. They are good at highlighting facts like homes traditionally appreciate over time and paying down their own mortgage is more financially sound than paying down someone else's through renting.

A numbers-oriented agent who can handle the uncomfortable elements of emotional conflict with clients are usually terrific listing agents. Their strengths are their strong command with CMAs and their ability to make logical arguments supported by the numbers of comparable sales. They make good negotiators because they look at everything from the perspective of the bottom line.

If this is the type of rockstar agent that calls to you, your best clients are investors and numbers-based clients who want to save or make money and grow wealth through real estate, because these clients are not tied emotionally to the process. When talking with leads, listen for mention of this aspect of real estate.

The People-Oriented Agent

The opposite of the rockstar numbers-oriented agent is the rockstar people-oriented agent. They are typically better with buyers than with sellers because these agents are better at hand-holding. They understand the enormous emotional strain a client will carry during a transaction and what their clients are feeling. A people-oriented agent can provide insightful, timely, and comforting advice just when the clients need it most.

These agents typically get complimentary reviews after the sale is complete. Most people underestimate the levels of our emotions, especially when under stress. People-oriented agents tend to be good at generating leads and usually have more clients at a time than numbers-oriented agents. Their pleasant personalities and emotional awareness make them lightning rods for clients looking to feel safe and comforted when worried about the homebuying process.

Because they work to keep people happy, these agents usually keep clients informed about where they are in the transaction and what's coming next. This type of communication can make a world of difference in the client's experience. The people-oriented agent also thinks first about the client's wants and needs and then about the client's budget. It's only when the client starts to care about the money that the agent makes that a priority.

These agents are often not as strong as numbers-oriented agents when it comes to listing homes, because their strength of reading feelings does not translate when it comes to negotiating with the other agent or reading a CMA. People-oriented agents are more likely to be conflict averse, but dealing with conflict is an important skill in servicing clients.

If you're aiming to be a rockstar people-oriented agent, you'll want to build a clientele around clients who want a supportive relationship. Seek out those who show strong feelings when it comes to buying or selling a home. These are the people who are clearly excited, clearly scared, or clearly apprehensive about the process and are looking for someone to address those emotions.

The Business-Oriented Agent

The rockstar business-oriented agent looks at the job of being a real estate agent as a business and thrives because of this. They tend to not take things personally and are often emotionally detached from the process of servicing clients. To them, everything is "just business." They are much more likely to recognize if they are hitting their sales goal for the year than if they have an unhappy client or if they botched some communication. Business-oriented agents look at things from a return-on-investment perspective.

Business-oriented agents often scale quickly and make good money, but only if they also have customer service skills. Many business-oriented agents are unaware that they can rub clients the wrong way and can make them feel more like a number than a person in the transaction. It doesn't take much to turn off a nervous client. However, business-minded clients will ask for your opinion of the market and respect your advice and the direction you provide in selling or buying a house.

If you're a business-oriented rockstar agent, you'll work best with clients who are efficient, productive, and appreciate someone who is also successful. Your clients are often successful in their own careers and respect others with similar accomplishments.

The Relationship-Oriented Agent

A relationship-oriented agent builds their business through the trust and authenticity they develop with those in their sphere of influence. They maintain high-touch contact in their customer service, build a strong foundation with the people in their database, and work to find win-win solutions. These agents first work to understand the goals of their clients, and these clients send referrals because of the agent's ability to build personal relationships. Relationship-oriented agents make it a priority to check in regularly with the people in their database. They frequently attend events or important milestones in the lives of their clients, know the names of their clients' children, and are aware of what is important— in both life and real estate—to those in their database.

If you are a rockstar relationship-oriented agent, you value the relationships you have with those in your database and strive to connect with more people. Your clients are likely to send you referrals for years to come. Because you're relationship-oriented, like-minded clientele will be concerned about your time, energy, and goals as well. You don't mind going the extra mile for your clients, and they reciprocate in kind.

If you're a relationship-oriented agent, you can generate leads by actively looking for those you easily relate to. You freely offer your expertise, knowledge, and insight, and the law of reciprocity helps you build a clientele of people who want to support you and your business. Through your ability to establish trust and build lasting personal bonds, your clients will help you build a large database of referrals.

The Volume-Oriented Agent

The volume-oriented agent is successful through sheer force of will. They are motivated by and place a premium on production levels. They know the numbers of their business and often talk about them with other agents. They know how many units they have sold, how many they are on track to sell for the year, what their gross sales volume is, where their average sales price is, and what their gross commission income is likely to be for the year.

Volume-oriented agents are successful because they push themselves hard and stay focused on the dollar-producing activities that create a flourishing business. They lead-generate well, push deals through, and often come up with creative solutions to keep things moving forward because they want one deal to close so they can move onto the next one. They are often competitive and compare themselves to other agents when it comes to production. A weak point is their profit margin, which is a reflection of efficiency, not volume. These rockstar agents often don't look at it very closely. They have a strong desire to "get it done" and will attract clients with a similar mentality as well as those impressed with production numbers and competition. Clients attracted to this type of agent work in sales jobs where volume equals skill. If prospects want an agent that closes the most deals, they will feel comfortable having this type of agent represent them.

If you're a volume-oriented agent, let people know how successful you are but remember to temper it by letting clients know you'll treat them as if they're your only client. You don't want leads feeling like they'll just be another cog in your money machine. Look for leads who care about results and aren't as concerned about the experience itself. Unlike the people-oriented agent, you'll do better with clients who need minimal hand-holding. Their goals are for you to get the job done.

In summary, to build the ideal clientele, it's important to know yourself. Leads who see a kindred spirit in you are much more likely to want to work with you. And the more people who turn into satisfied clients, the more they will refer you to others. That's the point where your lead generation allows your business to take off.

Develop Your Niche

Another area to consider is the niche you want to pursue, because "the riches are in the niches." Rockstar agents who focus both on a specific clientele and a niche can avoid many of the negative effects of real estate sales, including burnout, unhappy clients, and work with no payoff. Conversely, you'll find satisfaction and make real money as you gain a stellar reputation in a specific niche.

In *SKILL*, I explained the importance of owning market share in the minds of those in your database. When it comes to rockstar agent status, this principle is amplified. It is impossible to become the leader of all niches in real estate but quite possible to own a specific niche in your area. Knowing the type of clientele that you prefer is half the information you need. The other half is knowing your preferred niche. Do you like to work with house hackers, investors, first-time homebuyers, sellers, short sales, distressed properties, etc.? Being a rockstar in your category means owing that category in the minds of those in your database.

Niche success involves specialized knowledge, unique skill sets, and specific personality traits. The following six categories provide examples of niches.

Buyer's Agents

The easiest niche to build is being a buyer's agent. While this is normally an entry-level position for new agents, you can also be a rockstar agent in this niche and have a lucrative and rewarding career. Buyer's agents specialize in helping buyers find, negotiate, and close on properties another agent has listed.

This niche is usually a draw for people-oriented agents because they need to have patience and persistence and be available for their clients. It's common for a lead to ignore your phone calls, texts, or emails until they want to start shopping for a new house. When that happens, they want an immediate appointment with you. If you want to be a rockstar agent with buyers, you must have a flexible schedule.

In this niche, it's important to know as much about the buying process as possible, even the things you won't do yourself. This includes knowing about loan programs, low down payment options, title and escrow, and home inspections. The more you know, the safer your clients feel, and the more nuanced your negotiations will be. This knowledge you gather for clients about the buying process easily translates when speaking to leads about the buying process and what you can do for them.

You can make educational videos or write informational posts about the aspects of the homebuying process that scare buyers. These can be influential marketing tools and make you look like an expert to prospects. Share tips, tricks, and pieces of information to help people understand this process. This will give you a measure of frame control over leads and clients.

This niche will never run out of clients. It is one of the easiest niches to scale, especially after hiring admin assistants and showing agents. This is a great niche for rockstar agents who love the emotional side of real estate and want to be an intimate part of one of the biggest decisions their clients will ever make.

First-Time Homebuyer's Agents

A sub-niche of the buyer's agent is the first-time homebuyer's agent. Agents who specialize in this sub-niche are typically ultrasensitive to the needs of nervous buyers and find gratification in helping to calm those fears. Rockstar agents know about loan programs specifically designed for these clients and are skillful in explaining concepts to those who have never purchased real estate before.

Things like private mortgage insurance, tax and insurance impound accounts, earnest money deposits, appraisals, and inspection reports are overwhelming to the uninitiated. Agents who specialize in working with first-time homebuyers are adept at these conversations. Lead generation occurs in ways other agents don't think about. For example, lunch-and-learn seminars at places of employment can make attendees consider homeownership when they never thought it was possible.

Rockstar agents in this sub-niche often partner with lenders who also help first-time homebuyers feel confident about the process. For example, my mortgage company often helps Realtors in this sub-niche by pairing them with a loan officer to give a dual presentation that we support by scheduling the event, handling the logistics, and taking care of the administrative work. This is an easy win for rockstar agents who know how to convert leads and have a system for following up with the attendees. If your current lender is not doing something like this for you, it may be time to find someone who will.

Seller's Agents

Another niche for rockstar agents is working with sellers. The process tends to take less time to get to close than the buying process, which means that seller clients allow you to scale your business faster. The tasks are also easier to pass to your staff because they are more administrative in nature. Rockstar agents who focus on this niche typically have buyer's agents on their team to generate leads through open houses, sign calls, and other marketing on listings. For example, my team focuses on listings with the help of administrative assistants. They run CMAs, call agents about comparable properties' pending prices, schedule listing appointments, prepare marketing materials for my presentation appointments, enter listings into the MLS, schedule photos, and do other tasks as needed. After a property is in contract, the work passes to my transaction coordinator.

Leveraging all this work allows you to have multiple selling clients simultaneously and to market yourself as a listing expert. Clients want to feel their seller agent is a strong negotiator who won't back down to buyer demands. It's important to communicate your skills right from the listing presentation and make the sellers feel secure in your capabilities.

By marketing yourself as *the* agent who sells homes in a particular area, you'll receive a lot of attention from the homeowners who now live there. Although this was truer before internet browsing, word-of-mouth about you being the local neighborhood expert still works. Any type of marketing must include your track record for selling homes. Many rockstar agents make it a priority to knock on doors and meet the homeowners in the neighborhoods where they have listings, with the aim of getting more leads. This is particularly effective after neighbors see your signs around the area. Becoming a listing agent may not be as emotionally gratifying as being a buyer's or seller's agent, but it can be much more financially rewarding.

Real Estate Investor Agents

Real estate investors frequently complain about the lack of good agents to represent them. Most top-producing agents work with the largest pool of buyer or seller clients possible. However, because investors represent a smaller portion of clients, most agents do not have the experience or skills to service them well. This means this is a niche with a lot of growth potential. When you learn how to work with investors, you may have more clients than you have the bandwidth to handle. This is a much smaller niche, but it can be very lucrative.

It can also include more difficult clients, and this is especially true for new investors. One trait you must develop is the skill of "reading" who is a potential client versus who is looking for a free education. This will protect you from people who have no interest in hiring an agent. Also, investors are typically less motivated than primary residence owners.

Being a real estate investor yourself can make this niche easier to develop, because you already understand the needs of the clients, speak the language, and know what investors want: financial freedom, cash flow, and delayed gratification in return for building wealth. If you know how to connect your clients with the "core three"—that is, (1) a lender, (2) a property manager, and (3) a contractor—word will get around about you. If you know how to run the numbers to help clients determine a return on investment or what equity they can create, you'll also attract investors with money but without strong math skills. And if you know how to oversee a rehab, you'll be in even higher demand.

This niche is powerful because there is not much competition, you won't have to show as many properties, and you often can sell several properties to the same client. If you have an interest in real estate investing, this could be the perfect niche for you.

Local Market Expert Agents

Obviously, a rockstar agent who sells most of the properties in a neighborhood has an advantage over an agent who doesn't sell there as much. And while the internet allows buyers to see every house in a neighborhood and thus reduces the advantage of the buyer agent who knows the area well, it is still a useful niche.

If you are a buyer's agent who learns a particular market well, you can offer nuanced and specific information to your clients that other agents may not know and may not be available on websites. When you are a local market expert, you know about the best restaurants, the faster routes to avoid traffic, and the school districts with the most highly rated teachers. You may know which builders built the homes and even which flowers and vegetables grow best in that soil. This could be valuable information to those looking to buy in the area.

Most agents who are local market experts live in the area themselves. Where I live, the expert agents market themselves as knowing the best places for fishing and which docks to suggest to their clients with boats. Buyers here want specific information related to living on the water.

If you love the neighborhood you live in, market yourself as the local market expert and become top of mind for buyers in that area.

Probate Sales, Foreclosures, and Short Sales Agents

Agents in this niche are typically strong problem solvers who understand complex legal processes. They need a high degree of skill to read legal documents and to learn the unique systems of selling these types of properties. As with investor agents, this is a wide open and lucrative niche.

A probate sale occurs when the owner of a home dies without legal plans in place about who should acquire the title. When this occurs, the state administers the process of selling the home through an estate attorney or other representative of the court. The attorney then hires the real estate agent to facilitate the sale and complete the process. Agents who specialize in probate sales have relationships with attorneys who manage probate sales, have the knowledge to communicate with legal staff, and are aware of the unique paperwork and process associated with this type of sale.

A foreclosure is a property in which the title has been taken back by the lender. This property is defined as real estate owned (REO) on the bank's balance sheet, and the lender hires a real estate agent to facilitate the sale. The aim is for the sale to allow the lender to recoup as much of their investment as possible. REO agents have relationships with asset managers of financial institutions and often have large portfolios of lender-owned properties to sell. This can lead to a valuable inventory when other listings may be tough to find.

A short sale is when the owner of the home is selling the property for less than they owe to the bank. Since the amount is "short" of what is owed, the lender must approve the sale. These sales can take a long time to get to close because the lender obviously prefers not to register a loss on their initial investment. Because of this longer time frame, these homes are not a good option for buyers looking to buy quickly. Agents who specialize in these deals must be able to communicate clearly with lenders and have the patience to find a buyer to close on the deal.

If you target any of these niches, you will again find yourself in short company. Most agents are not trained to handle these deals, so that puts you at an advantage when it comes to owning the mindshare of those looking to hire these types of agents.

Rockstar agents understand the importance of setting themselves apart from their competitors and creating ways for their team members to participate in the deals they secure. Targeting an ideal clientele will help turn a top-producing agent into a rockstar and help push that boulder to the other side of the hill.

➡ KEY POINTS

- The fear of missing out on the "great" deal is stronger than the discipline to focus on a specific set of criteria.
- Targeting the wrong clientele for your business will prevent you from closing with the right ones.
- People want to do business with those they know, like, and trust.
- Frame control involves getting others to understand things from your perspective.
- Knowing your core strengths and where you shine the brightest will attract the type of clientele that will help build your business.
- The rockstar numbers-oriented agent is most comfortable working with all the numbers that make up a real estate transaction.
- People-oriented agents tend to be good at generating leads and usually have more clients at a time than numbers-oriented agents.
- Business-oriented agents often scale quickly and make good money, but only if they also have customer service skills.
- A relationship-oriented agent builds their business through the trust and authenticity they develop with those in their sphere of influence.
- The volume-oriented agent is successful through sheer force of will. They are motivated by and place a premium on production levels.
- You'll find satisfaction and make real money as you gain a stellar reputation in a specific niche.
- The easiest niche to build is being a buyer's agent.
- Rockstar agents understand the importance of setting themselves apart from their competitors and creating ways for their team members to participate in the deals they secure.

CHAPTER FIVE

HOW TO EXCEL WITH BUYERS

"If you want to make money, you have to help someone else make money."

—RUSSELL SIMMONS

Read the following chapter through the lens of a rockstar agent who will teach this to their team. Excelling with buyers is a first step, followed by teaching other agents how to do the same. This is the foundation upon which you will build a team at your brokerage agency or real estate business.

The Value of Buyers to Your Business

Many agents prefer not to work with buyers, but I believe this is a tactical error. While there may be some value in *you* not working with buyers, you absolutely want your team to work with them because buyers bring massive value to a business. When you were a new agent, buyers were your go-to client pool. As a top-producing agent, buyers helped you refine your systems, your scripts, and your ability to discern a serious lead from a poser.

When you are a rockstar agent, buyers will be the basis of the revenue you share with your team members. They also serve to help your newer agents learn the business, your systems, and their craft. The confidence your agents build working with buyer clients will be how they reach top-producing agent status themselves. It's through buyers that agents sharpen their skills. Buyers exert more control in a transaction than sellers, which makes them the trickier of the two sides to work with. Buyers are more emotional, prone to impulsive decisions, and likely to swing from one side of a decision to the other. Mastering working with buyers is important, and new agents can make up for their lack of experience by overcompensating with effort. Going the extra mile to let their clients know they really care can make up for mistakes made with paperwork, processes, or other areas where expertise will be missing.

Buyers are also easier to move from lead generation down the Sales Funnel. The process of buying or selling a home hinges on the decision to buy a new property. Sellers typically will not sell their home until they decide on which new home to buy. To convince a seller to sell, an agent must show them a home they would rather live in than the one they currently own. This can be done through photos of better-looking or bigger homes or house showings in a location they prefer. An agent who doesn't know how to convince a homeowner to become a buyer will only be left with homeowners who have already decided to sell.

It is also easier for agents to lead-generate buyers rather than sellers. Most people dream of owning a home. Even if they cannot afford it now, an agent can put them on the path of improving their financial position to finally owning something instead of renting. Buyer leads are common through other people—lenders, coworkers, and people in an agent's sphere of influence will know of someone who wants to buy a home, because the topic occurs more often in conversation. Sellers are less likely to notify others when they are considering the option to sell their home.

Buyers teach agents about the contract process because 70 percent to 80 percent of the work needed to sell a home is on the buyer's side. Securing a loan, getting the title and escrow, ordering and reviewing inspections, ordering and scheduling appraisals, seeking loan approvals, obtaining quotes for work that needs to be done, and handling any insurance and property taxes are all done by the buyer's agent. This will help your agents progress in their careers as they will be able to build their skills much faster than they would if they were only working with sellers.

Working with buyers also helps when working with sellers. The listing agent with a natural eye for what buyers will see when they walk through a home has a serious advantage over a listing agent who may be better with numbers and data but clueless to market demand. Working with buyer clients means agents learn the types of houses that sell the fastest, what design styles are trending, and what type of visceral reactions buyers are likely to have as they walk a home. This allows them to make small tweaks and corrections sooner in the process, which results in smoother transactions for their seller clients.

Agents without strong negotiation techniques benefit from working with buyers because they aren't negotiating their commission or jeopardizing the client-agent relationship over financial concerns. Buyer's agents have the luxury of focusing solely on the needs of their clients, not on business elements such as commissions, expenses, and listings that don't sell. When a seller's agent accepts a listing and either prices it too high or cannot convince a client to price it closer to what the market will allow, and the home doesn't sell, they lose capital. Professional pictures, marketing signage, and advertising all cost money. When a listing does not sell, an agent can lose $500 to $1,000 of upfront money. Buyer's agents don't have this problem.

Finally, working with buyers is the fastest way to a paycheck. If you have agents with slow months or your business hits an overall dry spell, agents can lead-generate by looking for people who are ready to buy houses. Using your database to make calls to find out who is still renting is a straightforward way to do this. For people who earn enough to qualify for a loan and do not yet own a house but want to, agents can break down the numbers to show them the path to homeownership. This isn't possible with sellers who may not want to sell or are overwhelmed by the idea of preparing a house to sell. Buyers can bridge the financial gap if your business is falling behind.

The final thing to consider is buyers may later become sellers. According to the National Association of Realtors, 90 percent of buyers would use their agent again to sell their home.[9] This is why it's so important for you

---

9   "2021 Profile of Home Buyers and Sellers," National Association of Realtors, November 2021, https://cdn.nar.realtor/sites/default/files/documents/2021-highlights-from-the-profile-of-home-buyers-and-sellers-11-11-2021.pdf.

and your agents to stay in touch with your clients. When a former buying client reaches out about selling, your agents can help them buy their next house (more on that in Chapter Seven). As you build your rockstar business, you should do so by working with buyers.

What Buyers Want

The first step in excelling with buyers is to learn what they want from their agent. There are certain things every buyer wants and other things only some want. I'll start with the five things every buyer *wants* and then explain the things many buyers don't *need*.

Buyers Want to Buy Homes

Every buyer clearly wants to buy a home. But there's one thing every experienced agent has already learned: Many buyers would avoid using agents if that were an option. Agents receive what appears to buyers as large commissions; we don't always answer our phones; and without us, they can't buy want they want: a house. If people could see homes without an agent, they would. If buying a home were as straightforward as buying a car, they would do it without us. If they understood all the processes, we'd be out of our jobs.

However, buying a house is scary, complicated, and stressful. Real estate agents are essential because there are too many moving pieces. We are necessary to explain options, guide the decision-making process, and provide the information clients need to feel comfortable. Our perceived and real value is our ability to calm our clients' roiling emotions. Even so, our clients don't work with us because they want to. We control the market via the MLS, where most listings are found along with valuable past sales data. We show homes. We have the forms and knowledge on how to write offers. We understand the law and the market and the nuances of title, escrow, and lending. Remembering we are one piece in a cumbersome process means never losing the desire to win over clients. By offering great customer service, fast response times, and sage advice, we can earn the goodwill of clients for years to come.

That being said, the goal isn't to make clients like us but to help them buy or sell a house. For example, a buyer's agent can show a client fifty homes, quickly answer every question they ask, do extensive due diligence on every property, and in the process provide them with a real estate education—but if the agent doesn't eventually close on a house, the client won't be happy. The agent will not have helped the client accomplish their goal. Not only will the agent not be paid, but there is also a high probability the agent will never get a referral from the client.

Teach your agents it is their job to be direct and to tell clients which properties are not right for them. Clients may not like them during the process, but they'll love them when it's over—if they close on a home. If one of your agents gets their clients the home they want, they'll consider the agent a hero. If the agent doesn't, they'll consider that agent a waste of their time. Tell your new agents to never push clients to buy something that is wrong for them or that they don't want. Also tell your agents not to be afraid to stand their ground and push back a little if they think a home is a good fit but the clients don't see it that way. Worrying about being accommodating won't close a deal on any house.

Buyers Want to Feel Agents Are on Their Side

As much as agents are aware they need to close on a home to be paid, clients are even more aware of that. Some clients will have been burned by agents in the past, even by fiduciaries like yourself. It's normal for some to distrust the advice you give. Clients with bad experiences with agents may show suspicion or cynicism in response to what you tell them. This isn't a reflection of you but of the past that formed their apprehension.

Tell your agents that they shouldn't take it personally with these types of clients. It's very common for clients to assume they are being given advice only to move the process forward toward the agent's commission. There is absolutely no reason for your agents not to admit they want their commissions. They (and you) do this job to earn a living. In the same way clients use an agent's services for their purposes, agents are being paid for closing on deals.

Nevertheless, all buyers want to feel that their agent is on their side. If they even *think* their buyer's agent is also working for the sellers (even when that's not true), the buyers will be distrustful. There are several things you can tell your agents to do to help clients feel their best interests are at the heart of an agent's work.

The first is to really listen to them. When a buyer tells their agent what they care about, listen! It's too easy to assume clients care about what you care about. If you are a numbers-oriented agent, you presume your clients care about the numbers in the deal. To some clients, though, the numbers only represent the boundaries within which they must operate. To these clients, finding a home that makes them feel happy and safe is much more important than getting the best deal. If you miss this fact, you can't satisfy them. If they think you're not listening to them, it will be harder for them to believe you're on their side. The same type of mistake can happen if you assume your clients, like you, want to take their time and think about every decision. Some clients prefer more options upfront so they can make a quick decision. All agents must represent their clients' interests, and that includes how they make decisions. You cannot stress enough to your agents how important it is that they listen to the clients.

Clients tell us everything about themselves and what they value, often in the first conversation. This is a crucial time to acknowledge their concerns and let them mold how the process will work moving forward. When clients understand that we value the same parts of the homebuying process that they do, they will believe we're on their side. It also helps when their feelings are validated. When a client is sad that they missed out on a house they liked, a good agent comforts them with the knowledge that other buyers in this situation feel that way too. When clients are excited about a property, a good agent acknowledges how important this decision is. Remind your agents that they can do all of this without getting emotional themselves.

Your agents can help your clients feel that everyone is on their side by letting them know they are a priority to your business. As a rockstar agent, your business will always have more than one client at a time, but no client must ever feel they are not important. Agents cannot tell a client they are too busy for them. Even when an agent needs some room to maneuver, they must never do it in a way that makes the client feel like they are not a priority.

To ensure that your staff also feel like a priority to you, you must teach them time management and both what to expect and how to communicate properly with clients and each other. This will prevent them from coming to you for all answers. You cannot control when leads or clients will reach out to agents with questions, and you don't want them to wait for responses. You need to teach your staff how to control the frequency and rhythm of communication. This can be as simple as teaching them to respond with "I'll text you sometime tomorrow afternoon to let you know what the seller said" or "Let me look up comps this weekend and get back to you on Monday." This creates the expectation the clients will be contacted and allows your agents some space to do their work. These are important steps to help both your agents and their clients always feel like they are a priority to your business.

Buyers Want the Process to Be as Painless as Possible

Your clients know buying a house is stressful and inconvenient, and they expect their buyer's agent to make this process as painless as possible, within reason. Uncertainty breeds anxiety. When clients don't know what to expect or how to interpret what they're being told by their agent, the result is anxiety on the client's part, and anxiety often brings out the worst in people. A good agent can avoid this by preparing clients, as much as possible, for what is to come.

In *SKILL*, I explain in detail that giving buyers a presentation before taking them on as clients allows an agent to show their knowledge, determine if they even want to work with the buyer, and, if so, how to prepare them for the process. In summary, my presentation covers topics from how my agents will show them homes to how contingencies work, how we protect their deposit, what a home inspection entails, and how appraisals work. I discuss the types of homes we will target, what a contract looks like, and how to communicate with my team throughout the process. I include every issue a buyer goes through that causes the most anxiety. By the end of the presentation, there is a visible difference in the clients: Their shoulders are more relaxed, their countenance is brighter, and they appear more eager to get started.

I tell them that the process for a buying client includes first sorting through the list of homes I'll send them. They will need to do the same on Zillow.com and Realtor.com. During this period, they'll come up with a list of questions they'll communicate to you or your team. They'll have to apply to lenders to see how much they'll be allowed to borrow. For the showings, if they have a young family, they either need to find a babysitter so they can look at homes with the assigned agent or bring the kids with them. This occurs over multiple weekends. Even for buyers without children, this is a time-consuming process. They then must consider each house individually to determine how they feel about it, and then they will compare the preferred home to the other homes they've seen. Once they've run through that gamut of emotions, they have to wait to learn what problems the house of choice may have, what research they still need to do (school systems, shopping areas, etc.), and the final price of the home. Does their loan amount give them the room to buy this property? They'll also be asking their friends, siblings, parents, and others to see the house to come to a consensus on whether the property is a good fit. If it is, then comes the sale and packing up of their current home.

In the same way that your showing agents don't love showing home after home after home, your clients don't like it either. So why do clients insist on seeing so many homes? It's the fear of missing out—that they will choose a house, then see a better one after they sign a contract. To make the process as painless as possible for your clients and your showing agents, you must have a process to show homes as efficiently as possible; this includes your showing agent's ability to earn the trust of your clients, find them the most suitable homes for them to consider, and direct them toward the house they can close on. (Efficiency is discussed in more detail below.)

One way to smooth out your clients' chaos is by assisting them with the moving process. Nobody likes moving. I tell my clients during the first meeting that my team will send moving boxes (branded with my logo and photo) to make packing easier. Before I reached rockstar status, I would even show up on moving day to help my clients load their moving truck. While there, I would call my assistant to order pizza for everyone and to ask her to deliver soda and beer. You can create similar ways to help your clients move.

I remind clients during the presentation that they'll need to change the utilities from their old address to the new one after they move in, and that my office will send them an email with the website addresses and phone numbers of the utility companies that service the new home. We also provide a list of the area's top restaurants, car mechanics, shopping centers, and other commercial spots. Gestures like this can make things much easier for your clients during a stressful time.

If your client asks for advice on homeowners insurance companies, send them a few quotes. If they are confused by something their lender said, offer to call the lender to help sort it out. If they mention not understanding the information the title company provided, guide them in interpreting this information. Actively looking for ways to make the process painless and telling them early in the process what you can do for them will lead to happy buyers and ensure referral business for you.

Buyers Want Agents to Save Them Money

This one should come as no surprise, and a large part of your job as a real estate agent is to negotiate well for your clients to save them money. When this happens, it clearly justifies your commission. Your clients expect you'll work to save them money. This can happen by negotiating a lower purchase price, but frequently that's not possible. When there are multiple offers, there's little flexibility related to price. It's what happens afterward when you can prove your worth.

For example, you can train your agents to save a buyer client's money by negotiating on a home's needed repairs. This requires the ability to interpret an inspection report. Your agent can get a quote from a licensed contractor on the costs to make the repair, negotiate that amount as a credit from the seller, then renegotiate with the contractor to reduce the price the buyer will pay. This works, for example, with pest reports (and I recommend using a licensed pest company to handle termite, rodent, or arachnid problems). However, there are many circumstances when you can use a general repair person for jobs such as removing dry rot. This can save your client thousands of dollars while you use the high repair quotes from the inspection report to negotiate the seller credit.

Another opportunity to save money is when the property appraises below market value, and your agent includes an appraisal contingency in all contracts. I prepare my clients for this game of "chicken" during the buyer's presentation, should the house they select appraise on the low side. The seller's immediate reaction will be to keep their price as is. If you can train your buyers to not walk away, every day that passes gives them more leverage. When a buyer doesn't back out but doesn't move forward, it puts pressure on the seller to make a decision on the price. In many cases, it makes more sense for the seller to reduce their price and move on rather than restart the process to sell the home to a new buyer and possibly risk the same outcome. With every day that passes, the sellers become more aware of the situation. Preparing your buying clients at presentation for this late-game scenario can teach them patience and help save them money.

Make it clear that you and your agents value your clients' hard-earned money. If they know you're actively looking to save them money, they'll appreciate your efforts.

Buyers Want Agents to Give Them Advice

Your clients will be looking to you for advice because you have the experience they don't have. Some people have an easier time than others asking for advice, but you can be sure everyone wants it. This is especially true in high-stress situations, such as when financial news is not good. The advice you give is directly related to how safe your clients feel about their purchase and about working with you. To be able to offer good advice, tell your agents (again) to listen to the clients to understand their goals. They do this by asking a lot of questions. The more they know about the client's goals, the better advice they can give.

Some clients want financial advice, such as choosing a loan, determining how much to pay in closing costs, or figuring out if they should remodel before moving in. Your ability to help them decipher if a kitchen remodel makes financial sense or decide if buying down the rate on their loan is the best move will increase their opinion of your agent's skills as a Realtor. This is when the ability to understand comparable sales in a neighborhood is needed. (I covered this process in detail in *SOLD*.)

Other clients want advice on how to negotiate the differences between partners, which happens most frequently between spouses, but there are other situations in which two people who will live together have conflicting opinions when it comes to buying a home. It's in your best interest to teach your agents the art of mediating both to help close deals and provide value to your clients.

Other clients will seek specific advice, such as insights on school districts, changes in gentrification patterns, or levels of property taxes in one part of town versus another. Clients will expect your agents to answer their questions and lower their anxiety. To excel with buyers requires that they get the information they need to make the decision that is right for them. I use the following sources to provide information to my clients.

Tools to Help Buyers

School Information

The Great Schools website (www.greatschools.org) provides school rankings within any community. While this metric will always be somewhat subjective and created by an algorithm from data that not every parent values equally, it is still useful for comparing one school to another. Your clients can check to see if scores are higher in one part of town compared with another and base their homebuying decision on that factor.

County Assessors' Information

County assessors' websites include the property tax amount for any particular property in that county as well as information on how those taxes are used. County assessors also provide statements with any special assessments assigned to the property and how they are applied. These assessments can cover funds allocated for schools, firefighting stations, police officers, or other community-related expenses that benefit all the homeowners in the area. Before writing an offer, my team will look up the property taxes for the house the client likes to let the client determine if that level is too high for them.

Rental Value Information

To check the estimated rental values for any properties your clients are considering buying, look at www.biggerpockets.com/rental-property-calculator or www.rentometer.com. These sites are primarily for investors, but house-hacking clients use them also. The sites take the rents from the houses, apartments, and housing units surrounding the subject property and average them to an estimated rental amount for the property your client is considering purchasing. I use these sites for my own rental decision making, such as when a unit becomes vacant or when a yearly lease expires. It helps you and your agents look like rockstars in front of your clients.

Analysis Information

To run a full analysis on any property under consideration, use BiggerPockets (BP) calculators (www.biggerpockets.com/calculators). This tool works best with investor clients, but some clients want to analyze a home from an investment perspective even if they plan on living in it for a few years before renting it out for income.

The BP calculators include a timeline of projected returns over a thirty-year timeframe. For example, the calculators can help your client know how much the property will ccash flow in five years. They can analyze for equity growth, loan paydown, expected rent increases, closing costs, capital expenditures, and projections of vacancy into return on investments. This analysis arrives in a colorful and easy-to-read PDF that you can show your clients to help them feel confident that they are making the right decision on their preferred house. The clients can then share this report with family members and friends if they want others' advice.

All these tools can be run by any administrator, assistant, or agent on your team. Having everyone on the team help with tasks means everyone is working to help the client feel good about moving forward, and who doesn't want that? Then you, as the rockstar agent, have the time to focus on the tasks that require your skills to run your business.

Teach your team how to use these tools, but let them know it should look like you created the reports for the clients. This will allow you to continue to showcase yourself as a high-value real estate rockstar and your business as organized and profitable. That's a win-win for you and your team!

Challenges with Buyers

Buyers, which represent the most emotionally rewarding aspect of real estate sales, are also widely considered to be the toughest. If you can win with buyers, you can build a business that will grow, provide referrals, and garner listings (most sellers only sell when they have the need to buy a new house). While there is no shortage of challenges when working with buyers, I'll highlight the big ones next as well as some techniques for mitigating them.

Buyers Lack Motivation

This appears to be a challenge of working with some buyers, but this is more often than not the agent's inability to figure out a lead's true motivation. No agent can make someone do something they do not want to do. Sometimes when hurdles arise that stop a buyer from taking action to complete a sale, they never wanted to complete the sale, and this was a decision made (even subconsciously) long before you entered the picture.

How do you avoid working with the buyers who don't really want to buy a home? You can't just ask them questions, as most buyers will tell you, and believe, that they want to buy a home. The key is to listen to the lead and then ask specific questions. This is crucial to avoiding working with the wrong clients. When you're first talking with a lead, pay attention to statements like those in the table below.

While these statements are not inherently problematic, they are red flags that warrant attention and further questioning. Your ability as the rockstar agent to ask the correct probing questions can help determine if the lead's statements should be taken at face value—which is better to know sooner rather than later—or if they reveal concerns you can work with and help the lead overcome.

RED FLAG STATEMENT	ROCKSTAR COUNTER QUESTION
I'm not in a rush to buy.	I don't want you to feel rushed either. To be honest, though, it's important that your motivation and my motivation match each other's. It doesn't make sense for our office to rush info to you if your homebuying motivation is lower than ours. Plus, the best properties do go quickly, and I'd hate for you to miss out on something you really want. Are you okay missing out on these properties, or are there some questions about the process we should cover before committing to this process seriously? If you're not in a hurry to write an offer on a property, would you feel more comfortable if we communicate primarily by email rather than by phone or text?
I can wait for the perfect deal.	That's great! I'm always looking for a great deal myself. Can you tell me what that perfect deal will look like, so my team can be on the lookout for you?
	When you say you can wait for the perfect deal, does that mean a deal that perfectly matches your ideal parameters, or a deal that is so good you couldn't say no even if you really wanted to say no?

I'm not going to overpay.	We are on the same page with that. In fact, my team will write an appraisal contingency into your offer to protect you against overpaying.

When it comes time to put an offer on a house, how will you determine what fair market value is so we know what to write at?

[If they don't know.]
Well, we should figure this out now before you are in the heat of the moment. Would it help to look at some comps for the neighborhood to see what other buyers are paying?

[If they plan to base it on a feeling.]
Okay. For me and my team to represent you, we need to know where this feeling comes from and what it's based on. Can you articulate for me how we can recognize what a deal looks like to you so we can avoid sending you to look at the wrong properties? This may also help us to realize that this isn't the right time for you to start this process. |
| I'm not going to pay over asking price. | Thank you for sharing that. What about the asking price is important to you? Many sellers price their house purposely low out of fear they won't get any activity, then they get an abundance of activity. If we find a house like that, we might have to write over asking price. Should we ignore it even if they think writing over asking price is still a great deal?

Would you feel better if we find houses that are priced too high for the neighborhood and we write under asking price, even if that's possibly still over market value? |

I don't want to feel rushed to make a decision.	I wouldn't want you to feel rushed either. We should take some time now to go over everything that goes into buying a house so you are prepared for the pace you'll need to move at and make decisions before we start the process.
I want to explore all my options.	I want you to as well! That's why we are getting so specific about the criteria that matters to you. Part of my job is to find you the houses that will work for you and save you the time from looking at the wrong ones. In essence, this is about exploring options for you. Would you prefer if my team doesn't do that but lets you look at everything yourself? If you'd feel more comfortable with that process, then we can let you do your own search and you can just come to our office when you find a house you want to write an offer on. —OR— I want you to also! In my experience, when someone says that, it often means they aren't quite sure what they want yet. Do you think that might be the case? If so, let's sit and talk about what kind of property would make you say, "That's the one!" That way we can ignore anything that doesn't affect you that way.
I'll know what I want when I see it.	That may be true. I find myself thinking the same way all the time. The problem is that it is impossible for us to be in your head to see what you see and feel what you feel. Can we talk a little about the types of properties that move you emotionally, so I can learn more about your unique taste?

It is imperative you learn if a client has not made the decision to buy a home before your agency commits to working with them. While working with a wrong client can cost a new agent their time, when you reach rockstar status, it costs you money. Each client you work with that does not close is time spent not lead-generating and not creating revenue. While "losing" a Client at the beginning of your Sales Funnel may seem like a terrible scenario, it's not. The terrible scenario is committing to the wrong Client, putting in all the work to bring them to the bottom of the funnel, then having them change their mind at the end!

Buyer Are Impulsive, Not Motivated

Many buyers will be impulsive at some point. While impulsivity is positive when a buyer is eager to proceed, it's negative when they change their mind and back out just as quickly. It is easy to confuse impulsivity with motivation at the beginning stages of a relationship. Both motivated and impulsive clients will contact you frequently, appear very excited, and ask a lot of questions. They will fill out lender preapproval forms, meet with you in person for the presentation, and sign whatever you put in front of them. Both want to get started ASAP. Even experienced buyer's agents can mistake an impulsive client for one that's truly motivated.

The difference is that impulsive clients are often led by their fear of changing their mind. Their emotions arrive suddenly and strongly, and they usually leave just as fast. An impulsive client will lose energy if progress isn't made quickly. This creates the confusing state of "rush, rush, rush, freeze, run away." This can adversely affect even the most levelheaded of agents.

When you suspect a client may be impulsive rather than motivated, ask straight out if this is a pattern in their life (this question also works well in the interview process for new team members). Many will admit that they are on the impulsive side. Then ask them directly about their fears of the real estate process to determine if these are driving their behavior. Questions to ask include:
- "What are you worried will happen?"
- "Why are you making decisions so quickly?"
- "Are you nervous if you don't decide right now someone else will buy this house?"

This will allow them to think about and express what they are feeling and why they are doing what they are doing.

While it may be tempting to ride out a wave of impulsivity and start showing houses right away, this is a dangerous wave to ride. Impulsive clients will back out when it's time to write an offer or commit to an escrow. Be cautious and thorough in addressing concerns and painting a clear picture of the process for these types of clients. Your agents can save themselves and impulsive clients a lot of time and effort once it's clear the relationship should never start or needs to end.

Buyers Don't Want to Follow Your Process

Some buyers want the reward of buying a home but don't want to follow your process. They consider the preapproval paperwork, speaking to your agent daily about available homes, and only seeing homes after due diligence is completed to be too much trouble. This kind of buyer will push your agents to move forward before they feel comfortable doing so. When your agents sense this, they have buyers who want to avoid the real estate process.

The cure is for the agents to become the leaders in the relationship. For the clients who want to bend your procedures and homebuying process to their will, your agents must convince them that they know what they're doing, and the client has no choice in the order of the steps. These steps are in your buyer's presentation, which sets the tone for your office's process. It will be up to your agents to establish themselves as the alpha in the relationship going forward. Once these clients see the agent in that position, they will be much more likely to follow the process you laid out for them.

Your agents can move the leadership needle in their direction by always explaining the reason behind every ask. Tell the client they need lender preapproval because otherwise sellers won't even consider their offers. Additionally, tell them that by seeking preapproval early, you can look for ways to improve their rate, which will make sellers very interested in their offers. Explain to them that if they skip your presentation, they'll still have to sign documents they won't understand, and, worse, your office won't be able to do its best negotiation if they don't attend because you won't really know each other. Explaining why you're asking them to invest their time now will make it easier to get increased client participation and effort later.

Buyers Think They Know More than the Agent

This isn't true with every client, but it is with many. The profession of real estate agent isn't well respected, and a lot of that is our own fault. Bad agents have created an environment where unprofessionalism flourishes.

Many buyers believe they know more than the agent, which creates havoc when the client needs to follow the agent's advice but doesn't or won't. This is especially important in a seller's market, where it is difficult to put buyers in contract. The more competition there is to land a listing, the more crucial your wise advice as an agent becomes. A buyer who controls the relationship will wield all the power but get no results. Agents need to ensure that clients recognize their knowledge, experience, and negotiating skills to reach close.

Rockstar Buyer Structure

As detailed earlier in the book, you'll need to create a system for your team to work together to efficiently push Leads down the Sales Funnel. This means hiring talented people who understand their role and excel in it and placing those people at specific points in the funnel. The following structure sets up your team so everyone is on the same page to consistently close deals. To reiterate: Putting buyers under contract at high volume with great service requires that you master the art of efficiency.

Clarity in Roles

I start with what I call the "road map," which is the list of tasks required to move a Lead down the Sales Funnel to Closing. The following list is the buyer's portion of the road map.

1. Administrative assistant schedules introductory call.
2. Assigned agent conducts initial introductory call.
3. Assistant enters call notes into our CRM (using the Brivity Platform) and Lead Board (software).
4. Assigned agent assigns showing assistant or deal finders to begin home search.
5. Assigned agent ensures Lead connects with lender.
6. Assigned agent obtains preapproval from lender and uploads to our CRM.
7. Assigned agent schedules my presentation.
8. Agent/Assistant sends buyer blueprint (marketing PDF).
9. Assigned agent prepares my materials for buyer's presentation (e.g., list of homes, add photo of client to presentation).
10. Assigned agent conducts presentation.

11. Assigned agent enters notes from presentation into our CRM and Lead Board sheet.
12. Team assistant creates listing alerts.
13. Team assistant obtains and uploads proof of funds letter into our CRM.
14. Team assistant assigns appropriate auto plan (discussed earlier in this book).
15. Team assistant moves Lead to "Active Buyers" tab in Lead Sheet.

This list is completed for each new lead, and the items are divided based on the nature of the task: Simply, either the task requires client interaction/communication or it doesn't.

All tasks that do not require interaction are assigned to different team members while tasks that do require client interaction are handled by the assigned agent in the transaction. This prevents the client from realizing the agent isn't doing all the work while everything is completed in a satisfactory manner. By sharing the tasks, your team members have the opportunity to learn more about your business while the more experienced team members carry out higher dollar-per-hour activities.

As noted earlier in the book, these tasks can be color-coded, with colors assigned to specific team members. This avoids confusion regarding which tasks are to be completed by which team members.

Excellence in Roles

It's your job as the rockstar agent to train your team to understand the road map and not just their part in it. This is the step that is lacking in most systems, yet it is vital to having a functioning one. It is equally important that you communicate what excellence looks like to you. For my team, excellence includes four factors:

1. **Know the result you're looking for.** Each team member needs to understand their goals. A showing assistant's goal, for example, is to get more buyers into contract. A listing assistant's goal is to get more listings ready for the MLS. A buyer's agent's goal is to close more buyer deals. An administrative assistant's goal is to aid their primary agent to do more business. Make it clear how they can know if they are successful in their roles or if they are falling behind.

2. **Do it quickly.** Part of excellence in this business is getting things done faster than others. Knowing the steps to put a listing in the MLS is important, but doing it rapidly means excellence. I started by timing myself performing the tasks I want my administrators to be able to accomplish. I have them practice until they can do it faster than me. This should not be difficult with a smaller number of repetitive tasks.

3. **Do it without making mistakes.** In addition to being done quickly, the work must also be done accurately. It's better to teach someone how to do something accurately first, then speed up how it's done. This is as true for buyer's agents putting buyers into contract faster and with few to no errors as for showing assistants helping buyers locate the perfect home without showing them too many wrong ones.

4. **Offer an elevated level of customer service.** Speed and excellence are only two ingredients; the third is ensuring every client experiences superior customer service. A team member can do a perfect job in a transaction, but if the client isn't happy with the service, your business loses a referral. Remind your team all three ingredients are needed to impress clients. For example, if three team members do amazing jobs but the fourth does not, the client will still be left underwhelmed. Everyone knows how hard we work to get leads and move them down the Sales Funnel, and we know our reputation is on the line with every client. It's too easy to treat the customer as part of the job instead of *the* job itself. As you manage your team, pay attention to how every single team member treats the clients. This is one area of your business that can get out of control faster than you might think.

Creating Clarity for the Client

In addition to your team members understanding their roles, it's important that the client be just as clear on their role. The best way to do this is to paint a picture for your clients of how the process is going to look, work, and feel during the buyer's presentation. I've broken down the components below.

Highlight How a Team Approach Benefits the Client
In this book you are learning the benefits of a team to your rockstar

business, but your leads are only concerned with how your team can benefit them, and rightly so. Highlight the biggest pain points in the industry, then showcase how the team approach helps eliminate them (see the table below). By showcasing the team model, you remove leads' worries that they'll be passed around to different people rather than being a priority to your business. You can point out that a team approach instead makes them *the priority* and allows the lead to get to close faster.

COMMON INDUSTRY PROBLEMS	WAYS YOUR TEAM COMBATS THE PROBLEM
Houses get sold quickly.	By having a team of showing assistants that can show homes at any time, your buying clients are always at the front of the line.
Too many buyer's agents call about listings.	By having a team of administrative assistants to take calls from buyer's agents, you get the info faster, identify which buyer's agents have serious clients, and get those agents in touch with the team's listing agents. For your selling clients, no leads or offers get missed.
Last-minute showings are problematic.	By having a team of showing assistants, one will be available to accommodate last-minute requests from your buyer clients.
Paperwork takes up time Realtors should be negotiating for their clients.	By having a team approach, someone will handle the paperwork while you can focus on making your client money.
There is so much due diligence that most Realtors skip the details.	By having a team approach, you don't miss the details because team researchers are completing the process.
It's easy to miss houses in the MLS.	By having a team approach, you have agents who scour the MLS daily looking for deals.
It takes a lot of time to open doors for inspectors, appraisers, and other vendors.	By having a team approach, someone will always be available, even to handle the logistics of an escrow.
Loan officers need to be watched closely.	By having a team approach, someone will follow up with loan officers to make sure they are hitting their timelines.
Marketing takes a lot of time.	By having a team approach, there is an entire staff to market their listing.

Your clients' primary concern with the team model will be that they lose access to you. Assure them that your team gives them more access to you, not less, by using the examples in the table above. The work the client really cares about is having things explained to them and finding the right house to buy.

Be Clear About How Your Clients Can Access You

Your clients will communicate with different people on your team. Most clients, however, will prefer to talk to you. You can address this hurdle by being clear at the beginning of the relationship about the best way to communicate. I have an hourglass theory in which the chaos of communication is pushed into a central location, where it can be controlled (there is much more on this in Chapter Nine).

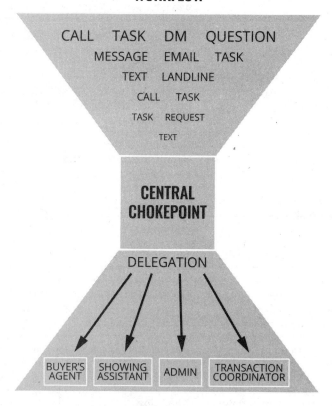

WORKFLOW

CALL   TASK   DM   QUESTION
MESSAGE   EMAIL   TASK
TEXT   LANDLINE
CALL   TASK
TASK   REQUEST
TEXT

CENTRAL CHOKEPOINT

DELEGATION

| BUYER'S AGENT | SHOWING ASSISTANT | ADMIN | TRANSACTION COORDINATOR |

As the rockstar agent, you get to decide what type of communication that will be. Whether it's email, text messages, phone calls, or a personal assistant, explain to your clients the best way for them to access you. Then have your team push through all those contacts and delegate who will respond as your representative.

Paint a Picture for How the Experience Should Feel

After you've determined the individual components of your system, your next task is to make it easy for clients to understand what they will experience. The following example explains how parts of the transaction will look and what the client can expect during that time. I include this story in my buyer's presentation, whether I present it or have a team member present it.

Flight Analogy

[Insert name], have you ever taken a flight to somewhere amazing, like Hawaii? The trip is equal parts exciting and nerve-racking. For those nervous about flying, though, sometimes it doesn't matter where you're traveling because you're always nervous during the flight.

On my team, I function as the pilot because that's the most important job. I ensure that you arrive safely in Hawaii. I help you determine the exact destination, and I chart the course, study the weather patterns, and practice for what I'd do if the worst-case scenario occurs and we have problems midflight. I'd like to point out the reason planes have pilots is because things can go wrong.

I've hired others to make the trip as comfortable as possible. These are my assistants, and they function like flight attendants. They will bring you pillows, blankets, food, and drinks. They'll remind you how long we have before we touch down, and what entertainment options are available. They are here to improve your experience.

Can you see how difficult it would be for me to focus on flying if I also had to be the flight attendant? Yet this is how most real estate agents work. They fly the plane, they pass out the peanuts, and they load your luggage too. Getting you to your destination safely is so important to me that I've hired others to help me while I focus solely on that. This cuts into my profit margins, but it provides you with a much better experience. That's important to me too.

During the flight, there will be times you'll have questions for me. That's totally normal. Sometimes I'll be able to answer them directly, but sometimes I'll have the flight attendants relay them to me. When I'm in meetings negotiating with other agents to get your offer accepted, I want to focus only on that. If you can tell my staff what your question is, they'll get it to me as soon as I've completed my task and can leave the cockpit. What's important is you make your needs known as soon as possible, so we can make you as comfortable as possible. I've put a whole team together to make that easier for you.

When my agents are showing you homes, looking up information, or doing research, I know what's going on. I'm often behind the scenes directing them on what to do or telling them what to relay to you. You can rest assured that I not only fly the plane, but I also own the airline! If you ever want to speak to me directly, please just tell a staff member or email me at [fill in email address].

Last, there will be times when you encounter turbulence. It is totally normal to freak out when this happens. Most people do. I'll remind you that a little shaking of the plane feels so scary because we're at 10,000 feet in the air. The same shaking at ground level would never concern you. Being in escrow feels like flying high in the sky. Unimportant things will feel significant, and your emotions will be all over the place. That's okay. Let me be the pilot. I'll tell you if we need to strap on our parachutes and jump out of the plane. I know the difference between turbulence and a real emergency. If I'm not freaking out, you don't need to either.

We'll experience this when we get an inspection report, an appraisal, or a hiccup with your loan. I exist as your agent to solve these problems, and I'm good at it. My staff will let you know what's going on and tell you what I need to fix it. Please keep that in mind when you want to panic from the turbulence. Everyone goes through it, but nobody remembers it when they land in Hawaii.

➡ KEY POINTS

- While there may be some value in *you* not working with buyers, you absolutely want your team to work with them because buyers bring massive value to a business.
- An agent who doesn't know how to convince a homeowner to become a buyer will only be left with homeowners who have already decided to sell.
- For people who earn enough to qualify for a loan and do not yet own a house but want to, agents can break down the numbers to show them the path to homeownership.
- Buyers can bridge the financial gap if your business is falling behind.
- The first step in excelling with buyers is to learn what they want from their agent. There are certain things every buyer wants and other things only some want.
- Uncertainty breeds anxiety. When clients don't know what to expect or how to interpret what they're being told by their agent, the result is anxiety on the client's part, and anxiety often brings out the worst in people.
- All tasks that do not require interaction are assigned to different team members while tasks that do require client interaction are handled by the assigned agent in the transaction. This prevents the client from realizing the agent isn't doing all the work.
- By showcasing the team model during your presentation, you remove leads' worries that they'll be passed around to different people rather than being a priority to your business.

CHAPTER SIX

EXCELLING WITH SELLERS

"Engaging people is about meeting their needs—not yours."

—TONY ROBBINS

While your team will spend most of their time working with buyers, ensuring a steady stream of listings is just as important—if not more so—for your team's success. Listings support your buyer's agents. They support your administrative staff by ensuring a predictable stream of workflow. Additionally, listing clients provide a much higher profit margin toward your bottom line than buyer clients.

Listings serve as the highest dollar-producing component of your business yet take less work than buyer clients; they therefore require fewer team members in the process. With fewer people working on closing a listing and with less time needed to close them, you spend less money on staff and keep a higher percentage of profit. This applies to more than just money; you'll also typically spend less effort to close them. Buyer clients will form your company's foundation, but listings will be where most of your money will be made. Don't ignore listings because buyers and buyer's agents demand your time and attention. This is an easy mistake to make.

In this chapter, I highlight how you can stay focused on taking more listings, how you can get your team to bring in more listings, how you can divide up the work required to close them, and how you can use your team's listings to acquire more buyers for your buyer's agents.

For those with established teams, have your team members read this chapter to see where they can incorporate the following into their workflow. For those building a team, read this chapter with the understanding that this is what it will look like as you hire and leverage work. For those on a team or who wish to join one, read this chapter with the understanding that this is what you want to start doing for your team leader. Regardless of where you are in the real estate sales spectrum, leveraging out the work and making the most of every listing is the best use of your time.

Working the Lead Funnel

There is a skill to converting Leads, and that is understanding the path, which is represented in the following graphic.

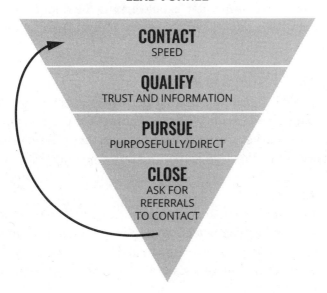

LEAD FUNNEL

CONTACT
SPEED

QUALIFY
TRUST AND INFORMATION

PURSUE
PURPOSEFULLY/DIRECT

CLOSE
ASK FOR
REFERRALS
TO CONTACT

1. **Contact.** The first step is to quickly contact the Lead and open the lines of communication. Speed to Lead is your friend.
2. **Qualify.** After successfully contacting the Lead, your next job is to determine the quality of the Lead. Determine if you can help the Lead (in this case, sell their house) by asking qualifying questions. The key to this is building trust while gathering info. The more the Lead trusts you, the more likely they are to answer your questions. Examples of questions to ask are:
   - "Are you ready to move now?"
   - "Do you have enough equity to sell?"
   - "Are you open to letting me sell your house for you?"
3. **Pursue.** If you qualify the Lead, your next goal is to pursue them. *Don't wait for the Lead to take the first step in initiating a business relationship.* You do this by being direct and clear that you want to sell their house, and you'd like to show them what you can offer them. This is usually done through a listing presentation. Keep your conversation centered on landing the Lead as a Client.
4. **Close.** After you have reached closing, your job is to ask for referrals. And you can't ask for referrals if you didn't keep the client happy and excel at your job. Happy clients become raving fans, which produces referrals. When they give you the name of someone, you contact that Lead immediately and restart the funnel. If you did a commendable job working the Client throughout the funnel, their referral will have that much more credibility.

The Value of Listings to a Team

Listings provide more value than just the commission and a high profit margin; they also provide work and income for you and your team. If you correctly market and work your listings, they can secure additional listings and leads plus free marketing for your company and agents.

Open Houses

Open houses are the obvious and easiest way to generate more clients from a listing. When your agents hold open houses, they meet new people to input into your database. As mentioned earlier, this is the first step in the Sales Funnel and the genesis of lead generation. Open houses offer a double benefit because these people not only expand your database but also are likely to qualify as serious leads. Many people at open houses are in the market to buy a house but not yet working with an agent. The key to successful open houses is to train your agents to perform at a high level and convert the leads they meet.

In *SOLD*, I offer details on how to conduct a robust open house and how to prepare and execute one. I also explain how to do lead follow-up and how to convert leads into clients (see Chapter Six in *SOLD* for the details). For this book, I want to focus on the information you need to hook the leads who walk in the door. I call hooks pieces of information that capture the person's attention, make them want to learn more about me, and, more importantly, learn what I can offer them. This can be done by sharing information about property taxes, private mortgage insurance, closing cost credits, off-market properties, and strategies that benefit buyers. If you can read your lead to understand their biggest anxiety or concern, you can figure out which hook to use. I also recommend using the acronym FORD to start conversations and build rapport with leads:

- **Family**: Ask the leads about their family, children, and their concerns regarding those individuals.
- **Occupation**: Ask what they do for work, where they work, or what they need in a home office.
- **Recreation**: Ask what they enjoy doing for fun and if they need space to store equipment for their hobbies. Do they need a side yard for their boat? Garage space for woodworking? A shed for their garden? Ask if the property needs to be located near the area they frequent for fun: the mountains, a lake, softball fields, and so on.
- **Dreams**: Ask what the client's dream home looks like or if this property will achieve their dream. Are they downsizing for retirement? Moving to an area with a good school district? Wanting more space for entertaining?

Have a minimum number of open houses that your selling agents need to hold, then review those numbers during your weekly check-ins with them. Providing your own team's listings and the listings of other Realtors in your office or sphere of influence for your agents to hold open will help your buyer's agents get more leads. By the way, as the rockstar, it's your job to secure access to these lists.

Open House Script

Agent: Welcome to my open house! Please come on in and sign up right over there.

Lead: Thank you. [Signs up.]

Agent: So, experience tells me people come to open houses for two reasons. They are in the market, or they are a neighbor checking out their neighbor's place. Which one are you?

Lead: Well, we aren't neighbors, but we are thinking about buying at some point. Just to be straightforward, we aren't serious and don't want to buy right now.

Agent: That's okay. It takes a significant amount of time and preparation before someone can feel comfortable knowing this is the right choice for them. Can I ask what it is about this place that caught your attention?

Lead: We really like the neighborhood and have always wanted to live here. Just not sure if we can afford it. Especially with the market being so hot.

Agent: Agreed. The market is definitely hot, and this is a premier neighborhood. There's a lot of demand for this neighborhood, but there might not be if people knew everything about it. It's kind of sad, really.

Lead: What do you mean?

Agent: Well, people drive by and see the amazing parks, new schools, and manicured lawns. It's certainly an eye-catcher. The problem is, nobody tells them where this comes from. At least, not until they sign the closing paperwork. By the time they realize what's going on, it's too late.

Lead: Really? What is really going on?

Agent: Eh, before I say anything else, are you committed to working with another agent? I don't want to step on anyone's toes or violate any fiduciary agreement you have with a buyer's agent. It's your agent's job to share this, not mine.

Lead: No, we have someone we've been talking to, but we aren't committed to them formally. We'd like to hear what you have to say.

Agent: Oh, that's good to hear. Many buyers know they need to vet the property they buy, but they don't do the same for the agent they choose. With my clients, I *always* make sure we sit down and go over the entire homebuying process, so they know exactly what they're getting into. More than that, I share some of the information you're asking about before we start the search. Do you still you want to hear more about the hidden surprises with this neighborhood?

Lead: Please!

Agent: When these newer, nicer neighborhoods are built, the city doesn't want to pay for all the amenities they insist on including. That means someone else must pay for them. The way this works is the builder borrows money, usually through a financial vehicle like a municipal bond. They use that money to build the streets, lights, sewers, parks, and all the infrastructure needed to develop a community. Rather than build that cost into the home itself, the builder passes it off through property taxes. If the price was built into the home, nobody could afford to buy it. Instead, the bond is paid back over time through homeowners' property taxes as a special assessment. The homes in this neighborhood are $300 to $400 a month higher in taxes than homes across town. When you sign your closing paperwork, it gets snuck in there. By the time you realize it, it's too late. At today's interest rates, you can borrow an additional $80,000 for $400 a month. When I represent my clients, I advise them to buy the more expensive house and put the $80,000 toward that. That's much wiser than buying a home where you're paying extra in property taxes instead of the mortgage. It's just too bad most people don't know that. Check out this listing I printed off before coming to host this home. You can get this house, a much larger lot, and more square footage for $50,000 less than this one. It will be a smaller mortgage too!

Lead: We had no idea!

Agent: Most people don't. Can I ask another question?

Lead: Of course.

Agent: Would you like to meet me in my office later today or tomorrow? You seem like nice folks who may want to be homeowners someday. I'd feel better if I could give you my presentation and share more info like this. There's no charge and no obligation, but I could get you up to speed and educate you on this process.

Lead: We'd love that!

Agent: Great! Let me just verify the information on the sign-in sheet to make sure I have your correct information and we'll get that scheduled ASAP. I'm so glad you guys came in today! It's been great speaking with you.

Would you mind if I show you around this place a little? I'd love to get a feel for what you like.

Lead: Absolutely!

Agent: Let's go. By the way, tell me more about your family. Do you have kids or plans for kids?

Sign Calls

The phrase "sign call" comes from those who call the phone number on the front yard listing sign, but in today's world, most leads see your information online. Regardless, the purpose is the same: Generate leads through those who call asking about your listing and try to convert them into clients for your team. Provide training to your agents and have them practice this. Again, the key is to find the right hook to use with the lead. Many of the hooks used at open houses will work for the sign call method as well. The aim is to get the lead to see your agents as having information they need but may not have known before the call.

The lead will be asking about the listing, but your selling agent's goal is to find out why the listing caught their attention in the first place and to obtain clues to pass to the buyer's agents in your office. If they can figure out what those are, they can use them to build rapport and create a relationship to the point where they can follow up in the future to set an appointment and try to secure them as a client. The following questions can help your buyer's agents learn more about the lead:

- "What about this listing got you the most excited? Was it the property itself or its location?"
- "What made this property stand out among the others you've seen?"
- "Have you had any luck writing offers on other properties yet?" (This will let your agents know if the lead already has an agent without having to ask directly.)
- "If I could get you access to see this property, would you want to right away, or is this more of just a curiosity thing?"
- [For those highly interested in the property]: "I'll look into this property for you. Can I ask, what is most important to you in the agent you choose to represent your interests here?"

Your team's assigned buyer's agent should contact this lead quickly, because a lead's interest will wane if they aren't contacted immediately. They will simply talk to another Realtor to get what they need. Consider having a dedicated number that goes to your internal sales assistant or another agent to answer sign calls.

Sign Call Script

Agent: Good morning [or afternoon], I see you're inquiring about 123 Main Street. How can I help you?

Lead: Hello. I wanted to know if this house is still on the market and what you think it will sell for.

Agent: I know the house is on the market now, but I'll have to speak to the seller for more details about the price. Did you have a number in mind, or were you asking to determine if you might get a great deal on it?

Lead: Yeah. I just wanted to see if they might sell it cheap. I think it's out of my price range.

Agent: I'll inquire about that price for you. Can I ask how you determined what your price range is? Has a lender preapproved you for an amount yet?

Lead: Oh, no. I just feel like anything over $400,000 is too expensive for me.

Agent: Ah, perfect! Well, we definitely don't want you to have a payment higher than what you're comfortable with. I'm happy to run some numbers for you when we are finished here to determine what the monthly payment on a house like this would be. Would that give you more clarity than you have now?

Lead: Yes. But I just want to know about this house now.

Agent: Of course. What's the best email for me to send some information to once I talk to the seller? I'll include some additional homes in the area and what they sold for, so you can have some context on the market for yourself. Happy to do it.

Lead: Wow, thanks. I wasn't expecting that.

Agent: Yup. To make sure I look at the right houses, can you tell me a little more about why you liked this property? Was it the property itself or the geographical area?

Lead: It's the area. It's close to my work and my kids go to school near there. I'm getting divorced, so I need a new place to live, and I want to stay close to my kids. I don't want to disrupt their lives too much.

Agent: That's very honorable of you. I'm so glad that you reached out to our office. I'll make sure I only look up houses in this school district. How many kids do you have? How many bedrooms would you need?

Lead: Two kids. Boy and a girl. I need at least three bedrooms, but four would be ideal.

Agent: Okay, great. What grades are they in? Do you need extra parking for additional vehicles?

Lead: No. They are young. Third and fifth grade.

Agent: Okay. I'll spend a little time looking for properties that have a big enough backyard to play in and spaces where they can ride their bikes. That's such a fun age. You're going to make a ton of memories in this next house. I'm excited to see how I can help you.

Lead: Thank you for that. That's very cool of you. Honestly, I don't really know what to do to get started. I was just looking at houses online.

Agent: That's not a problem. That's where everyone starts these days. Here's what I'd like to do. I'll do a little more research, then get a little better feel for what you like and what you want. I'm assuming you don't have another agent so I'm not stepping on anybody's toes. [If the answer is no.] Once I have more info, let's schedule a meeting so I can share with you what goes on in the process and how we can make sure you're making the right move for your family. This is an important one. After we meet, we can decide if buying is best or if you should wait. You'll have a much better feel about me as well by then. We can figure out the next steps from there.

Lead: That sounds good to me. I feel better talking to you already. What was your name again?

Off-Market Opportunities to Show Buyer Clients

When you have a listing in "coming soon" status, you can share that information with the buyer's agents on your team to help them market to their own clients or, even better, leads they have not been able to convert yet. Who doesn't want to hear about exclusive off-market properties? This can be a powerfully persuasive tool for your agents to use to secure leads and get appointments with them.

Train your agents to share all off-market property photos and information with their leads, whether they are sign call leads, open house leads, or online leads. Agents can use this information as a hook into leads who want to know more. Showing agents can arrange for showings to build rapport and establish trust and credibility with interested leads.

Off-Market Property Script

Agent: Hi [Name]. I just came across a property that made me think of you. I remember you had mentioned you love one-story houses, but we don't see them very often. Are you in the middle of anything right now?

Lead: Nope. Whatcha got?

Agent: We're taking a new listing that isn't on the market yet. Nobody has seen it. We're currently working with the sellers to get it ready for pictures, so it's not in its best shape, but that doesn't matter. This place is a gem. Someone's gonna get lucky here.

Lead: Really?

Agent: I have the seller's permission to show it to my clients before it goes live, but only because they trust me. I'm not showing it to any outside buyers. When this property hits the market, it's going to get a ton of interest. I'd love to show you this place, and if you like it, see what I can do to help you get it before the bidding war happens. Where's your comfort level with me when it comes to me helping you and your wife buy your next place?

Lead: To be honest, I haven't thought about it much. I know my wife really liked you. I've just been busy with work and a little discouraged by how hot the market is.

Agent: I thought that might be the case. That's why I'm reaching out. Part of winning in an environment like this is finding the deal *before* the rush. That's why I called you. There's simply no one better than me at working to find deals like this for my clients. It seems like we hit it off. Are you okay to sign the paperwork to have me represent you? Then I can make the arrangements to show you and your wife the property. You don't have to buy it, but if you like it, you have a chance to wrap it up before anyone else.

Lead: Sure. Send that over and I'll let my wife know. She's gonna be thrilled.

Free Marketing of Listing

Your team should market every client's listing to their SOI. This is a powerful factor to sway sellers to decide to list with you. Most agents get business and receive referrals by staying top of mind to their SOI. With a team of five agents and three administrative assistants, for example, you have eight people sharing listings on their social media and with their email base. This not only brings value to your sellers but also to your team. When the agents on your team share these listings to their individual SOIs, it looks like it's their listing. More team listings means more opportunities for team members to generate business for themselves; this not only builds your team members' confidence but it also converts to revenue for your company. As each SOI sees that agent doing more business, it communicates to them that the agent knows the business and can be trusted with referrals. I encourage all the agents on my team to post everyone's listings to their SOI to help everyone generate more business for each other. Several agents on my team use both of our pictures to market to their database. The following picture is an example.

Just Listed

1952 Josephine Ave, San Jose CA

David Greene 925-626-8237
Krista Keller 209-204-1319
www.davidgreene24.com

THE DAVIDGREENE TEAM

What Sellers Want

Having your team understand what matters to sellers will net more listings. The aim is to show sellers that you and your team can help them get out of their home for the price that they want.

Sellers want three things, in order of priority:

1. To know their property will sell.
2. To get top dollar for their property.
3. To have as smooth and pain-free an experience as possible.

To win sellers over, these concerns have to be addressed in this order. The first can be addressed by having your agents tell sellers how they will get their house sold faster than other agents. After the sellers' interest is piqued, your agents shift the conversation to how they can get a better price than other agents. Finally, your agents share how they've helped past clients make this process smoother.

Using Your Team to Market Listings

Your sellers aren't just hiring you as the rockstar agent; they are also hiring your entire team. During listing presentations, share how the entire team works together to sell the client's listing. Highlight that this team works with dozens of buyers at a time, and these buyers will all be shown their listing before other houses for sale. This should address the fear that their house will not sell.

Faster Task Completion

During the presentation, also tell the lead that the entire team helps get the listings ready for market. That means your listings are ready faster than those from agents who work alone. This teamwork includes finalizing paperwork and ordering signs, photos, and cleaning services. One straightforward way to show teamwork is to ensure an assistant is ready to answer their phone while you're in the appointment. After explaining how important speed and leverage are in getting results, send your assistant a voice message requesting something like comparable properties or paperwork to sign. In a few minutes, you'll receive the information via email. This showcases your team's efficiency.

Faster Communication With Client

The No. 1 complaint in our industry is poor communication by agents.[10] Realtors are often accused of not answering their phones, and thus not caring about their clients. The reality, though, is that real estate agents are often already on their phones or in meetings doing the work required of them as a fiduciary. Now, many agents do answer their phones, but these are usually agents with fewer clients. The more skills an agent has, the busier they are. The dilemma is that sellers want the best agents, but these agents never have much availability to answer their phone.

This problem is explained in the presentation, along with the solution: an assistant who fields your calls. This assures your clients that they will experience excellent customer service every time they call. Whether it is you or a team member presenting this information, highlight how you, as the rockstar agent, will remain focused on negotiations, finding the right buyer for their house, locating the right new house for themselves,

---

10 Margaret Horton, "What Is the Biggest Complaint That Buyers or Sellers Have About Realtors?", Realty Times, November 6, 2017, https://realtytimes.com/advicefromtheexpert/item/1006688-what-is-the-biggest-complaint-that-buyers-or-sellers-have-about-realtors.

and anticipating any problems before they arise. You can do all of this while a message is never lost.

Higher Volume Equals More Skill

The more you do anything, the better you get at it. This principle is also true in real estate. Tell the listing leads that with the team approach, your agency sells more houses because every member of the team gets better with every experience.

Sellers shouldn't be expected to know what's involved in creating the lead preparation, doing the marketing, negotiating for better prices, etc. "Get my house sold" is all they're thinking. It's your job to present that the team approach gets more houses sold, which is the highest value for sellers.

More Help Getting Listing Ready for Market

Getting a listing agreement signed is the hard part, but getting a listing ready for the market is the long part. It requires scheduling of yard signs, photos to be taken and uploaded, cleaning of the home, gathering information for the MLS, and so on. This work can be assigned to a new team member. Having staff to prepare listings for the market is one of the top ways clients benefit, as do you as the rockstar agent.

More Eyeballs on "Coming Soon" Properties

I'm not the best person to catch everything that should be improved in a property that I'm listing. I won't notice a rug that clashes with curtains or some paint that needs to be freshened up. Because of this, I have my team members check my listings to catch as many imperfections as possible. This quality control is beneficial for the seller and gives me peace of mind.

More Leads for the Team

More listings equals more sign calls, more online leads, and more overall opportunities for your team members to generate new business. In a hot market, many of my buyer's agents can sell our team's listings to their clients, so their offers are accepted faster. This is also a benefit for our sellers because we make sure our agent's offer is the most competitive. It's the rockstar agent's job to produce leads, and that is done with more listings.

Creating a Rockstar Listing System

Many agents know how to secure a listing, but a rockstar agent must secure more of them while spending less time working on them. Reducing the drag listings takes on your rockstar productivity is vital. I'll next highlight the ways my team members shoulder most of the listing responsibilities to put me in a position to excel with sellers.

The six stages are as follows:

1. Preappointment

The goal of the preappointment is to allow me to be as successful as possible during the listing presentation. My staff does this by building trust and rapport with the lead and gathering information.

My administrative assistant stays in close touch with leads between initial contact and the listing presentation. My listing assistant gathers information on the state of mind of the seller, which prevents me from having to ask sensitive questions that may hurt my relationship with the lead during the presentation. The questions posed include:

- Do you intend to use David as your agent, or are you still interviewing other agents?
- What is most important to you in the Realtor you use?
- How much do you believe your home is worth or will sell for?
- How much do you currently owe on your home?
- Have there been any recent updates or upgrades completed on the property?
- Does the home have any solar and, if so, how much is the balance/what is the monthly payment?
- Do you plan on doing a 1031 exchange?
- Do you plan on using this sale to fund your next purchase?
- Do you have any photos of the interior/exterior that you can send us for comps?
- Can you do me a favor and have two extra key copies made for David?
- What is most important about you for us to know?
- What is most important for you regarding communication?

The listing assistant also:

- Runs and saves a CMA in the MLS for me to review.
- Prints a copy of the CMA and calls every agent with an active and pending listing to ask:
  - How many offers did your listing receive?
  - Can you share the price you went pending for?
  - How many showings is your listing currently getting?
  - Do you feel you priced the home well?
  - Where would you price it if you were to list it again?
- Makes notes on the CMA with the above information and with other information, such as the condition of comparable homes, and similarities and differences for me to review with the lead.
- Gets an opinion from our preferred appraiser on what the home might appraise for.
- Prints the email from the appraiser to include in the listing packet.
- Confirms that the seller's name on the tax records is the same as the lead's and determines if there are additional owners on record.
- Investigates if the house is held in a trust or other form of title and prints the proper forms.
- Prints the required seller disclosure forms.
- Puts together the presentation's listing folder, which includes:
  - Seller disclosures
  - Listing agreement paperwork
  - Team blueprint marketing material
  - Branded PopSocket
  - Branded pen
  - CMA with notes
  - Printed email from appraiser
  - A copy of my book *Sell Your Home for Top Dollar*
- Schedules the listing presentation.
- Enters the listing presentation date into my calendar.
- Calls the lead the day before to confirm the appointment.

With this information available, I should have no trouble crushing the appointment, making an indelible impression, and securing the signed paperwork. Once you start training your listing agents to handle presentations, your support staff will do this for them too.

2. Listing Appointment

During the appointment, I focus on delivering an excellent presentation and keying in on the emotions of the sellers. As noted earlier, I have one assistant ready to answer the phone to send what I need, which allows the leads to see the responsiveness of my team for themselves.

3. Coming Soon

During the "coming soon" phase, my staff focuses on four things:
1. Getting the listing ready to hit the market.
2. Keeping close communication with the seller.
3. Marketing the property to generate public interest.
4. Marketing the property to generate leads for your team.

My administrative assistant does most of the work to prepare a listing for the market. This includes:
- Uploading signed paperwork to the file storage software.
- Ensuring seller disclosures are filled out and received.
- Ordering the sign for the yard.
- Confirming the seller is doing the necessary work to show the house (e.g., painting, cleaning, packing).
- Ordering moving boxes.
- Scheduling marketing photos.
- Coordinating inspections and making copies of the inspection reports.
- Scheduling a time to review the inspection reports with the seller.
- Paying the vendors.
- Posting "coming soon" marketing pictures on social media.
- Entering the required information into the MLS and uploading the marketing pictures.
- Writing the property description.
- Putting a lock box on the property.

My listing assistants follow up every day with the clients via email or phone to communicate what progress we're making.

4. Active Listing

Once the listing is active, my listing assistants are responsible for:

- Preparing me for my own weekly call with the client (e.g., number of showings).
- Fielding calls from buyer's agents, answering what they legally can, and passing to me what they cannot answer.
- Scheduling showings with the seller for interested buyers.
- Following up with showing agents to gauge buyers' interest to share with the seller.
- Checking my inbox for inquiries about the property.
- Collecting and reviewing offers and inputting the information into a Google Sheet for me to review.
- Completing administrative tasks as needed.

The goal of the listing assistant is to make sure no buyer leads are missed, that the showing agents have all the necessary information, and I'm not fielding questions they can answer to keep the process moving forward.

5. Pending Listing

When the listing goes pending, I ensure that my transaction coordinator has all the necessary paperwork to manage the transaction. This includes the offer, any counteroffers and addendums, and the appropriate legal disclosures. I communicate with the buyer's agent to make sure the following tasks are completed from the buyer's side:

- Inspections are ordered.
- Appraisal is ordered.
- Loan due diligence is completed.
- Lender is sent the documents they need.
- All contingencies are on track to be removed by the buyers.
- Property is marked as "pending" in the MLS.

The listing assistant communicates with the seller to ensure:

- The seller is signing and returning documents to the transaction coordinator.
- The seller understands the information provided by the title company.

The listing agent also confirms:

- Whether the seller needs assistance with the logistics of moving.
- The seller knows to turn off the utilities currently held in their name.
- The seller remembers to contact the post office about their change of address.

6. Sold Listing

The listing assistant's job for a sold listing is to wrap up the details. When a listing is closed, the listing assistant:

- Closes out the file and the "coming soon" work.
- Markets the sold closing on social media.
- Removes the lock box from the property.
- Has the yard sign removed.
- Marks the property as "sold" in the MLS and in the CRM.
- Collects a testimonial from the seller.
- Sends the seller a gift.
- Ensures all belongings are removed from the house.
- Confirms all paperwork is collected for compliance purposes.
- Puts the seller on a follow-up auto plan in the CRM.
- Asks the seller for referrals.

Team Listing Goals

The goal of your listing team is to leverage listings to get more business. Use the strategies in this chapter so that your listing agents are providing leads and opportunities for your buyer's agents. Your listing assistants' responsibilities allow your listing agents more time to find more business, and the cycle begins over again. Ideally, your listing assistants should eventually get licensed to become listing agents themselves. Your buyer's agents should learn from your listing agents how they can win their own listings, and your listing agents should learn from your buyer's agents how they can gain more buyer clients.

Excelling in real estate sales requires experience and, more importantly, the confidence that comes with it. Having team members participate in the work means they gain that experience at a much faster rate. As your agents gain top-producing agent traits, more deals will close and there will be more raving reviews of your staff.

This momentum, in turn, creates opportunities for you, such as scaling your business more or earning passive income. The two options offer different values. Scaling obviously keeps your business growing. However, some rockstar agents prefer the passive approach so they can focus only on the parts of the job they love. This improves quality of life and quality of service and allows for a longer and happier career. Others take it to work only the hours they like and use the rest of their time for other pursuits. Either way, your team is what allows you to grow your business to the point where you get to decide.

➡ KEY POINTS

- Listings support your buyer's agents and your administrative staff by ensuring a predictable stream of workflow; they also serve as the highest dollar-producing component of your business despite taking less work than buyers.
- Don't ignore listings because buyers and buyer's agents demand your time and attention. This is an easy mistake to make.
- The Lead funnel:
  - Contact with speed
  - Qualify through obtaining information
  - Pursue directly
  - Close and ask for referrals
- Open houses are the obvious and easiest way to generate more clients from a listing.
- The key to successful open houses is to train your agents to perform at a high level and convert the leads they meet.
- To build rapport, remember the acronym FORD:
  - Family
  - Occupation
  - Recreation
  - Dreams
- Your team should market every client's listing to their SOI. This is a powerful factor to sway sellers to decide to list with you.
- The No. 1 complaint in our industry is poor communication by agents.
- Ideally, your listing assistants should eventually get licensed to become listing agents themselves.

CHAPTER ▶ SEVEN

SUCCEEDING IN DIFFERENT MARKETS

"Buy land, they're not making it anymore."

—MARK TWAIN

This chapter will help you to identify a seller market and a buyer market and explain the strategies needed to succeed in either one. The most successful businesses don't use the same strategies year after year but adapt to economic, political, and technological shifts. This is why some businesses stay afloat while others don't, and some increase profits while others stagnate. As a real estate rockstar, you're running a business. Your team depends on you to guide them through both markets and remain profitable.

Types of Markets

The two markets are the buyer's market and the seller's market. A buyer's market refers to a real estate environment in which market conditions and supply favor the buyer. This market is affiliated with significant inventory, lower demand for housing, and buyers with a lower sense of urgency. Conversely, a seller's market has limited inventory, a high demand for housing, and buyers who are motivated to make aggressive offers.

Either way, it is the buyers who determine these markets, which I elaborate on later in this chapter.

Each market requires different skills. Additionally, the prevailing factors that determine each market will affect the strategies you employ. Having a firm understanding of these influential factors will help you explain the situation to your clients, help you gain their trust, and help you consistently put them in contract. Earlier in this book I discussed frame control. This knowledge of the markets will give you frame control and help you develop the local star power Oren Klaff describes in *Pitch Anything*.

What Drives Markets

Real estate markets are driven primarily by supply and demand, fiscal policy, world events, and the psychology of following the herd. I'll explain these in the following sections.

Supply and Demand

This is by far the most crucial factor because it drives economic markets. In fact, the other three factors all find their relevance in this first factor.

Economist Adam Smith is credited with the creation of the concept of supply and demand in his 1776 work, *The Wealth of Nations*. Known as the father of economics, Smith likened the concept of supply and demand to an "invisible hand" that naturally guided the economy.[11]

Supply refers to the available amount of any given product or service. Demand refers to how much desire there is at any given point in time for that product or service. When there is a short supply of something and a strong demand, the price will increase as the buyers compete to obtain it. This fuels "bubbles" in the economy. It also leads to more of the supply, such as building more homes or raising more money to invest in real estate. What will set you apart from your competition will be (1) your ability to articulate this concept to your clients and obtain their trust and buy-in, and (2) your ability to foresee changes in the relationship between real estate supply and demand and get in front of the curve.

---

11 "The Origins of the Law of Supply and Demand," Investopedia, September 21, 2021, https://www. investopedia.com/ask/answers/030415/who-discovered-law-supply-and-demand.asp.

A seller's market is one in which there is more demand for housing than available supply. Houses will sell faster, for more money, and with conditions more favorable for the seller. In this market, you'll need to employ strategies that keep your business running at its peak performance. I highlight these strategies later in this chapter.

Supply and demand has everything to do with how real estate is *valued*. Many people struggle with the concept of value because they think it and price are connected, but they aren't. Take, for example, the cost of building a home from the ground up versus one that's already built. In a strong market with limited inventory, established homes will sell for much more than it would cost to build new ones. The land itself under an established home is often more valuable than the land under a new home. That means it makes sense for builders to construct new homes.

Conversely, in buyer's markets, someone can buy a house for much less than what it costs to build one. Under these conditions, builders will likely not build new homes, and new construction will be severely limited. One strategy for a buyer's market is to have preexisting relationships with builders to sell their existing inventory, but you'll need to quickly recognize the change in markets and adjust your marketing efforts accordingly.

It's very important for real estate professionals to understand the difference between price and value. Your clients will often be confused about this differentiation and will rely on you to provide clarity. Real estate can be valued in many ways, such as:

1. The income it produces
2. The replacement cost of rebuilding it
3. How it stacks up to comparable properties
4. Its sentimental value
5. Its proximity to valuable amenities

Fiscal Policy

The U.S. economy and how the government manipulates currency play massive roles in which real estate market the country experiences. This should come as no surprise because of the relationship between real estate and debt. Because most homeowners borrow to buy their homes, the amount borrowed and the cost of real estate debt factor into which properties clients can afford to buy.

When a prospective home buyer applies for a loan, the selected residential mortgage lender looks at the person's income and debts to calculate a debt-to-income (DTI) ratio. This ratio is how the lender determines how much of the person's paycheck will be left over after debt service. The more income left over, the higher the amount the lender will let them borrow.

The other component to the lender's fiscal formula is the interest rate on the debt. A lender calculates the amount of mortgage a borrower can afford to pay each month, based on the DTI, then factors in the current interest rate. This is the amount the lender is willing to lend. For a borrower, lower interest rates mean higher loan amounts, and that means they can shop for higher-priced houses and still stay within their DTI.

When the federal government plays with the country's currency, it affects mortgage interest rates. When interest rates increase, homes tend to become harder to afford, so home prices are forced downward. When rates decrease, the opposite happens. The federal government tends to be less interested in the price of homes as they are with other metrics such as the prime rate, bond prices, and the stock market. Wise real estate investors pay attention to current fiscal policy to try to figure out how the government's decisions may affect local real estate markets.

In 2008, the U.S. government started its quantitative easing (QE) program. During QE, a government buys its own bonds and other debt, thereby increasing the amount of money in circulation to keep the economy afloat. While this isn't the same as printing dollars, the effect is similar. As more currency enters circulation, the economy gains momentum and inflation takes effect. In 2008, this led to a sharp increase in home prices in the United States.

As noted in Jett International Ltd., in a post titled "Quantitative Easing and Real Estate Review & Outlook": "The logic behind the connection of QE and real estate prices is straightforward. Presuming QE has made homes more affordable through its effect on interest rates, consequently home prices have experienced a boost."[12] Since 2008, the real estate market has shifted from a buyer's market to a seller's market. Those who bought between 2008 and 2022 typically did very well. Those who waited, not so much.

Mortgage interest rates are largely determined by demand for mortgage-backed securities (MBS). An MBS is a security you can buy that is made

---

12 "Quantitative Easing and Real Estate Review & Outlook," Jett International Ltd., accessed July 22, 2022, http://jettinternational.com/heading-1-2/.

up of thousands of mortgages packaged together. The same investors who buy MBSs also often buy Treasury notes. Because of this, the ten-year Treasury note is often closely tied to mortgage interest rates.[13] When the government makes decisions that affect bond rates, MBSs are affected. As MBS prices adjust, so do the interest rates on the homes the common consumer is looking to buy. After you understand how the pieces fit together, it's easy to see the role fiscal policy plays in home affordability. This affordability affects supply and demand and influences the type of market we find ourselves in. Following fiscal policy allows you to peer into the future of real estate markets.

Because we make our income selling properties, it's important to understand the relationship between the financing of real estate and the values of the properties.

World Events

World events are highly likely to impact U.S. fiscal policy, so they too are something real estate agents pay attention to, because they can foreshadow a shift in the markets. Influential world events impact most national economies.

Bonds frequently compete with stocks for buyers, and as the bond market becomes more attractive, firms that are marketing bonds can offer lower interest rates and still sell their products. If the stock market wants to compete, it must offer a more attractive product. The same works in reverse: The more popular the stock market is, the higher the rates the bond market has to offer to compete. In general, investors favor the stock market during periods of confidence and bonds during periods of uncertainty.

Specific world events like war or terrorist activity, or even rumors of a possible recession, have negative impacts on the world economy. Investors in their own countries, for example, may stop buying bonds in their local markets and start buying them in U.S. markets. As money flows into the U.S. bond market, those selling bonds offer lower interest rates. This, in turn, pushes mortgage rates lower, which leads to increases in the value of real estate. World events can affect real estate markets in more ways than just interest rates. Rumors of wars lead many U.S. investors to assume the economy will slow down. A slower economy sees fewer people

---

13 Elizabeth Weintraub, "How Are Mortgage Rates Determined?", The Balance, June 18, 2022, https://www.thebalance.com/how-are-mortgage-rates-determined-1798392.

wanting to buy homes in anticipation that home prices will likely drop as the economy sinks. As buyers pull back from shopping for homes, the market shifts from a seller's market to a buyer's market.

These same economics affect things like the prices of materials needed to build homes. When China, for example, has a booming construction market—typically found in a seller's market—it may use a considerable amount of the world's supply of wood or concrete. When the supply of these products becomes limited worldwide, but the demand continues to increase, prices skyrocket. This makes construction more expensive and prices for houses go up.

The globe is growing ever more connected, so assume events in one part of the world will affect events in others. Therefore, the wise real estate agent pays attention to world events to decipher how that may impact local real estate markets.

Psychologically Following the Herd

In *Psychology Today*, in "The Science Behind Why People Follow the Crowd," Rob Henderson writes, "In his book *Influence*, [Robert] Cialdini ... notes that consumers often use a simple heuristic: Popular is good. Following the crowd allows us to function in a complicated environment. Most of us do not have time to increase our knowledge of all merchandise and research every advertised item to measure its usefulness."[14] Henderson goes on to explain how the rising popularity of something catches our attention.

This attention then creates a herd mentality, and the real estate market is no exception. When many people are buying homes, it appears that homeownership is a smarter option than renting. This lowers days on market (DOM), increases home prices, and the herd creates a seller's market.

Conversely, when homeowners see lots of homes for sale, or worry the economy may be shifting and fear their home may lose its value, they are also more likely to sell. As more homes hit the market, inventory increases, leading to a higher DOM. This drives home prices lower and creates a buyer's market. As noted above, lowering the price of new construction forces homeowners to lower the price of their existing homes

---

14 Rob Henderson, "The Science Behind Why People Follow the Crowd," *Psychology Today*, May 24, 2017, https://www.psychologytoday.com/us/blog/after-service/201705/the-science-behind-why-people-follow-the-crowd.

as well. When the buying herd sees this, they hold off on buying to see how low prices may fall.

Markets can spiral in either direction quickly when buying or selling clients find comfort following what others are doing. As with stocks, investors are drawn to a rising market. While an argument can be made that the worst time to buy is when everyone else is buying, stock market investors are herd animals. Wise real estate agents understand this mentality and caution their clients to take the opposite action in the housing market.

In early 2020, COVID-19 concerns caused local governments in the San Francisco Bay Area (and in many other areas) to issue "shelter in place" edicts. As the federal government worried that many citizens would lose their jobs or not be able to work, a moratorium was set on banks foreclosing on homeowners. This caused lenders to be concerned that new borrowers would stop making their mortgage payments. Their immediate response was to increase reserve requirements, acceptable credit scores, and the cost of loans. As you can imagine, this led many buyers in contract to back out. It also prevented many borrowers from being eligible for loans they had already been approved for. The mortgage market and real estate market felt immediate and severe effects.

At the time, my team had twenty-eight properties in escrow. I advised my clients that their investments were solid and made financial sense despite the current market volatility. My real estate knowledge allowed me to anticipate that this was not a recession but herd mentality at its finest. One year later, the clients who stayed in contract have averaged almost six figures in equity as the market became scalding hot. The shelter in place edicts became a golden opportunity for buyers to get deals they normally would not qualify for. Other agents' failure to understand that this was a temporary buyer's market in the middle of a seller's market allowed my clients to win big.

Succeeding in a Seller's Market

Now let's talk about how to use this information to increase your business. The way to win in a seller's market is to (1) get more listings, and (2) put your buyers in contract.

Get More Listings

The easiest way to do well in a seller's market is to get more listings. When there is limited inventory and high demand, whoever controls the inventory controls the game. Every agent knows they need listings even when there's little inventory. Where most agents get it wrong is in the way they go about getting listings. For one thing, looking for listings through the sellers themselves will rarely get you their listings. Here's why:

1. **Sellers are harder to find**: There are no open houses to find sellers. We find buyers because they are looking at houses, and we are between them and the inventory. Open houses, sign calls, search engine optimization, and IDX squeeze pages are some of the ways a buyer finds an agent for what they really want: a house. It's much more difficult to land a seller because they are seeking one agent. The one counter to this is to buy leads from websites/companies where home sellers are seeking listing agents.

2. **Sellers want you to compete with other agents**: If a seller does contact you, they are usually also contacting other agents. (The exception is when it's someone from your SOI.) If a seller finds you online, they typically want you to reduce your commission, or pay for things like staging, or put your money into fixing their home to prepare it for the market. Clearly, these are not the types of clients a rockstar agent wants to work with.

3. **Sellers may not trust you**: When you don't already have a relationship with the seller, it is more difficult to get their buy-in. When they hear that their house is worth less than they expected, it's natural for them to be disappointed and doubt you. The same is true with hiccups during the escrow process or when a buyer makes requests the seller doesn't like. Working with sellers who don't know you and trust you is tough.

4. **Sellers who are FSBO or have expired listings**: Many Realtors make a living calling For Sale by Owners and expired listings. This is a viable strategy for those with the requisite skill set. However, if a house expired as a listing or can't sell as an FSBO, it may not be a house you can sell either.

The best way to find listings during a seller's market is to do what no one else is doing: Look for buyers.

Most home sellers don't want to sell their home until they have a new one to move into, so they aren't going to start the process of looking for a listing agent until they have the next house they want to buy. If you can find homeowners when they are in their own homebuying phase, you can likely help them with both buying and selling. And if you don't want to take them on as a buyer's agent, you can refer them to someone else and focus on the listing.

The key to finding sellers in a seller's market is to find sellers who want to buy first. This knowledge gives you a massive advantage over other agents.

Put Your Buyers in Contract

The other knowledge you need is how to put your buyers into contract in a seller's market. When there is competition among buyers for each listing, it is vital that your buyers are first choice for the sellers. Remember that being the second-best offer is the same as being the worst offer. When it comes to getting your offer accepted, remember the words of Ricky Bobby from the movie *Talladega Nights*: "If you ain't first, you're last." Your goal in a seller's market is simple. Prepare your buyer client for the level of commitment they'll need, identify the property they can close on, and pursue it with everything you have. If you can do this, you can win buyers in a seller's market. Here's how.

Build Rapport and Trust with the Listing Agent

Sellers care about two things: (1) the selling price of their home, and (2) getting to close. Paramount to your success is your ability to convince the listing agent that your buyer wants the house so much that they won't back out.

If you have three team members speaking with the listing agent, which one is building the rapport needed to secure the deal? Make sure there is one lead buyer's agent and that person contacts the listing agent and communicates consistently and frequently. This starts immediately after the showing assistants identify your buyer as interested in the property. Using flattery doesn't hurt here. The goal of your lead agent is to convince the listing agent to present your buyer's offer as the best option for the sellers. One way to do this is to write the best terms, of course, but another is to have your lead convince the listing agent you're the agent they want to work with the most, and your clients are the buyers their sellers want to work with the most.

It's common in a seller's market for buyer's agents to email the offer to the listing agent and do nothing more. There are no phone calls or efforts to pitch their buying clients. If a buyer's agent shows this little effort in getting the offer accepted, how hard should the listing agent expect them to work to keep the buyer in contract? It's far better to overcommunicate with the listing agent than to risk not communicating enough.

When it comes to communicating with listing agents, I recommend being straightforward and direct. I tell listing agents that my team has the buyer for their house, the buyer has been prepared for the emotional swings of an escrow, and the buyer wants the house so much that they won't back out. I then ask what concerns the listing agent has about the escrow and about moving. I use this insight to craft an offer that will address the seller's fears. Making the listing agent believe you're the best option and writing an offer that settles the seller's concerns will get your buyer the house.

Be Fast

It's a mistake to assume every seller will wait for multiple offers before they decide on a buyer. In a seller's market, you must do everything to give your buyer the best chance to get the house they want. One way to do this is to get your offer in quickly and make frequent follow-up calls to the listing agent to see if the seller accepts. This pressure can sometimes work in your favor. Granted, it's not a foolproof approach, but it does tend to work when there are two specific types of people in the deal, and that's an inexperienced listing agent or anxious sellers.

When listing agents are inexperienced, they convey your pressure to their clients, leading the sellers to believe if they don't accept your offer, their house won't sell. In situations with a more experienced listing agent but with anxious sellers, they may accept your buyer's offer just to relieve themselves of the worry that their house won't sell. (And some sellers who seriously need or want to move on may accept just to keep their own process on track.)

Handle Due Diligence

Most of a buyer's due diligence is typically conducted during the escrow process to keep the buyer from wasting their time or money on a deal they can't qualify for. However, a seller's market is not a typical market. Some processes such as title insurance cannot reasonably be conducted before going into escrow, but many others can. If your buyer likes a house enough to present an offer without contingencies, here are four steps to help them do so safely.

1. Order inspections before your offer is accepted.
2. Ask the seller if they have inspections from when they bought the house (especially if it wasn't that long ago).
3. Ask your lender to conduct full underwriting approval, not just conditional approval or preapproval.
4. Ask your lender for an appraisal waiver.

These can help you write a competitive offer without forcing your buyer to take on the risk associated with waiving contingencies.

Use Your Loan Officer

Part of being a rockstar agent is leveraging your team, and loan officers are often forgotten members of your team—but they can be a huge advocate to put your buyer in contract. When your buyer doesn't get the house, you don't get the commission, and the borrower doesn't get the loan, so everyone loses. Because of this, you should have strong working relationships with loan officers to create mutually beneficial outcomes.

At minimum, as you prepare to send the offer, the loan officer should call the listing agent to discuss the strength of the buyer's lending position. They should also highlight the problems they *don't* anticipate happening based on the documentation provided by the borrower and on their own preliminary approval work. The dual and consistent communication should provide the listing agent and sellers assurances that your client is their best choice.

Reminding the lender to call the listing agent can be easily delegated to a team member; simply include this step in the list of to-dos associated with submitting an offer.

Find Mutual Wins

During a seller's market, your buyers may secretly think you are working for the seller instead. You may need to write such strong offers that it's an easy conclusion to make. While offers undoubtedly need to be strong in this market, it's important to make every effort to make offers that are advantageous to the sellers without negatively impacting your buyers.

For example, it's understandable that a seller would be worried about finding their next place once their current home sells. A seller's ego cares about price and terms while their crocodile brain worries about the logistics of the next move. You can be sure their croc brain is screaming loudly: "I don't want to accept any offers until I know where I'm moving to!" (There's more on croc brain in Chapter Nine.) As the buyer's agent, you make it easy for the seller to accept your clients' offer by providing a solution to this fear. If the listing agent shares that their client is nervous about the timeline, offer things like the following in your offer:

- **Sellers to rent back from buyers at buyer's principal, interest, taxes, and insurance (plus private mortgage insurance if applicable) for up to twenty-nine days after the close of escrow**: This gives the sellers the full escrow period to look for their next home plus an additional twenty-nine days if they want it. It also prevents them from being required to pay for a full month's rent if they don't need it. This option works best when your buyer has a flexible timeline.
- **Closing costs in exchange for higher price**: Many sellers care most about the price they get for their house. It's easier to understand dollar amounts than variables such as who pays the escrow fees, warranties, inspections, and lender closing costs. This "price" thinking means a solid strategy is to write your offer so the seller gets the highest sales price possible. This method also benefits your buyer client, although it sounds counterintuitive for the buyer to receive credits in exchange for a higher purchase price. This is more easily understood when you consider that low interest rates make borrowing more money better for the borrower.

  Consider this scenario: An offer of $550,000 will get your buyer the house. If you increase this offer to $570,000, with the seller crediting $20,000 in closing costs, this will save your buyer $20,000 (which is not chump change). The buyer pays approximately $84 more on the monthly payments (3 percent interest rate amortized over thirty years). If your buyer puts 10 percent down (i.e., borrowing $513,000 on the loan), the principal and interest on the loan will be $2,163 per month. Were your buyer to borrow $20,000 less, the payment is reduced only to $2,079. Is there a practical difference between these two amounts for most buyers?

Now consider what your buyer can do with an additional $20,000:

- Make improvements to the new home to turn it into their dream home or to gain immediate equity.
- Invest in the stock market at a much higher return than the 3 percent due on the loan.
- Pay off other debt they owe that has a much higher interest than the 3 percent due on the loan.
- Keep it as a rainy day or emergency fund.
- Buy a new car if they need one.

Clearly, your buyer has more options with this $20,000 than to put it down on a property's closing costs to save 3 percent. This becomes a win-win for the seller and your buyer.

- **Allowing the seller to keep certain belongings**: Many home sellers have items in the home they are emotionally attached to and would like to keep. They don't always say so because they assume everything is part of the sale of the house. In a seller's market, you can ask the listing agent about items the sellers might like to keep. Many listing agents don't think about this or are afraid to broach the topic. By having them ask their clients, you can get insights into pain points the seller is having, which you can then address in your offer. This gets the seller's attention and sets your offer apart when multiple offers are involved. Sellers may want to keep family heirlooms, such as permanent light fixtures they inherited from their grandmother, or sentimental items such as a chandelier they received as a wedding present. Writing into the offer the items that the seller can keep costs your buyer nothing and makes your offer stronger.

- **Offering shorter or longer escrow periods**: The standard escrow period is currently about thirty days, and many agents assume this is the only option. However, before my team writes an offer, they ask the listing agent what timeline will work best for their sellers. In most cases, a shorter escrow period is better for sellers. When your buyer can accommodate this, let the listing agent know that your buyer can offer a fifteen-day escrow. Some sellers prefer a longer escrow period because it gives them more time to find their next property, or to close on the next deal, or to facilitate the logistics of their move. When you know the date of the close of escrow, your buyer may be able to accommodate a shorter or longer escrow timeline.

Preparing Your Buyer Clients for a Seller's Market

Of course, the art of negotiating isn't only with the listing agent but also with your own buyers. To get a deal made, you need an offer that works for both parties, and the party that you have the most influence over is your own clients. Preparing your clients with what they need to know and do to win in a seller's market is 100 percent your responsibility. Here are the four steps to take to prepare your buyer client for a seller's market.

Step One: Timing

If you wait to explain why you may need to write an offer over list price until the moment of the offer, the news will not be well received, and you are much more likely to be seen as someone more interested in your commission than your client's best interests. To avoid this, share information about pricing and markets in your initial presentation.

Step Two: Evidence

In the moment of the offer, don't say that you may have to write an offer without contingencies and likely over asking price and expect them to believe you. Because they won't. It's better to use the triangle theory to let the data and evidence make your case for you. It is most natural to deliver this news during the buyer's presentation. At the end of your main presentation, pull up a previously prepared CMA to show your lead the list price and sell price of the properties that have sold over the last three months. If it's a seller's market, it shouldn't be hard to find comps to support this. Now is the time to explain how comparables work, so they understand later why you're advising an offer for more than what they hoped to pay.

Step Three: Relationship

It's natural for your buyers to want to control your relationship. As noted earlier in the book, the problem is that they don't know what they don't know. Allowing your clients to send you information on houses they are interested in or you researching every question they have about them can waste a lot of your time on homes they have no realistic shot of getting.

It's better for you both if your client understands that you're the expert in this relationship and that they are better off letting you select the houses they have the best chance of getting in contract. When you have this control, you can send them to listings that have been sitting on the market longer or are receiving less attention rather than the "hot home" online that has massive interest. This also protects their stamina (no buyer can continue pursuing homes without eventually getting one). Additionally, it allows you to prove your value as the agent when you guide them in the right direction.

Step Four: The Right Properties

When you have a team, the responsibility of looking for the best properties for a buyer should be delegated to a showing assistant or an administrative assistant. With a little training, they can find the right homes for you to review with your client. Train your showing assistants or admin assistant to look for the following home attributes:

- **High days on market (DOM)**: The longer a home has been on the market, the less likely it will get multiple offers. This does not guarantee you can get the house, though, so don't let your buyers postpone seeing it. Houses that have been on the market for forty days can have an offer come in the same day the buyer sees it.
- **Fallen out of contract**: Many houses will show a low DOM but a higher CDOM (cumulative days on market). This is usually a sign a property had been in contract but then fell through. For a seller in a hot market, this can be a terrible turn of events. The property is no longer showing up in searches as a new home, so finding it means specifically looking for it in existing inventory. Even if there is nothing wrong with the home, it will get less attention. Finding a property like this can showcase your value as an agent.
- **Poor marketing**: Discount selling agents are popular in a seller's market when it's easier to sell a home. When an agent agrees to a reduced commission, they usually skimp on marketing costs, which is not in the best interest of the seller. And the amount a seller saves on a lower agent commission is more than lost in reduced interest and, ultimately, reduced price for their home. One sign a discount broker is representing the seller is poor marketing photos. My team targets listings with pictures taken with a phone or that otherwise don't look professional. These properties garner less interest (good for our buyers) and are often represented by less skilled agents (also good for our buyers).
- **Inaccurate information**: Many agents pull information for their listings directly from the tax assessors' info. Others use the same

information from the last time the house sold. This can be problematic for sellers if remodeling was done to change the house's layout or increase the square footage. This isn't reflected in these databases. I have my team look for properties with abnormally low square footage for the area and then review the photos to determine if there may be more square footage than the record reflects. This could be a second story that's been added or a garage that's been converted to living space. Train your agents to notice when a property's bedroom count (say, four to five) doesn't make sense for the property's square footage (say, 1,200 square feet). This is indicative of a property with more square footage than is being advertised, and other buyers are likely passing it over as too small.

- **Unique properties**: Properties with functional obsolescence or funky floor plans are often ignored by buyers. Even in a hot market, buyers don't want a bathroom attached to the kitchen or one where they must walk through one bedroom to get to another bedroom. If you have a buyer who can afford to remodel, then layout isn't a problem. For those with the capital to do so, it makes sense to propose this as a strategy during the buyer's presentation. This is an especially powerful strategy for homes in coveted neighborhoods. If your client is open to this strategy, tell them this also adds significant equity immediately.

Marketing

Remember, marketing matters, and how you market yourself in a seller's market can gain you clients when other agents are having trouble.

One way to market yourself to sellers in a seller's market is to highlight that you have what they need: buyers. If you have a lot of buyers, highlight this in your marketing.

Conversely, marketing to buyers in a seller's market requires you to address their fears. Most buyers are afraid of two things in a seller's market: (1) not getting a home at all, or (2) overpaying for one.

When you put your buyers in contract, share their success in your marketing. When you get someone in contract under list price, advertise that fact. The goal is to have nervous leads reach out to you because you're doing something different. Then you can set them up with a presentation appointment to share strategies that will work in the current market. That means targeting these two fears through your success stories.

Success in a Buyer's Market

Success in a buyer's market requires different strategies than those used in a seller's market. Buyers have different options, different concerns, and different desires than buyers in a seller's market. You can provide value by understanding these differences. Finding buyers is the key to success and where you should focus your efforts.

Finding Buyers in a Buyer's Market

A buyer's market is usually due to economic conditions independent of the real estate market, but it affects potential buyers' ability to obtain financing or their psychology, so they don't want to buy in this type of market. Your team will need to target a demographic that normally wouldn't consider buying homes. Agents can obtain clients with the following strategies.

Targeting Renters

Many who bought in the last buyer's market, which was between 2009 and 2012, were those who never thought they would be homeowners. However, home prices dropped to the point where it was just as cheap, or cheaper, to buy than to continue paying rent. These types of buyers aren't likely to worry if the market will continue to decrease or how long it may take for the market to recover. Their thinking is that if they can buy a house and the payment will be lower than their rent, it makes financial sense to buy. For these clients, your team needs to focus on the practical advice that they'll face raising rents and can own their home instead of paying off someone else's.

Targeting Those with Steady Employment

When the economy is hurting, many who would like to buy a home won't qualify because of their unemployment situation. Thus, those with steady employment are attractive to lenders. Most recessions are caused by job losses in a specific sector that spread throughout the market in general. In the 1990s, this was the tech sector. In 2010, it was the real estate/lending/sales sector. For those who work in weakened industries, buying a home becomes nearly impossible. As a rockstar agent, you need to push your marketing efforts toward those with employment in safer jobs.

First responders, teachers, and those who work in the federal government or utility companies usually keep their jobs even when everyone else is losing theirs. With lowered home prices, these groups are more likely to consider buying or moving to a bigger house. This is especially true in expensive markets. Buying will be easier for this cohort than for homeowners whose homes have lost equity.

Targeting Experienced Investors

Experienced Realtors know that what goes up must come down, and they also know it will go up again. In 2013, I was closely watching Northern California home prices, hoping they would continue to drop. While the standard homeowner was doing the opposite, investors recognized the opportunity to buy properties that would have cash flow on day one with zero rehab needed.

As these investors jumped into the market, houses started selling, prices stopped falling, and regular people followed the investors. In a very short span of time, the market changed from too much inventory and dropping prices to houses selling in a matter of weeks. While the would-be investors waited for prices to drop even further, the experienced investors recognized when the price-to-rent ratio was favorable and bought all the best inventory. The trick as a rockstar agent is to market yourself as someone who can help investors, then go find them where they are. Don't simply advertise your listing as a home; also advertise how it would perform as an investment. You'll catch the attention of those looking for properties as investment vehicles.

Targeting Those with Properties That Have Lost Equity

This may sound counterintuitive, but many homeowners who lost equity in their properties, and know they can't sell them, will be open to buying another property at a lower price. This gives them the option to move into the new property and to turn their original property into a rental, or decide to sell one to rework their loan with the bank. Don't assume that a homeowner wouldn't buy a second home in a buyer's market. Targeting this group will allow you to find buyers in a niche that other agents haven't considered.

Finding Sellers in a Buyer's Market

Finding sellers isn't difficult in a buyer's market; they should be everywhere. The key is finding the right homes. Selling listings in this market requires you to find properties with the following traits.

They Have the Equity Required

A homeowner willing to sell in a buyer's market may find themselves "under water" (i.e., they owe more than they can sell the house for). If a lead approaches you about selling their home, make sure there's sufficient equity to sell it at current market value.

They Can Be a Short Sale if They Don't Have the Equity

For homes without the equity needed to sell, a "short sale" is an option (i.e., the bank agrees to take less than what the owner owes and pays off the note in full). This makes the transaction more complicated, so know ahead if this is a viable option and what price the bank will accept.

They Are Unique

Unique properties can still sell in a buyer's market. While homes that don't stand apart, like tract homes, don't garner much interest, those with interesting traits can still sell at strong prices. They may even warrant a price war. Unique properties can be homes:

- In exclusive neighborhoods with limited inventory.
- With boat docks, RV access, workshops, hangars, or large garages.
- That have incredible views.
- That are located on larger lots or with two homes on one lot.
- With accessory dwelling units.

They Have Owners Motivated to Sell in the Current Market

Determine the seller's motivation early on to ensure it is high enough for them to sell in this environment.

Offers That Work

For Sellers

As a listing agent, your job is to do what the seller expects. How you set these expectations will impact both the quality of your career and the happiness of your clients. All sellers will look to you for guidance and to advise them on the merits of the offers from potential buyers. You can make your job easier by having influence over the offers you present to your clients. This can be as simple as discussing with the buyer's agents what your seller is looking for and what they hope to avoid. This works best in a seller's market or, more specifically, when you have negotiation leverage because there is a demand for your client's property. When this is the case, ask buyer's agents to submit offers that are more desirable for your client. Some things that will always matter:

- Price
- Shortened or removed contingency periods
- Financially strong buyers
- Few contingencies (that is, ways for buyers to back out or negotiate a better price)
- More of the closing costs paid to the buyer

Some things that will matter to some sellers, but not to others:

- Longer escrow periods (i.e., sellers need time to find their next property)
- Option to rent back the property
- Specific loan type (i.e., prefer VA financing or conventional options)
- Retain certain items (as discussed above)

A good listing agent understands what their seller wants and doesn't want and puts that in the contract. You must talk with your client to be able to do this well.

For Buyers

In a buyer's market, most of your effort will be convincing your client to move forward on a property. It is common for a buyer to want to make ridiculously low offers or believe there is a better deal if they wait just a little longer. You must balance the goals of your buyer client to get the best property available that they can afford with the goals of your business to be efficient and trustworthy.

Choosing the right buyer client is important here. You want motivated clients with a solid sense of what is reasonable. Be disciplined in your selection. Invest your time and your team's time into buyers who are preapproved and have some level of need to buy a property. Emphasize the ways your clients can save capital and perhaps buy even more real estate. If your buyer can't decide between House A and House B, show them how they can buy House A and then House B. This can be done by:

- Using low down payment loans.
- Asking for loan programs that give buyers a credit.

- Asking loan officers about grant money for buyers.
- Writing a higher offer price in exchange for a large amount of closing costs (discussed above).
- Asking the sellers to pay more of the closing costs themselves.
- Having your clients buy properties in the names of their businesses or retirement accounts, where applicable.

In a seller's market, success will come down to two things: (1) your ability to get your client to write the strongest offer; and (2) your ability to win the trust of the listing agent.

I offer our buyers this piece of advice when we are operating in a seller's market: "You aren't competing against the seller here. You are competing against the other thirteen buyers who want this house." This helps them understand that I can't out-negotiate the seller because it's not the seller they are competing against. It's crucial that you find a home your buyer absolutely loves. I understand because I buy a lot of real estate for myself. When I find a house that I like but don't love, I write a less competitive offer at a price I'm willing to pay. This is a natural response, but it doesn't work in a seller's market. Someone else will like that house more and offer more for it.

This losing of bids leads your buyers to experience fatigue and emotional turmoil. Too many "swings and misses" and your client will emotionally check out. Protect them, and yourself, by encouraging them to pursue only properties they absolutely love. If they must pay more than they want for the property, they need to know it's worth it to them.

Explaining the Market to Your Client

It's important that your clients understand the market. A major source of frustration in real estate is when clients offer opinions on the market that agents know are wrong. For example, clients may want to keep writing offers that are too low even though the market is hot and extremely competitive. This conflict is a problem for us and for the client, which is why the market is part of my initial presentation.

Pricing is a sensitive area when we must tell our clients something they don't want to hear. Because everyone knows we only get paid if a house closes, assume your motives are always in question. This can include everything from telling clients they need to be preapproved before looking at houses to needing to write offers far over listing price for the property they want.

In *SKILL*, I explain the concept of "triangle theory." This tool allows you to align yourself with the party you are negotiating with by creating a common adversary you are joined against. This common adversary can be the agent on the other side, an unreasonable client, or the market itself. If this is your first time being exposed to the idea, consider the following image.

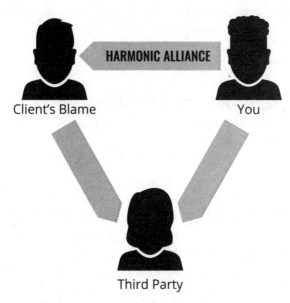

The following are some of the techniques I use to explain the market before I invest time in a lead's home buying or selling process. I use as many facts and incorporate triangle theory as much as possible. The less it's about my opinion and the more it's about objective data, the less often I need to qualify my advice to clients during the process.

For Buyers

Understanding How Fast Homes Sell in Hot Markets
Buying a home is a huge decision for our clients, and finding the right one, of course, matters. There are a lot of other buyers who are all also trying to make the right decision for themselves, so the last thing an agent wants is for their client to arrive at a "make an offer" decision only

to find someone beat us to it. As of this writing in 2022, we are facing a housing shortage. Here is one way I explain this to my leads:

> Here's a CMA of the city you're looking in, at the price range you're approved for. As you can see, the average time a home sits on the market is 14 days. This means the best homes will move even faster than that. I want to put you in a position to be as successful as possible. Let's discuss the factors that will weigh into your decision now, so when the time comes to place an offer, we'll be prepared.

Understanding the Price They Need to Pay

I then explain about pricing to get the lead adjusted to the sticker shock that comes with hot markets:

> This CMA shows what the price the homes in your price range were listed for and what they sold for. As you can see, the sales price is often significantly higher than the list price. This happens when homes receive multiple offers, because there are more people looking to buy than there are homes for sale. Sellers see this same data and expect similar, or better, offers. The way I see it, we have two options. We can look for properties in a different area or in a different condition to avoid paying over list price, or we can make an offer that's 3 percent to 5 percent over list price. Which of these is more appealing to you?

Understanding They're Not Overpaying

I then move my presentation to break the lead's presumption that offering over list price is overpaying:

> It's easy to think that paying over the asking price is overpaying. Let me offer you a little insight into how

homes are priced by listing agents that may change your perspective on that.

1. Many listing agents purposely price homes lower than the comps to encourage a bidding war.
2. A property is ultimately worth what someone is going to pay for it. The listing price is more of a suggestion of what the seller and listing agent think that will be.
3. The bank's valuation of a property is based on the appraisal, not the asking price.
4. The asking price is usually determined by comps, but those comps are a moving target. Many of the properties on the market now were at one point valued much, much lower.
5. It's common to pay over list price and still have the property appraise for more than your offer.
6. The list price is an indication of the property's value now, but you aren't buying it just for now—you're buying it for the next thirty to fifty years.
7. If a property sat on the market for a year without offers, would you have a problem offering less because you believe the property's value to be less than the asking price? This property has been on the market for five days. It's not unreasonable to think its value may be higher than what it's listed at.

Understanding the Need to Be Preapproved at the Start

Many leads want to house-hunt right away, even when they don't know the prices of houses they can afford. This next section enlightens the leads on the order of the process:

I understand. Nobody likes to go through the hassle of a preapproval. Here are a few reasons why it's better for you to do that anyway.

1. Sellers won't consider offers from buyers who are not already preapproved, and I advise my sellers the very same thing.

2. If you aren't preapproved, you may fall in love with a house you won't qualify to buy.

3. If you aren't preapproved, we may miss ways we can improve your finances to get you a better and lower-rate loan.

4. If we do find a house you like, it'll be a mad scramble to get you preapproved. It's entirely possible we'll miss out on a house you love because we have to wait on a preapproval.

5. Your credit score will take a minimal impact, not nearly as much as you think. If this is something you're worried about, let's get on the phone with my lender now, or email them, and we can go through this together.[15]

Understanding Why You Have a Preferred Lender

It is quite probable that because this is a presentation and no trust has yet been built, the lead will wonder why you have a preferred lender.

Hey, I get it. Maybe somebody offered you a better rate. If so, that's terrific. But not all rates are equal, and many times a lender will dangle a teaser rate you can never get. Or worse, you aren't told how much you'll have to pay to get that rate. I have a loan officer I trust. At least let them look at your estimate to see if anything seems fishy. I also feel comfortable that my lending partner can make sure we get to close. Having a "better" rate or low fees means nothing if they can't make sure you get the funds. How would you feel about having a phone call with my loan officer so we can compare the two options and see which seems like the best overall fit?

---

15 Consult my team if you need support on this step at www.TheOneBrokerage.com.

Understanding Why They Can't Wait Too Long to Write an Offer

Some leads will let you know they have a tough time moving quickly on decisions, or the leads are first-time homebuyers who underestimate the speed of decision making required in a hot market.

> The last thing I want is to rush you into making a decision. The second to last thing I want is for you to miss out on your dream home because of analysis paralysis. Here's what I propose. We sit down, pick out any house online, and pretend like you love it and want to buy it. I'll make a list of everything that concerns or scares you and what questions pop up as you consider buying it. Then, we will go through that list together to discuss what we can do to avoid problems in those areas when the real time arrives. It's a way to overcome any fears you may have when you find the house you really do love.

Understanding Unreasonable Seller Concessions

In a hot buyer's market, it seems like you can ask for a lot of seller concessions with an offer, but that's not realistic.

> Everyone wants a good deal. Me included! And I'll definitely get you every dollar I can. The thing is, we are in a very competitive buyer's market. I've spoken to the listing agent, and they've said that there are other buyers who are waiting for us to back out of this deal so they can buy it. The listing agent thinks they can sell it for more than you have it under contract for. You're contractually protected at this point, but once our contingency timelines expire, the seller can sell to someone else. If we don't get those concessions, are you okay with losing the house?

Understanding Market Concerns

When the leads are reading about the economy when it's not doing well, their first concern will be about buying during a crash.

> This is a legitimate concern. No one wants to buy before a market crash! Let me ask you a few questions to help make sure this is the right time for you to buy a home. First, what makes you think a crash is coming? [Common replies include "It happened the last time the market was hot" and "My family told me to wait."] Dig deeper into their logic by asking the following questions:
> 1. What do you think made the last crash happen?
> 2. Are you taking out a loan you can't afford?
> 3. If a crash did happen, would there be anything forcing you to sell at that time?
> 4. What expertise does your family member have in this arena?
> 5. If we went back five years and took your family's advice, would it be good advice considering where the market is now?
> 6. If a worst-case scenario arose, could you rent out any bedrooms? Could you rent out the whole house and rent somewhere else?
> 7. What happens if the market doesn't crash and homes continue to appreciate?

Understanding Why "Off-Market" Deals Aren't the Answer

Some leads will want to shop off-market, if they even know what that is, but they won't know why it's not a wise idea.

> I respect you believe you can find something off-market, but the problem is you'd have to pay me yourself. I'd really like to avoid that. If we continue to look on market, it will be the seller who pays me, and you can keep your money for investing in more real estate. Additionally, off-market deals are not often the best deals. Sellers usually expect more than market value

because they are giving up the opportunity to create a bidding war. Let's talk more about why you want to find off-market deals. What are you hoping for?

For Sellers

I also hold initial presentations for seller leads to make sure we're on the same page and they understand all the steps of the process.

Understanding the Listing Price

Clearly, every seller wants top dollar for their home, but what they want may not be realistic.

You and I are on the same side, and I want to sell your home for as much as possible. I don't set the price for your home; the buyer does. We get your house in the best shape possible, market it expertly, and do all that's within our power. The point is to make buyers *want* your home, then see how much they are willing to pay for it. Buyers make that decision based on the other neighborhood homes available for sale, which are called comps. In addition, the buyers will order an appraisal that will affect the lender's valuation. These factors together determine the market value of your property, which buyers use to decide how much they are willing to pay. I've got a CMA here to show you how much other comps have sold for, which buyers also use to make their pricing decision. Can we go over this together?

Understanding Paying a Higher Price for Their Replacement Home

Most sellers sell their home with the intention of buying a new home to either expand or downsize their living situation. This will not be an even amount.

The age-old dilemma in real estate is that if we want to sell high, then we have to buy high too. And if we want to buy low, we must also sell low. We mitigate this when interest rates are low, which happens in a strong market. If we sell now, while the market is hot, we may have to pay more for your next home, but the ultimate cost of that money will be less because of lower interest rates. We can get the best of both worlds by selling now.

Understanding Capital Gains Taxes

This part of the presentation is for leads who are selling their **primary residence** to buy another primary residence home, not for first-time homebuyers:

Since you've lived in your home for two out of the last five years, we may be able to get an exception toward the capital gains because this is your primary residence. Let's talk to your CPA to find out if you'll have to pay capital gains when you sell.

If the lead is looking for an **investment property**, the information I share is different:

While it's true you may have to pay some capital gains on a sale, we can also avoid those if we conduct a 1031 like-kind exchange. We'll run this by your CPA, but if we reinvest the proceeds according to the correct guidelines, we can likely defer the taxes you would owe. In addition, we probably won't have to reinvest your initial capital, so if you had plans for the equity in this place, we'll have to determine how much money you don't have to reinvest and see if that is enough for what you're looking to do with the money in this property.

If there's no way to shield the lead from taxes, the script again changes:

I get it that nobody likes paying taxes. However, if you owe taxes, that means you did very well with this investment. It can be easy to focus on the taxes we owe instead of the money we made, but why do that? We pay taxes on income at work, and it doesn't make you want to quit your job, right? These tax rates will likely be lower than what you pay on your income. Additionally, there are some write-offs you can include, such as any money you reinvested into the property, realtor fees, closing costs, and others. Let's see what your CPA says before we let the idea of taxes ruin for you how well this investment worked for you.

Understanding Wanting to Sell but Then Waiting for the Crash Before They Buy

This idea is very common. Playing the market can be appealing and lures a lot of people in. Here's why that scares me though: no one knows for certain when a crash is coming or even if there is one looming. You may wait on the sidelines for so long that you can't get back into the housing game at all. Is there any objective data that leads you to believe we'll be seeing a crash? Even if there is a crash and you lose your job, you can rent out the rooms of a house you already own, but you won't be able to buy a new house if you're unemployed. And if a crash doesn't come, the housing market may not let you buy at all.

Understanding Not Using the "House Down the Street" As a Comp

A lot of sellers think they can use any home for sale in their neighborhood as a comparison, but that's not the way comps work.

I would love to sell your house for as much as that home, and I think in some ways your home is superior. Here's the problem though. Real estate appraisers won't value it based on the components of your home that you've mentioned, even if we agree those components are valuable. If the appraiser doesn't include those in the value, then the lender's valuation of what they think the house can sell for will be affected. Appraisers look at components like square footage, lot size, view, and upgrades. Now, based on the information in this CMA, these are the homes that compare best to yours. Of these properties, which do you think has the most in common with your property?

Understanding Adding Value to a Seller's Home

Sellers are usually interested in knowing what they can do to add value to their home in order to get the highest price. Value, however, has two meanings. Let's take crown molding as an example.

There are two ways to look at this. One way is the molding will add value as far as how desirable the property is to a buyer. Buyers may be more likely to choose your home over another home, but it won't add value as far as how much your home will appraise for. If you invest your capital into crown molding, it likely won't get you the return you are looking for. We can clearly see from looking at this list of previously sold homes that there was no difference in price between those with crown molding and those without. I suggest that we focus on spending as little as possible to get your home as close to the comparable sales.

Understanding the Level of "Hot"

Many sellers will be in a hurry to hit the "hot" market, but the market might not be that hot where they live.

I get it. The news is constantly saying that the market is hot. The problem is that real estate markets are hyperlocal, and individual markets don't behave the same way. The best way to determine the market in your area is to look at the numbers. On this CMA, you can see how long homes waited before they went pending. That means this market isn't the same as those you hear about on TV. These numbers clearly show what buyers here are willing to pay and how long houses sit before a buyer writes an offer. Based on this information, does it still make sense for you to sell?

Understanding Repairs and Staging in a Hot Market

Many sellers think that because they are in a hot market, they don't need to do any repairs or staging to make their house more attractive to buyers.

I don't blame you for wanting to save money and save headaches in getting your house ready for the market. However, I know the return repairs and staging can net you. When interest rates are this low, buyers are willing to pay more for a house that is move-in ready. That's because the cost of borrowing from the bank is much less when rates are low, so buyers can borrow more. If we take care of all issues for the new buyer, they'll pay a premium for your home. From an investment perspective, you're spending a little to make more money. Knowing how buyers will look at your house, do you value making more money or doing less work?

 **KEY POINTS**

- Buyers drive markets.
- The most successful businesses don't use the same strategies year after year but adapt to economic, political, and technological shifts.
- Real estate markets are driven primarily by supply and demand, fiscal policy, world events, and the psychology of following the herd.
- Because most homeowners borrow to buy their homes, the amount borrowed and the cost of real estate debt factor into which properties clients can afford to buy.
- Because we make our income selling properties, it's important to understand the relationship between the financing of real estate and the values of the properties.

- The way to win in a seller's market is to (1) get more listings, and (2) put your buyers in contract.
- When there is limited inventory and high demand, whoever controls the inventory controls the game.
- The best way to find listings during a seller's market is to do what no one else is doing: look for buyers.
- Your goal in a seller's market is simple. Prepare your buyer client for the level of commitment they'll need, identify the property they can close on, and pursue it with everything you have.
- At minimum, as you prepare to send an offer, the loan officer should call the listing agent to discuss the strength of the buyer's lending position.
- In a seller's market, success will come down to two things: (1) your ability to get your client to write the strongest offer; and (2) your ability to win the trust of the listing agent.

CHAPTER EIGHT

IMPROVING EFFICIENCY

"Efficiency is doing better what is already being done."

—PETER DRUCKER

As a rockstar agent, it will come as no surprise that as your volume increases, so should the efficiency with which you accomplish tasks, communicate with your team, and overcome obstacles. The more weight you can carry, the more money you can make—but if you can't handle the load, your business won't succeed.

It's important to know that there are five pillars that will support your business and allow you to hire more agents and staff and take on more clients. As you build your rockstar team, focus on these pillars:

1. Preparation (Front-Loading Your Process)
2. Urgency
3. Focus
4. Priorities
5. Oversight

Preparation (Front-Loading Your Process)

Create the Path and Vision

The first step is to paint a clear picture for your team of what you expect from them. Each member needs to understand their role and how to know when that role is done well. Your responsibility is to create those roles, hire the right people, and set expectations. The clearer you paint the picture, the faster your team members will excel.

This principle works with your clients as well before you start the home buying or selling process. Buyers must look at several homes, go through conflicting emotions, get excited then rejected, and have disagreements with their spouse or partner. These steps should be discussed in the presentation so they know what to expect and you can determine what a "win" looks like for them.

Meanwhile, sellers will have their own set of expectations, and you'll never be able to meet them without a clear discussion at the presentation. Do they know what a "fair price" means to them? How long do they think it will take their home to sell? Do they understand buyers may back out of the contract? By talking with them about what success looks like for them, you can shorten the road to get there.

Your job as the rockstar agent is to guide your clients with a map at the very start. They'll be nervous and anxious, so the clearer the picture you can paint, the faster you will reach your goal of getting to contract and the happier they will be.

Answer Objections Early

Seek clarity early on. If you answer your clients' questions quickly, you'll end their concerns that you're just commission-oriented, and they'll receive your information better. Waiting until there is a major problem will reduce your credibility of council with the client (e.g., waiting to tell them that "we are only looking at big ticket items" *after* receiving an inspection report that scares them). Expectations determine results. If your client expects an outcome you can't give them, they'll be disappointed in you and the experience. If you set realistic expectations at the beginning, they'll let you guide them throughout the complicated process. Here are some examples of issues to discuss early on:

- **Price reductions**: Don't wait until a house isn't selling to explain the timing of price reductions. Discuss this as soon as the listing agreement is signed. Have a plan in place if the price will need to be reduced, and by how much.

- **Repairs and staging**: Don't wait until there is a lack of showings to advise the client to fix up their home. Discuss repairs and staging before the house is placed on the MLS.
- **Asking price**: Don't wait until the client finds their dream house before discussing the reality of needing to offer over asking price.
- **Closing costs**: Explain loan closing costs before the lender sends out paperwork; that means not waiting until just before the close of escrow.
- **Clean lines of credit**: Tell clients not to open additional lines of credit before they are in escrow.
- **Teamwork**: During the buyer's presentation, before the client asks to see a property, explain that you use showing assistants. Then clearly define your expectations for your showing assistants so you and they are not working at cross purposes.

Take Advantage of "Wet Concrete"

You set the relationship in the initial stages of working with your clients. This is when your influence is most powerful. Not setting a relationship upfront is akin to trying to change concrete after it has dried. You can do it, but it's incredibly difficult.

At my second listing in my career, when I was very green, I agreed to take a listing at a price much higher than the comps showed. I explained to the clients the house would not sell at this price but that we could "try it out" and adjust later. I didn't know to put a plan in my listing agreement that clients would have to follow. When the home didn't receive much interest, the clients blamed me. They didn't renew the listing with me because of the lack of showings, and I knew this was directly related to the price being too high. However, by the time this became an issue, it looked like I was making excuses by blaming the price instead of myself. I learned a hard lesson, and now I set expectations at the presentation when I have a good degree of influence over the client.

This principle is true for your team too. Many new agents get into real estate sales because of what they see on HGTV, but they have no realistic idea about the demands of the profession. You and they are much better off when at hiring you give them specifics on the tasks they are expected to perform, the irregular hours that may be needed to meet buyer and seller schedules, and the frustrations they will experience with any process.

Tiered System

I developed the tiered system to help reduce clients' FOMO. It allows me to remove unreasonable expectations and the fear of missing out on a potentially better deal. Here's a common scenario:

Client: I'd like a multifamily property I can house-hack, in the best school district, in a very competitive price range, with 20 percent equity in the property and a motivated seller.

Agent: Well, that's going to be nearly impossible to find, especially in a competitive market like this one. Because of all that you want in this property, the seller won't be motivated to sell or even offer concessions. And everyone would love a property like this.

Client: I know. But that's why I have you!

In this scenario, if I let the client dictate the terms of the home search, everyone loses. I won't sell them a house, my showing assistants won't get a commission, and the client won't start building wealth. If I directly tell them this plan won't work, they are likely to hire a different agency. To avoid that, in the presentation, I investigate the why behind what they want and present them with a plan that will allow them to pursue their top-tier desires while preparing them to write an offer on something more realistic.

Agent: Let's discuss your wish list. What's most important to you?

Client: Well, it needs to be a multifamily so I can house-hack. I don't want to pay the full mortgage. I was told homes in the best school districts appreciate the fastest, so I want that. I'm only approved up to $400,000 so that's all I can spend, and I really want built-in equity because I've been told to buy right. I also want a motivated seller so I can pay less than asking price.

Agent: I see. Of these factors, which would you say is the *most* important?

Client: Eh, I guess it would be a multifamily property that's in my price range.

Agent: Okay, great. I really want to help you get everything you want, but my fear is that we won't find a property that has everything, and that will cause you to miss out on the right property that has the most important features to you. We can't always hit home runs; sometimes it's best to just get on base. What if we try this? I'll set up a search for multifamily properties in your price range. We'll send you information on those every day [first-tier want]. I'll keep an eye out for those in the best school districts and those which may have some hidden equity potential [second-tier wants]. When I find a property that matches these criteria, I'll see how motivated the seller is by asking the listing agent before I schedule a time to have you see the property [third-tier want]. This way, we make sure we don't leave any stone unturned, but we also don't miss out on a solid property because we are waiting for a unicorn that may never show up. Sound good?

Client: Yeah, that does. I understand now that my expectations may be unrealistic, but I still want to try, you know? I don't want to give up on the dream.

Agent: Absolutely. I want to find you the best deal possible. I'll unicorn-hunt, but if we find something in that process that makes sense for you, I really want you to buy it. Once you close, we'll start the hunt for the next unicorn again. Deal?

Client: Deal!

Presenting a game plan allows the client to hold out hope they'll get the deal of the century but also be happy when they find a solid deal that suits their most important needs. It satisfies their FOMO and keeps you in charge of the process and relationship.

Urgency

Rockstar agents operate from a natural state of urgency and don't even realize it's a part of our personality. Urgency here does not mean hurry or panic. Urgency means we value our time in handling a high volume of sales but also in handling the roller coaster of client emotions. Emotions can change frequently and oftentimes without warning. Sellers can go from incredibly excited to sell to equally fearful and even to seemingly apathetic. This could come from something they hear on the news, from advice they receive from a friend, or from life changes when something becomes a bigger priority to them.

Rockstar agents and their team put a high value on urgency. On my team, as soon as a lead expresses interest in selling their home (the highest priority of any agent's business), someone immediately books an appointment for the next day, looks up comps, and maintains consistent communication via text, email, or phone with the lead. We want to ignite the lead's desire to sell.

Your Team

As your volume increases, so does the temptation to spend time doing things that aren't productive for a rockstar agent. As your team and volume grow, so does the chance for team members to not meet expectations. Everyone on your team should operate out of a sense of urgency all day. Preaching the following points in meetings can help cultivate this culture:

- We don't know how long the real estate market will stay strong.
- We don't know if politicians and policymakers will affect our ability to earn a living through commissions.
- We don't know when a newer and hungrier agency might try to take our market share.
- We don't know when interest rates may rise.
- We don't know if income taxes will be increased.
- We don't know if another disaster, like a pandemic, could affect our ability to produce income for ourselves.

- Given these unknowns, we need to approach every day with respect and our desire to get as much out of it as possible.

Three Days in One

On episode 433 of the BiggerPockets podcast, I interviewed entrepreneur Ed Mylett, who has a theory about getting three days out of one day. He wrote in a post about it on his website: "Imagine that in one month, you got 90-days' worth of work done. Think about what would happen in your life. And you stack that up over a year or three years. How different would your life be?"[16]

This is a fantastic concept. Most of us vastly underperform to our potential. This is especially true when we consider the lack of accountability inherent in real estate sales and commission work in general. Let your sales leaders and your staff know that you expect they will do their best to get three days out of every workday, just like you do.

Compound Effect of Daily Tasks Taking Too Much Time

As I was working on this book, I became aware of how I lacked urgency in my writing. I took frequent breaks to check my text messages and direct messaging on social media, and I checked my email inbox too often. This made the process of writing take much longer than necessary. I am now more aware of how I lack urgency when I write, but this is by no means the only time the lack of urgency plagues me.

In the real estate office, I thought about how often we stop to have a conversation about nothing with another agent in the office and take breaks to get coffee that we don't really want. When your administrative assistant has a question for a lender or title officer, do they ask in a way that allows a yes or no answer? Or do they write a too-long message that forces the vendor to figure out what's being asked? These types of small tasks performed without urgency become expensive by the end of the day. Real estate sales involve a million small tasks leading to the one big goal of selling a house. The more tasks that are involved, the more opportunities for a lack of urgency. Work performed without urgency leads to drowning in wasted time. Set the example for your staff. When we operate with urgency, so will they.

---

[16] Ed Mylett, "The Top 5 Secrets of Time Management and Productivity," EdMylett.com, January 28, 2019, https://www.edmylett.com/podcast/the-top-5-secrets-of-time-management-and-productivity/.

Gamify

To make urgency less daunting and more fun, consider making it a game. I frequently set challenges in which team members see how fast they can complete a task without making a mistake. Or I have one team member close their eyes and verbally explain how to navigate web pages while another team member clicks on the buttons they describe. This focuses the team member on the process to anticipate what comes next, thereby increasing the speed at which they operate and the overall urgency of their work efforts. Gamifying important key metrics can change your staff's perception of you from just their boss to a game show host. Consider gamifying tasks like:

- Who can put an MLS search together the fastest?
- Who can show the most homes in a five-hour period, or who can make the most sales calls in a two-hour period?
- Who can put a property in the MLS, fill out an offer sheet, or input a new lead into our CRM the fastest?
- Who can open a file in our transaction coordinator software for a new client the fastest?

Your Clients

Urgency turns leads from window shoppers into determined clients. Consider the difference between a casual stroll through a store on Sunday versus a Black Friday bonanza. On Black Friday, we understand time is urgent because others are looking to buy the same limited number of products. This same phenomenon occurs with our clients. If a seller has no urgency to sell, they have no reason to list their home at fair market value. If a buyer feels no urgency, they will always look for a better deal. If we want to snap our clients to reach their goals, we must introduce urgency into the process.

Adding Pressure to Create Urgency

People don't like the pressure that creates urgency, but it can help break clients out of their analysis paralysis. A buyer who does not feel the urgency of decision making can be lulled into a false sense of security. If buyers take their time because they have no urgency, home values could steadily increase before they make an offer.

Sellers can experience the same problem. The longer they don't act with urgency, the longer their home sits on the MLS with the DOM increasing, and the more their negotiating power decreases. Not feeling the pressure can hurt your clients. This is, of course, no excuse for creating artificial pressure to influence our clients to make bad decisions. The point is to correctly convey the reality of the situation. A healthy dose of urgency can do that. Remind your clients that:

- If your buyer takes too long to be preapproved or make an offer, another buyer can get the property.
- If your buyer waits too long, a hot market can limit the amount of inventory they can look at.
- If your seller takes too long to put their house on the market, interest rates may increase, affecting the offers they receive.
- If your seller takes too long to choose a contractor to complete repairs, that contractor may accept other work and become unavailable.

Removing Pressure After Acting

After a client has taken action, it's important that you remove the pressure they may still be carrying. This is important because of the psychological impact pressure has on the psyche. Pressure serves a purpose, but we are not intended to live that way all the time. A client can relax after:

- A listing agreement is signed and the house is ready to go on the MLS. Tell the client to relax, and you'll take it from here.
- A buyer puts a property in contract. Tell them they can relax until the inspection report is received.
- A lender gives lending approval. Tell them they can relax about funding.

Focus

Focus means having a crystal-clear vision; the more we focus on our business, the better we operate. For example, texting and emailing made me lose focus while I should have been writing this book. Maintaining a high degree of focus on tasks and ensuring we are working on the most important next thing is the difference between a productive and unproductive day.

Visualizing Tasks

I develop focus by visualizing the tasks I need to complete, which I learned while playing sports and in my last career before becoming a real estate agent. I closed my eyes to visualize myself running the play and responding to my defender in the moment. I continued this same practice in law enforcement. Running potential scenarios in my mind prepared my subconscious for how I would respond if they occurred. It shortened the time between making a decision and acting on it in the moment.

Real estate works the same way. There are a lot of tasks we perform on any given day, so visualizing how to do them saves time. Let's use the example of a purchase agreement. When you review offers on your listing, how long does it take for you to know where the information is that you need to present to your client? On which page is the inspection period listed, and where are the boxes that may be checked if contingencies are waived? Visualizing this information will shorten the time it takes to explain the offer fully to your client.

No Wasted Steps

Athletes train to perform their skill in as few steps as possible to increase efficiency. These movements, referred to as fundamentals, are practiced over and over until they can be performed incredibly quickly and with very little conscious thought. In an industry that requires so many small tasks to be completed, why wouldn't we take the same approach to save steps? When a team member logs onto a database, they should enter all the data at the same time. Don't start the process without completing it. When your listing agent is waiting for someone to call back with information, make sure they get everything they need in that one return call. Look for ways to increase your efficiency and your teams' efficiency.

Deep Work

In marketing his book *Deep Work: Rules for Focused Success in a Distracted World*, Cal Newport states:

> Deep work is the ability to focus without distraction on a cognitively demanding task. It's a skill that allows you to quickly master complicated information and produce better results in less time. Deep work will make you better at what you do and provide the sense of true fulfillment that comes from craftsmanship. In short,

deep work is like a superpower in our increasingly competitive twenty-first-century economy.[17]

Deep work occurs when you remove all distractions that prevent you from entering that state. This is when we are at our most productive. Deep work means your productivity increases, as does your confidence. This also leads to improved profitability. When my team started selling more than $100 million in gross sales a year, too many team members were interrupting my work with questions someone else could answer. I moved my office to decrease access to me, which increased my focus to keep growing the business. You need deep work to grow your rockstar agency and make more money for you and your team.

Priorities

Being efficient is only half the battle; the other half is being effective. I once hired a manager for my real estate portfolio. I told them what result I wanted and clearly explained (so I thought) how they could achieve it. I then made the mistake of not checking in on the manager. Six months later, I had the most comprehensive and detailed Excel spreadsheet I had ever seen. Unfortunately, I had a host of problems in my properties that were accurately noted on the spreadsheet but were not being resolved. I hadn't explained clearly enough that the job was to fix the problems, not just document them.

If you don't have a clear understanding of your business priorities, this can happen to you too. This is especially true for your team's and clients' priorities.

Understanding Key Metrics

Not all tasks are the same. For example, not all events generate the same amount of revenue. Which are the most profitable? Well, taking listings is directly related to the highest profit margins in real estate. That means hiring quality staff will earn you a large return on investment. Communicating with leads to eliminate lead bleed is vital, as is closing buyer units at higher price points. My advice is to make sure you are spending the most time on the activities that increase your key metrics.

---

17 Cal Newport, *Deep Work: Rules for Focused Success in a Distracted World* (New York: Grand Central Publishing, 2016).

Sticking to the Correct KPIs

We need to focus on our key performance indicators (KPIs). It is easy to stay "busy" in this business, but you want business, not "busyness." Focusing on KPIs means our business remains profitable. This includes gross commission income, houses in escrow, leads being generated, and more. This is especially important for your team to understand because they likely came from jobs where they were paid by the hour, not by the completion of a huge process—like having someone sell or buy their home. They didn't have to feel the pressure of urgency to make a living. This mindset is hard to break. Giving clear KPIs and expecting accountability will help until they create new work habits for the real estate industry. Some examples of KPI metrics include:

- CMAs sent to former seller clients.
- Listing appointments attended.
- Contacts made when business was expressly discussed.
- Touches to the database.
- Offers written.
- Lead presentations.

Avoiding Distractions

Rockstar agents recognize the reality that no matter how often we train our team, they will always be vulnerable to distractions. We can help by limiting how many distractions there are in the workplace. For example:

- Prevent team members from walking unannounced into someone's office to ask a question, because this interrupts deep work. Train members to email first to allow the other person to prioritize when they respond.
- If the problem is urgent, texting first is an option.
- If the problem is massive, set up a meeting and have all data ready to deliver a concise message or question.
- As much as possible, ask yes or no questions.
- Ask non-sales members to leave their phones in a desk drawer or across the room.
- Create a protocol in which team members ask three other people for help before going to a senior leader, and only if the question remains unanswered.

- When a staff member is out of the office (e.g., showing houses, meeting an inspector), create a buddy system in which a colleague in the office can look up information quickly. Someone in the office at a desk with a computer can accomplish a task in thirty seconds that someone on the road with a phone may need twenty minutes to do.

Oversight

Many people avoid oversight, but the most successful people seek it out. For example, someone who hires a personal trainer wants oversight, as does the medical school student who signs up for the most difficult courses and the person who seeks out a peer group for personal growth. These are all examples of people who expect the most out of themselves and realize they need oversight from someone they respect and trust. As your team's rockstar agent, that's the role you play.

Keeping Your Team on Task

Your team members will (or certainly should) want to contribute to your agency's success but don't know how to do it. I remember being in that position early on. I was ready to do whatever was needed, but I needed someone to guide me. If I didn't get it from my leader, I modeled myself after other senior people. Your team members will do the same. If you don't provide direction, someone else will—and that person may not be who you want them to model. When your business has grown to the point where you can't provide that direction yourself, promote staff who display the work ethic, skill, and qualities you want emulated. Remember, if you don't do this, your newer team members may not be trained in your preferred style.

Conducting Meetings

I conduct oversight via meetings, which are also good training opportunities. I recognize they are largely unpopular events, but they are the best way to share information quickly. When two parties go too long between meetings, they can significantly drift apart, and it is unproductive to have to spend time getting back on track. My team holds multiple types of meetings. For example, I hold hourlong weekly whole team meetings and weekly meetings just with the sales leaders; there are also daily meetings for the sales leaders and their showing assistants and administrative assistants. I discuss meetings in detail in Chapter Eleven, but for now, I'll show you the types of metrics that we share.

These figures show where we are in reaching our yearly volume goals and our current metrics. In weekly meetings with the sales leaders, they display their own information. We discuss what went well in the previous week, what needs improvement, and what their plans are to either catch up to their goal or stay ahead of it. The sales leaders offer each other assistance, advice, and resources.

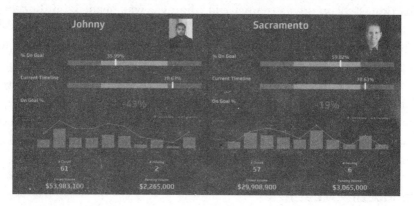

Using Dashboards

As the CEO, I use a dashboard that provides me with the information I need to provide the oversight and direction my team needs. This dashboard contains snapshots of:

- Team total closed volume.
- Team pending volume.
- Number of properties in contract.

- Number of Leads moved down the Sales Funnel.
- Number of leads contacted.
- Number of leads assigned to sales leaders in the previous week.
- Number of current active buyers under each sales leader's control.
- Number of escrows each sales leader currently has.

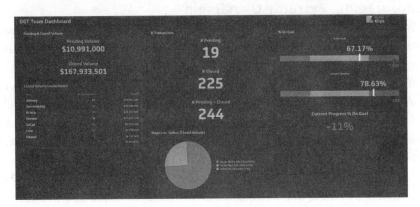

This dashboard provides a high-level overview of how my team is performing. If I see a number drop below what I'm accustomed to seeing, I dig into why that may be. When I see a sales leader performing better than before, I ask them what additional support they may need.

Implementing the 80/20 Rule

"The Pareto Principle, named after esteemed economist Vilfredo Pareto, specifies that 80% of consequences come from 20% of the causes, asserting an unequal relationship between inputs and outputs."[18] This means that 80 percent of your results come from 20 percent of your efforts. As the rockstar agent, it's your responsibility to make sure your team is sticking to those percentages, which is related to my earlier comment that KPIs are an important metric.

Knowing Good Is the Enemy of Great

This is true because good allows us to stop moving forward. In a new job, our priority is to "not be bad" at it. When we start to become good at it, we like our job better and usually start to make more money. Good stops us from achieving our potential as human beings, as professionals, and

---

18 Investopedia, "Pareto Principle," April 7, 2022, https://www.investopedia.com/terms/p/paretoprinciple.asp.

as business owners. Those who achieved greatness were not content just to be good. They aimed higher because they knew they had more inside of them. Don't let your team stop at being good. Help them to find their own greatness.

Encouraging "Extreme Ownership"

This is a term coined by Jocko Willink in his book by the same name. When someone practices extreme ownership, they are constantly evolving and aiming to become better at what they do. This is particularly important for team leaders. Let's say one of your buyer's agents fails to put a property under contract when they could have, and the agent blames the client for not offering a high enough bid. It's tempting to leave it at that, but that won't fix the problem. When you trace the situation, you find that the client only wanted to pay a set amount. The buyer's agent should have better prepared the client for what to expect. To avoid this issue in the future, the team leader must do a better job of training the buyer's agent on how to prepare clients.

In extreme ownership, the leader takes on the yoke of responsibility, which in turn allows them to experience growth as a leader. Not taking extreme ownership prevents you and your team leaders from becoming as efficient and effective as possible.

Having the Right "Heart Soil"

This expression means the emotional condition of a heart. What drives your team members to work for your agency? Rules, standards, and policies can provide expectations and state what is allowed or not allowed, but what motivates your team members to work for you and your clients? Is it the policies in place or the desire for your clients to succeed in buying or selling (or both) their homes? The latter comes from good heart soil. When you sow the right staff in good heart soil, they will grow as team members and help you grow your business. A team member who needs constant supervision, correction, or oversight has the wrong motivation, such as doing the job only for the money, thinking the job is easier than it really is, or putting their ego before the business. Better than putting rules in place is hiring the right people with the right motives and with healthy soil in their heart.

Socializing with Purpose

Humans need to socialize, and it's a healthy component of any business. However, it becomes problematic when we isolate socializing from the goals of our business. In an ideal sales world, socializing combines with focused business efforts to amplify sales income, not detract from it. If you allow it, your team members could spend time complaining about clients rather than working toward success. This will have troubling effects on your bottom line. When they socialize in the office, expect that the conversations will be on how to improve performance or how to lift up others to reduce the stressful nature of the industry. Success in this industry, as with any industry, is about raising standards. Create a culture where people feel that elevated level of urgency described in detail above. Individual members will then focus on helping themselves and others achieve individual and team goals and less on gossiping or complaining.

Being Prepared

Abraham Lincoln said, "If I only had an hour to chop down a tree, I would spend the first 45 minutes sharpening my axe." This maxim highlights the connection of being prepared and saving time. By preparing a presentation, for example, I know what I'm going to say before I start speaking. I can deliver a much more concise message than if I begin speaking contemporaneously and try to figure out what I'm saying in the middle of it. Your business works the same way. Setting clear expectations, offering training to staff, and autofilling cover sheets for every buyer client, for instance, saves you time via preparation. It also eliminates mistakes. Preparation takes less time than fixing the mistakes that come with being unprepared.

Working Together

The COVID-19 pandemic required technological advancements to keep businesses open virtually. That lead to working from home becoming more popular than ever. The common argument is that someone working remotely is more productive because they don't spend as much time commuting and can instead focus on the work. The problem is that working from home is fraught with distractions that reduce productivity. When your team is in the office, efficiency is increased in several ways:

- Staff learn from each other by overhearing scripts and how to handle objections on the phone, as well as from observing each other.

- Staff also observe the differences between top-producing agents and less successful agents in their work habits.
- There is social pressure not to slack off, such as not taking a longer lunch.
- There is no social media or television—or family—creating distractions.
- Information is disseminated in real time, and peers are around to ask questions.

Human nature means most of us get our ideas about what is acceptable and unacceptable from each other. We subconsciously emulate the standards and habits of those around us, and those in turn determine our success and guide our behavior. Being around others who work hard raises expectations. Another reason to have staff work on-site is that everyone together will raise up the level of the status quo.

 **KEY POINTS**

- It should come as no surprise that as your volume increases, so should the efficiency with which you accomplish tasks, communicate with your team, and overcome obstacles.
- Five pillars will support your business and allow you to hire
  - Preparation (front-loading your process)
  - Urgency
  - Focus
  - Priorities
  - Oversight
- Not setting a relationship upfront is akin to trying to change concrete after it has dried. You can do it, but it's incredibly difficult.
- Real estate sales involve a million small tasks leading to the one big goal of selling a house. The more tasks that are involved, the more opportunities for a lack of urgency.
- Gamifying important key metrics can change your staff's perception of you and increase productivity.
- If a buyer feels no urgency, they will always look for a better deal. If we want to snap our clients to reach their goals, we must introduce urgency into the process.

- People don't like the pressure that creates urgency, but it can help break clients out of their analysis paralysis.
- Visualizing information will shorten the time it takes to explain the offer fully to your client.
- Deep work occurs when you remove all distractions that prevent you from entering that state. This is when we are at our most productive.
- Make sure you are spending the most time on the activities that increase your key metrics.
- When someone practices extreme ownership, they are constantly evolving and aiming to become better at what they do. This is particularly important for team leaders.
- Preparation takes less time than fixing the mistakes that come with being unprepared.

CHAPTER NINE

EXPERT COMMUNICATION

"To effectively communicate, we must realize that we are all different in the way we perceive the world and use this understanding as a guide to our communication with others."

—TONY ROBBINS

Hearing the Heart Behind the Words

One major problem that agents face when communicating is sharing information in the way they think, not in the way the lead or client thinks. Communication is more than just sharing information. At its heart, it is the art of downloading your emotions, thoughts, and expressions into the other person. Successful agents help their clients regulate their fears and excitement by how they communicate. The agent's calmness and confidence are transferred to the client through words, tone, and actions.

While it seems counterintuitive, not responding with an answer to every question a client asks will do wonders for your communication skills. Many times, the appropriate response is to answer a question with a question:

Lead: "Do you think the market is going to crash soon?"

Agent: "What do you think would cause it to crash?"

Responding in this way helps the client voice their concern and put it into perspective for themselves. Humans are prone to listen to our own advice and emotions over someone else's. Your leads and clients are seldom seeking literal advice. Rather, they are looking to have their fears or desires validated. Good communicators recognize this and reply accordingly.

This chapter will provide you with tools to:

- Understand different personalities so you can communicate in ways that matter to them.
- Understand the meaning behind actions.
- Understand how the human brain processes information.
- Use these three together to tailor communication with your clients and team members.
- Create a system to streamline communication and thus reduce mistakes.

Hourglass Communication Model

In Chapter Five, I described one communication model as an hourglass. Agents with a low volume level of closings may have sloppy or unstructured communication. In running an agency, this causes major problems. Agents (or even yourself) may mask this issue as being "too busy." It would be more accurate to describe this situation as being inefficient.

When you can no longer keep up with communication, the first step is to organize how it comes to you. If you can't control how communication is received, it will control you. Consider all the ways communication occurs: cell phone calls, landline calls, Zoom meetings, Slack notifications, text messages, voicemails, social media DMs, emails, etc. It's exhausting and feels like a never-ending game of Whac-A-Mole. It's only a matter of time before moles get missed.

The answer is to push your communication to one central chokepoint, where it can be evaluated and delegated.

Let's use the analogy of a sheep rancher who must vaccinate his flock.

The sheep are in a large, fenced pen as they graze. The veterinarian could walk from sheep to sheep to administer the vaccine, but as the sheep move around, it is easy to confuse the vaccinated sheep with the unvaccinated sheep. There's less planning time needed, but it will take much longer and some sheep will be missed. The wiser rancher herds all the sheep into one gateway leading out of the pen, and the vet administers the vaccine as each sheep passes through. Now, consider if some sheep need additional medication. The rancher sends those sheep down a different lane, where the vet can them give the extra care they need. In this system, no sheep is missed.

In your situation as the rockstar agent, your administrative assistants flow all communication into the central area and delegate them as appropriate. This system means your agency never misses any contact from leads or clients. The figure below explains how this works.

WORKFLOW

CALL   TASK   DM   QUESTION
MESSAGE   EMAIL   TASK
TEXT   LANDLINE
CALL   TASK
TASK   REQUEST
TEXT

CENTRAL CHOKEPOINT

DELEGATION

| BUYER'S AGENT | SHOWING ASSISTANT | ADMIN | TRANSACTION COORDINATOR |

This hourglass takes the communication that is coming from scattered directions and pushes it to one central chokepoint. The information is then evaluated and delegated to the proper lane of buying agent, showing assistant, administrative assistant, or transaction coordinator.

The Three Levels of Hourglass Communication

First Level: Workflow means the format your clients or leads use to communicate (e.g., phone call, email, DM). This is the top of the hourglass.

Second Level: The central chokepoint can be designed the way it will work best for your office. Perhaps one assistant oversees all communication with new leads while a transaction coordinator manages all communication with clients in escrow. Alternatively, you can have your personal assistant manage the delegation of communication.

In my office, we use a combination of techniques. For example, when I receive a phone call from a client while I'm driving, there is a high likelihood that I will forget to follow up with the client when I'm back in the office. My standard response before getting off the phone is to say to the client: "Hey, I want to make sure I follow up with you on what we just discussed, but I'm driving. Would you mind emailing me at [my email address] so I can make sure I get to this once I'm in the office?"

Who hasn't gotten off the phone with one client only to immediately have a call from another client that makes you forget what you promised to do on the first call? This script helps me avoid forgetting, for example, to call a listing agent or research a property. The email reminder puts the task in one central location where my assistant or I can take care of the question quickly and efficiently. I use a similar script when someone sends me a text message or a DM. I start my day by creating a message that reads, "Hey! Thanks for this. I want to make sure it doesn't slip between the cracks. Mind emailing me this at [my email address]?" I then paste it into whatever correspondence format that my client used.

Third Level: Delegation occurs after the information is in the central chokepoint and requires a trusted decision maker. Whoever it is must decide who is the appropriate source for the communication. The person could delegate via your CRM, spreadsheet, or whiteboard. The point is to push the information down the hourglass to the right lane. Implementing this hourglass will lead to fewer mistakes, dropped leads, and unhappy clients.

The Six Human Needs Theory

I first learned of the six human needs theory from Tony Robbins, who explains this concept on his website:

> All dysfunctional behaviors arise from the inability to consistently meet these [six] core needs. But people's needs aren't just behind the bad decisions we make—they are also behind all of the great things humans accomplish. Understanding your own needs and psychology can not only help you avoid toxic behaviors and habits but can also help you achieve your goals.[19]

He explains it's not only dysfunctional behavior but, in fact, all behavior that is linked to gratifying one of these six basic needs. I explain these basic needs in the following sections.

Certainty

Certainty can be expressed as needing reliability, predictability, or safety. For example, I need to know I will be able to eat today. If I don't believe that need will be met, I will feel anxious about food. If I am continually in an environment where food is not guaranteed, I will move until I find an environment more likely to have food. This is one reason why food insecurity is a grave concern worldwide. Not everyone has the ability or option to move to meet this need.

Most of the stress you encounter in your clients will come from the inherent lack of certainty in real estate sales.

- Will my home sell?
- Will the buyer back out?
- Will the seller take my offer?
- Will I find a home I like?
- Will interest rates go up?
- Will I find a tenant for my house?
- Will I find something wrong with this house?
- Will the appraisal be low?
- What will the rehab cost?

---

19 Tony Robbins, "Discover the 6 Human Needs," March 4, 2019, https://www.tonyrobbins.com/mind-meaning/do-you-need-to-feel-significant/.

The list goes on. In this environment, the human need for certainty is constantly being challenged. The result is stress and anxiety in our clients, and the remedy is to provide the certainty via our communication, demeanor, and persona.

Understanding this need is also crucial in your hiring practices. Some interviewees will not do well working in a purely commission-based model and would be better off in a job that offers the certainty of a predictable paycheck.

Variety

The need for variety counterbalances the need for certainty. My clients want to buy an affordable home, but they don't want a cookie-cutter house. People either skew toward certainty or variety. In the case of hiring, interviewees with a high need for certainty should choose a traditional career path. Interviewees with a higher need for variety are drawn to your entrepreneurial venture.

You want to know if your client leans toward variety or certainty, because you'll want to cater to that. For a variety client, don't show them tract homes, but look for houses with unique features like outdoor spaces, creative decor, or unusual floor plans. It's easy to assume everyone has the same tastes as us, but that's definitely not the case.

The same is true in your team members. If someone prefers to know what to expect every day while another needs a variety of tasks to energize them, you must understand this to create an environment where they can do their best work.

Significance

Some clients will show a strong need for significance, and you'll want to cater your communication toward that need. For example, some people want a home that is bigger than those of their friends, or they want to live in a prestigious gated community. Don't bother showing properties that check every other box but don't have a "wow" factor.

Investor clients seek significance via a better ROI than what they believe is the market average. This can often be expressed when a client insists on writing offers that are below asking price when it's clear that won't work, even after explaining to them the logic of writing a higher offer. Instead, you'll have to find a way to cater to their need for significance. When you recognize your investor client is stuck in their need for significance, you can change your approach to honor that. You could try, for example:

> There are five other buyers trying to get this house. I know you don't want to pay over asking price, but are you okay if someone else lands this flagship property and we have to settle for something a little more routine?

> There are not many buyers preapproved for the amount you are. You've worked so hard to get to this point. Don't you want a property that illustrates this?

> I understand the seller is being ridiculous and should give in, but he probably can't afford to sell it for less because he's up to his eyeballs in debt and is stuck. You're much, much better at managing your money than he is. I think you've already proven you're the better person here.

Connection

The need for connection is built into human nature. Many who are drawn to this career need to connect with others. In fact, top agents who are so good at establishing rapport and connection have this strong need for it in themselves. These agents excel at open houses, happy hours, and other in-person events.

This is often why some clients prefer to live in a condo or in a downtown area near other people. They value the community offered by these properties and find comfort in the proximity to their neighbors. Trying to sell them a solitary house overlooking a valley is a mistake. Relying on email instead of phone calls could be a mistake as well. These clients want to develop a working relationship with *you* beyond a handshake and a business transaction.

This is an important need to understand in your staff as well. Some team members might crave being a part of a team more than they crave contributing toward the team's goals. If you find yourself with a team member who doesn't perform up to par, even though they have a terrific team attitude, this is often why. This is also a primary cause of excessive socializing in the workplace and frequent loss of focus. If a team member works for a connection rather than with focus and urgency on tasks, you'll find yourself with a nice person but an unproductive contributor.

Contribution
These last two components—contribution and growth—counterbalance each other in the workplace. Most of us have a desire to give back, which is stronger in various stages of life. Some team members will be more motivated by this need, so it's wise to tailor your communication to them. Contributors make excellent administrative and support staff because they thrive on contributing to the greater good.

Growth
The need for growth is the counterweight to contribution. Your team leaders probably favor growth over contribution because it allows them to push through the obstacles that a thriving business produces. The opposite is often true of your administrative and support staff who tend to prefer contribution over growth. However, if a support person's need for growth is high, they won't feel gratified for very long simply supporting you. If you don't recognize this and don't promote them into roles that offer growth, they will probably leave for better opportunities elsewhere.

DiSC Styles
DiSC is a personality assessment tool that fosters better communication with others.[20] It is an acronym for Dominance/Decisiveness, Influence, Stability/Steadiness, and Conscientiousness/Compliance, which are components of personalities. Most of us have one or two dominant personality traits that express themselves in our communication, and these reveal what we tend to value the most. Understanding the DiSC profile will help your business in two ways.

1. It will help you to better understand your clients and what they value. You'll communicate better with them as individuals, which will give you a higher probability of doing well in the areas most important to them.

---

20 "What is DiSC?", DiscProfile.com, accessed July 22, 2022, https://www.discprofile.com/what-is-disc.

2. It will help you to better understand your team members and what they value. You'll be able to cater your training and communication toward what each member values and determine which roles they would do best in.

The DiSC profile reveals my team members' strengths and weaknesses. This is akin to the way a coach uses a player's physical attributes; no good football coach would use a tall, skinny, fast body where a large, sturdy, and slower body is more useful. As a rockstar agent, if you put the wrong people in the wrong positions, you'll get both frustrated players and a team that performs poorly. The DiSC profile helps you determine where to best use your team members in the company.

Dominance/Decisiveness

The D score measures how comfortable an individual is at making decisions in an area they are unfamiliar with. While everyone is comfortable making decisions in a familiar environment, the high-scoring D is also comfortable when faced with a new challenge, situation, or circumstance. A low D score means the person most likely has a high C score (Conscientiousness/Compliance). Those with a high D score tend toward positions of leadership, as well as entrepreneurship. If you are looking to be a rockstar agent, odds are you have a high D score. Traits of those who score high on D include:

- **Goals**: Bottom-line results, victory
- **Fears**: Being taken advantage of or appearing weak
- **Influences others by**: Assertiveness, insistence, competition
- **Overuses**: The need to win, resulting in win/lose dichotomy
- **In conflict**: Speaks up about problems, looks to even the score
- **Would increase effectiveness through**: Patience, empathy[21]

A high score on D includes people who are results-driven and goal-oriented and value quick, factual, to-the-point communication. They are often perceived as rude or blunt by others because they value time over other social norms, such as politeness, curiosity, and openness.

The incorrect way to communicate with a high D is to start with lots of background information because they will perceive you as inconsiderate

---

21 DiSC styles, "What is the DiSC D style personality?", DiscProfiles.com, August 13, 2019, https://www.discprofiles.com/blog/2019/08/what-is-the-disc-d-style/#.YXsI8BDMLOQ.

and taking up their time. Instead, open with the point of the conversation ("We need to determine if we are going to go with venue A or venue B") and then let them ask the questions they feel are most relevant to help them make the best decision. They often prefer to lead the conversation, not wait for you to get to the point before they speak.

With high D clients, showcase your boldness, fearlessness, and results. High-scoring D clients want to hear about your sales accolades and production status. They are also more likely to want you to handle more of the transaction and have them do less; once they trust you, they may not want to be kept in the loop. Frequent updates or phone calls that don't require their input will be seen as a waste of their time and make you look inept in their eyes.

With high-scoring D employees, let them know how they can succeed. If you assist them in achieving their goals, they will work hard for you in return. These team members will gravitate to those who help them achieve results and are drawn to those who exude confidence, clarity, and strength. They are harder to offend than others but will often offend others without realizing it. As mentioned above, they do well in leadership and sales roles where there are no ceilings to stop their growth. If you have a problem, a high D is usually up for the challenge to solve it.

Because they move so quickly through life and work, a high-scoring D knows that they don't watch their own back very closely, which makes them fearful of being taken advantage of. As a rockstar agent, never go back on your word. Don't tell a D team member that they'll get a raise when they hit a certain goal and then not give the raise. This isn't good etiquette at any time, but it is especially bad to do to a D team member. When praising them, mention their accomplishments and always support them so that they can keep skyrocketing.

Influence

The i score measures how much someone values influencing others. A high-level i is usually the most popular person in the room and the social butterfly who loves to persuade others. They make you feel good, are fun to be around, and excel at being encouraging and complimentary. Their gregariousness and charisma sparkle in social environments. Most top-producing Realtors are a combination of high D and high i, so their drive mixed with their love of people put them a class above other types of agent personalities. Traits of those who score high on i include:

- **Goals**: Popularity, approval, excitement
- **Fears**: Rejection, not being heard
- **Influences others through**: Charm, optimism, energy
- **Overuses**: Optimism, praise
- **In conflict**: Expresses feelings, gossips
- **Would increase effectiveness through**: Being more objective; following through on tasks
- **Biggest fear:** Not being liked[22]

A high i often makes a great salesperson because of their natural ability to make connections, network, and influence others through charisma and charm. When communicating with a high i, avoid starting conversations with business talk. They'll first want to know about you as a person. Most importantly, at your first conversation, they'll want to figure out how to make you like them. The high i person is easily bored. They are impulsive and crave energy, so bring your own energy or they will find someone else to talk to. I filmed an episode for HGTV's *House Hunters* specifically to communicate better with high i clients because I could bring it up in conversations. This opened doors for me to share my values as a Realtor and build the connections needed to secure them as clients.

Compliment their appearance, their style, or their personality, and watch their eyes light up with excitement and feel their energy connect with you. Do not criticize a high i, even in jest, until they are quite comfortable in their relationship with you. While the D may perceive a critical comment as bold and impressive, the i will go find someone else to connect with. When meeting a high i lead, be liberal with compliments about their house, their taste, and themselves as a person.

As an employee, a high i will not do well in a cubicle working alone on computer screen. They also won't do well during a performance review if they receive criticism that's not sprinkled with praise. This "praise sandwich" (praise, criticism, praise) helps them avoid their fear that you don't like them anymore and makes it easier for them to hear your message. This technique works for your high i clients as well. For example, sandwich any negative feedback their home received during showings with positive news.

---

22 DiSC styles, "What is the DiSC i style?", DiscProfiles.com, August 16, 2019, https://www.discprofiles. com/blog/2019/08/the-disc-i-style/#.YtXPsuzMLUI.

The high i team member will be most productive and happiest spreading the good news of your company. Send them to social events, parties, BBQs, and so on, and prepare them with stories about happy clients and closed deals. They will come back with leads, which is exactly what your business needs.

Stability/Steadiness

The S score indicates how much stability, predictability, and familiarity someone prefers in their life. When faced with a new circumstance or environment, they tend either to clam up or push back because they prefer repetition. For work, the high-level S person gravitates toward positions of personal or administrative support; they don't like the pressure of making tough or new decisions. The high-level Ss make loyal employees and place value on maintaining harmony. Traits of those who score high on S include:

- **Goals**: Harmony, stability
- **Fears**: Letting people down, rapid change
- **Influences others through**: Accommodating others, consistent performance
- **Overuses**: Modesty, passive resistance, compromise
- **In conflict**: Listens to others' perspectives, doesn't speak up about own needs
- **Would increase effectiveness through**: Displaying self-confidence, revealing true feelings
- **Biggest fear**: Change[23]

A high-level S rarely gets bored doing the same thing every day at work; in fact, they prefer the stability. Because of this, they won't do well in commission-based work and will feel more comfortable with a steady hourly income.

They are often cheerful, love being a part of a team, and like to help people. Because of this natural trait, they gravitate toward win-win scenarios and place a high value on everyone being happy. Unfortunately, because people with this personality trait rarely speak up for themselves, a high-level S team member may reduce their commission to keep the client happy, offer to do the work of others, or make concessions just to keep

---

23 DiSC styles, "What is the DiSC S style?", DiscProfiles.com, August 29, 2019, https://www.discprofiles.com/blog/2019/08/what-is-the-disc-s-style/#.YtXReOzMLUI.

the peace. The issue is that this can eventually lead to unreleased feelings of resentment that boil over at inopportune and unexpected moments. Your office manager and team leaders must check in with high-level S members to make sure they aren't harboring any feelings of animosity or resentment. They need to praise your high-level S members for their contributions to the team, especially because they won't ask for it.

These team members are often the bedrock of your office because of their loyalty, attitude, and willingness to get the job done. Additionally, people feel comfortable talking with a high-level S person, which means they often play the role of peacemaker and know who might be unhappy or what drama may be brewing in your office.

The biggest fear for an S is change; they avoid surprises and being caught off guard. When change is necessary, give your high-level S members ample notice and time to process their thoughts. Expect resistance at first and then compliance after they've accepted that the change is inevitable.

This advice applies to high-level S clients. They will need information delivered in bite-sized chunks and be given the time to think about it. When meeting with a high-level S lead to sell their house, don't start with a discussion on commission or a marketing plan. Ask about the memories that were made in the home and how they feel about selling it. They may experience some anger or frustration as they work through these emotions, most likely because this is the first time they've processed them. Be patient and give them time before moving to the next phase.

After a high-level S client accepts they are selling their home, the next question to ask is: "What are your biggest fears when it comes to moving?" Let them process these emotions. They will want to be kept in the loop and will want feedback from open houses, including numbers of showings and what they can do differently or better to help show the home. A satisfied high-level S client will refer their SOI to you and remain a loyal customer.

Conscientiousness/Compliance

The C score measures how high someone values details, accuracy, and thoroughness. The high-level C is conscientious and seeks compliance and accuracy. Doctors, lawyers, engineers, and similar professionals are filled with people who score high on the C trait. The high-level C person likes to memorize protocols, policies, and procedures to avoid making mistakes, and they tend to be good at analysis and creating order out of chaos. Traits of those who score high on C include:

- **Goals**: Accuracy, objective processes
- **Fears**: Being wrong, strong displays of emotion
- **Influences others through**: Logic, exacting standards
- **Overuses**: Analysis, restraint
- **In conflict**: Focuses on logic and objectivity; overpowers with logic and facts
- **Would increase effectiveness through**: Acknowledging others' feelings, looking beyond data
- **Biggest fear**: Being considered sloppy or incapable/unreliable[24]

Your high C is a stereotypical "numbers person." They place a high emphasis on accomplishing tasks and do less well with people. It is this personality trait that can lead doctors to lack a bedside manor or engineers to show up to a meeting with crumbs on their shirt. More important than appearance is the quality of their work. This trait can make high-level C members a challenge on your team. They deliver extremely high-quality work with very few errors and gravitate toward the more complex problems and analysis that other personality traits shy away from. A high-level C shines when it comes to analyzing properties, reviewing documentation, and ensuring legal compliance. They don't do well with work that requires emotional intelligence, interpersonal interactions, or quick responses and will struggle in conversations with highly emotional clientele. For example, because they value accuracy, they won't be able to provide answers at a pace fast enough to satisfy an upset or excited client. A reliance on communicating through emails rather than phone calls will strike at the heart of their sales numbers. Even though a C team member is highly analytical, to an emotional client they can seem unaware, incapable, or as though they are making excuses. A high-level C needs time to produce quality work and won't do well if pushed to "fly by the seat of their pants."

The high-level D and I have a hard time remembering this when working with a high-level C and can pressure them to provide results faster than the C is capable of doing. High-level Cs work more comfortably in the commercial sales space or with a real estate investor than as salesperson.

---

24 DiSC styles, "What is the DiSC C type?", DiscProfiles.com, September 5, 2019, https://www.discprofiles.com/blog/2019/09/what-is-the-disc-c-style/#.YtXULOzMLUI.

Their biggest fear is being perceived as sloppy or inept. Mistakes, even small ones, can crush the confidence of a high-level C, and they will often worry needlessly about the minutest of errors. If a C does make a mistake, reassure them that it won't create tension on the team.

When dealing with high-level C clients, you are judged on your accuracy and attention to detail, every time. These are the clients who lose trust in you if you make one small mistake on a form or state their house was built in 1978 when it was 1979. These clients are often measured in their communication and speak at a pace that reflects this. If possible, allow them to communicate via email and be very straightforward about what is and isn't important. Make it clear what you need, or you'll likely get every piece of data they can think of.

The Three Levels of Mental Processing

In *Pitch Anything*, Oren Klaff breaks down the three levels of the human brain's processing system. When information, or stimuli, enters the brain, it begins in the first stage and is analyzed before moving on to the next stage. Each stage is responsible for determining a specific threat level and making this known to us before passing the information on to the next stage.

Consider these stages as three levels of security you must pass through before you make it in front of the decision maker. Recognizing the patterns found throughout this security system will help you earn trust and make your way to the decision maker faster, more efficiently, and more often than if you don't understand the security protocols you'll be confronted with. Great communicators tailor their approach to these three security levels.

The Crocodile Brain

I discussed this concept in *SKILL*, but I think it's so important that it warrants further discussion. Scientists discovered that the crocodile brain, also referred to as the reptilian brain, was developed for one purpose: to keep you alive. The croc brain analyzes every unknown stimulus we receive through the lens of "Could this hurt me?" It is not a nuanced or long analysis. If the croc brain decides something may hurt you, it activates your fight-or-flight response. If it determines the stimulus won't hurt you, it deactivates it. For example, every time we jump at a loud noise—think of a glass breaking in a restaurant—that's our croc brain in action. Adrenaline pulses through our system and our muscles tighten. The croc brain is our security center. You may notice a handful of diners who don't jump. These are people who have worked in restaurants and are accustomed to hearing glass break within this context, so their croc brain doesn't activate: There is nothing for them to worry about.

The croc brain evaluates new incoming information with a level of mis-trust. When we meet a new person trying to sell us something, we think, "What is their angle?" That ends when it is determined they are trust-worthy. This is why leads initially view agents from a commission-angle perspective: Is the commission all we want? Until we silence their croc brain, it won't change their opinion of us. Respect the croc brain and the role it plays, and don't discuss any plans before the lead trusts you.

New clients won't trust you until they feel safe enough choosing you as their Realtor. Do this by being nonthreatening in your value proposition. Likewise, new team members may have an adjustment period before buying into your work culture. Avoid difficult conversations until they see the value of their work and your team.

Ways to win over the croc brain:

- Show you care about the leads' interests before asking for anything that would benefit you. Begin a presentation by asking what they are most concerned about and clearly spell out what the lead can expect and what the journey will look like.
- Meet with a lead in person rather than over the phone so they can read your body language and facial expressions and see your work environment if meeting in the office.
- Include testimonials from clients on your website and social media.
- Try to determine a lead's DiSC profile to speak to them so they will hear you.
- Make sure your team members understand they serve the client, not the other way around.

The Midbrain

After the croc brain deactivates, it sends information to the midbrain, which is the second security system. The midbrain takes the information and evaluates it within the context of the social setting or environment. Many agents make the mistake of neglecting both the croc brain of leads and the midbrain of clients. If the agent gets past the lead's croc brain and the lead hires them, the agent then does extensive research, finds the perfect home for the client at the first showing, and then is bewildered when the client won't immediately write an offer. The reason is simple: The client's midbrain is screaming, "I can't tell if this is a good deal because I have nothing to compare it to!" Were the agent to show the client several homes and *then* show the perfect one, the client's midbrain would be much more likely to allow this information to pass to the next stage in the process, which is the neocortex.

To win over the midbrain:

- Show the client more than one property so they can develop context.
- If you don't show many properties, review over Zoom or a phone call the properties you've looked at and disqualified on the client's behalf.
- Share what other clients did to be successful in their home search.
- Describe home prices from thirty years ago so they can compare the decision they are making today to decisions others made in the past.
- Highlight the traditional return on investment that real estate offers compared to other investment vehicles.

The Neocortex

The neocortex is responsible for analyzing stimulus through a lens of logic and reason. Problems are thought through more thoroughly and rationally, and multiple potential outcomes are processed. As you read this book, your neocortex is activated. You read the words, digest them, and decide whether you believe them. As you consider how your business is run compared to the models in this book, you decide if you should change your model or if it's good as it stands. The neocortex helps you make these determinations.

It is obvious why we perceive information through these three security levels; the problem arises when we disrespect the order. If you tailor your first message to include logic, reason, and rationale but the person receiving it has no context, the nuance of your communication will be completely lost. The lead will perceive initial information in their croc brain, so communicate to the croc brain. Don't lay out a plan before the lead is using their midbrain and can process your higher-level information. Then it's on to communicating with the lead's neocortex:

- Don't present the return on investment on a potential property until the client has considered all asset classes, compared them to each other, and decided they want to buy a certain asset class.

- When presenting seller clients with an offer that is less than ideal, give them time to work up to their neocortex thinking before they can make a decision.
- When telling buyer clients that they need to write an offer higher than they had anticipated, also give them time to get to neocortex thinking (from "I'm being ripped off!" to "What if there is a better house out there for less money?" to "How much higher do I need to offer?").
- Respect that when clients get feedback from family members or friends who contradict your counsel, they will need time to work through the conflicting information.

Communication Rhythm

As you put the information in this chapter into play, you'll develop a rhythm to the communication between you and your clients as well as you and your staff. Becoming an expert communicator will save you time (allowing you to do more deals) and make you a better leader (allowing you to manage a larger team). The steps for becoming an expert communicator are next.

Listen Before You Speak

This will always be a problem for rockstar agents. When you become highly successful, people will defer to your judgment most of the time. This can create a habit where you speak first, speak longer, and end the conversation before the other side has had a chance to share. With your clients, you want to do the exact opposite. Even if the lead doesn't speak up fully, their croc brain will share what it's feeling because it always reveals fears.

Elevated heart rates, widened pupils, and lumps in the throat are universal signs of heightened emotion, and often of fear. Asking careful questions will help you navigate leads or clients through their thoughts until they can articulate their fears into words. Your job is to help your leads and clients get all these fears spoken and then guide them to lower their emotions. Only after this will the croc brain be satisfied, and you can share your perspective.

Hear the Human Need

When your client is highly emotional, it can be tempting to just answer their questions outright. A wiser approach is to consider what is behind the question and speak to that instead:

- **Client question:** "When am I going to receive an offer on my house?"
  - **Human need behind the question:** Certainty. This client is afraid the house won't sell.
  - **The wrong answer:** "Offers will come when they come. We can't force the market."
  - **The right answer:** "Your house is in fantastic condition, in a desirable location, and has excellent marketing. The right buyer is out there, and we'll find them. I'm not surprised at all that we haven't received an offer based on the average DOM we discussed. It's just a matter of the perfect person finding your home."
- **Lead question:** "I'm sure you do a fine job as an agent, but I am really interested in Acme Brokerage. Did you hear about their new client-concierge-iMarket-disruption-progressive-game-changing program?"
  - **Human need behind the question:** Variety. This person wants something exciting and new.
  - **The wrong answer:** "If you want all the bells and whistles, that's fine. But I can sell your home just as well without those."
  - **The right answer:** "Sounds like you have your finger on the pulse of the market! Yes, I have heard of their program. It looked cool to me too when I first heard about it. But I realized after looking into it that it's the same things all Realtors do but packaged to appear fresh and new. Would you mind if I shared how I'd use a combination of internet marketing and CRM technology to get your home in front of people?"
- **Lead statement:** "I'm really looking for a Realtor who is involved in the local community here. I don't want to be just another deal in their rearview mirror."
  - **Human need behind the statement:** Connection. This person wants to develop a meaningful relationship with their Realtor.
  - **The wrong answer:** "I don't live here, but I know how to represent a buyer. You'll be fine with me."
  - **The right answer:** "I feel the same way! I hate when a client just wants me for my knowledge, skill, and expertise. I can help

anybody in real estate, but what I really want is a repeat client for life! Real estate is about more than just paperwork and legal hurdles. It's about making memories, building wealth, and getting to know another person."

- **Lead question:** "My wife and I have been preapproved for a $1 million loan. No offense, but have you sold million-dollar homes?"
  - **Human need behind the question:** Significance. This person wants to have their standing recognized.
  - **The wrong answer:** "Million-dollar homes are the same as $100,000 homes. There's no difference in the transaction, and it's the same work."
  - **The right answer:** "A million-dollar purchase is quite the accomplishment! I would be honored to help you with this purchase. I can assure you there is no other Realtor that would take this responsibility as seriously as me. You will be my top priority for as long as it takes to get you the amazing home you have worked so hard to deserve."
- **Lead question:** "Which causes are you most passionate about? I really like to do business with those who support the causes I believe in."
  - **Human need behind the question:** Contribution. This person wants to feel their real estate agent's commission will also go toward supporting something worthy.
  - **The wrong answer:** "What does that matter? I'm not asking you which causes you care about. Let's keep business, business."
  - **The right answer:** "I can see you care deeply about giving back to others! I admire that about you. Your heart really wants to serve and give back. The best way I can help you do that is by taking on as many time-consuming elements of this transaction as possible so you can focus on continuing to support others. When I find you the right house, you'll be able to plan events and have meetings. I'm excited about making that happen for you."
- **Lead question:** "I've bought real estate before, and I think I want to take on a commercial property. I'm thinking I need to raise $10 million to go big! I've been playing too small in life so far. Can you connect me with people you know who want to invest?"
  - **Human need behind the question:** Growth. This person wants to feel like they are succeeding in their goals.

- **The wrong answer:** "I couldn't introduce you to people to lend you money in good conscience. You don't know anything about this asset class, and it may be over your head."
- **The right answer:** "Going for it! I love growth-oriented individuals because I'm the same way. One thing I've learned about growth is it needs to be a continual exercise. If I make a decision that backfires, it stifles my growth instead of promotes it. What if we look to grow your finances before we raise money from others? That way, you will have a strong track record before trying to raise funds."

When you speak to the human need behind your leads' and clients' questions and comments, you'll be able to address their real concerns and move them forward without offending them.

Tailor Your Communication to the DiSC Profile

Before I learned about the DiSC profile and how to tailor my communication, I was often visibly frustrated by leads, clients, and team members thinking the "wrong way." When I learned they were not wrong but that we simply valued different things, I stopped assuming their actions and their communication methods were a waste of my time. I learned to refocus on what they deemed the most valuable. Why was I so easily irritated? Because only 3 percent of the population have high D scores like mine.[25] With so few people sharing my value system, it became obvious as to why I rarely clicked with others.

Once I could diagnose other people's personalities on the DiSC scale and could tailor my communication accordingly, I was suddenly less frustrated. The DiSC profile is the Rosetta Stone to me in understanding how to communicate. Communication became much more efficient, which a high-level D like me finds important. The number of conversions with clients increased, my time spent communicating decreased, and my team members felt less intimidated by me.

My advice to you as a rockstar agent is to become well versed in DiSC. Consider it like a textbook for running your company. It will not only help you to communicate better with others, but also it will shine a light on

---

25 Michael Whatmore, "DiSC Personality Series: Spotlight On High-D," Executive Coaching San Francisco, September 10, 2013, https://executivecoachingsanfrancisco.com/disc-high-d-personality-profile-spotlight/.

your own narcissism and presumption that everyone should think like you do. This will make you a more effective, more influential, and more efficient leader.

Respect the Way Information Is Processed

As noted above, there are many ways humans process and hear information. Understanding these will help you provide information to leads, clients, and team members in a way that they will hear you and allow them to reach decisions faster. The real estate agent's game is based on the ability to make decisions rapidly, so getting those you communicate with to have a faster process helps everyone.

The Speed at Which We Process

Some people, like me, process information very rapidly and make communication into a game. I frequently catch myself piecing together the information someone is sharing to figure out where they are going with it. At best, this helps me save time in the conversation. At worst, I interrupt and appear pushy, selfish, and rude. This was a hard habit to break until I learned the DiSC profiles.

Have you ever been in a heated argument with someone who seems to articulate their point so clearly in the moment and knows all the right things to say? This is incredibly frustrating for people who don't think clearly when they are angry. Many people need time after an argument or a period of heated emotions to gather their thoughts and determine how they want to respond. One reason problems seldomly get resolved in the heat of the moment is because it takes time for the croc brain-mid-brain-neocortex process to work.

Your clients and your team members are individuals. Some will process faster than you. Others will need more time. The DiSC will reveal how to talk to all of them.

As a reminder, high-level D people want you to get to the point quickly. They prefer to ask the questions and may be frustrated if the pace of the conversation or work is slower than they like. They also prefer you to start with the bottom line and fill in the pieces for how to get there later.

High-level i people seek to be influential. Before they can process the specific question you ask, they may need time to be assured you're not mad at them, it's not personal, and you aren't asking for ulterior reasons. Make extra effort to reassure a high i you are pleased with their performance and want feedback on your idea, not on them. You can win over high i's by complimenting something unique about them, such as their clothing, personality, style, or other personal choices they've made.

The high-level S dislikes change and needs more time to process it than other personalities. If you rush a high-level S to make a decision before they are ready, they will likely to do so but then change their mind or backtrack after they've had time to truly consider the decision. Provide information in bite-sized chunks.

The high-level C is most concerned about being accurate and correct, which leads them to carefully consider their responses and actions. They process information slowly, especially if it's on a subject that they are unfamiliar with. You can help these leads by presenting them with the information you'd like to discuss before your initial meeting. This will give them time to research the topic and prepare answers to your queries.

More Ways We Process Information

Some people prefer to write out their thoughts in journals. The act of putting pen to paper and transcribing thoughts into written words helps them think more clearly. For these folks, encourage them to take notes during meetings and give them time to review these notes before asking for any decisions.

Others process information by talking about it. These people need to *hear* themselves speak out loud to make order of the thoughts and feelings they are experiencing. For these people, start a conversation and let them speak uninterrupted until they have nothing left to say. In many cases, you can have a team member do this because it can be time consuming, and these folks are rarely looking for advice. They just need to process their thoughts out loud.

Finally, others need alone time to process their thoughts. These folks are often introverted and need time away from other people and possibly from outside stimuli to come to any decisions. When they are distracted, they have a harder time working through options. For these individuals, give them space by asking how much time they'll need to work through their options.

The Order in Which We Handle Information

A byproduct of everyone valuing different things means we don't all handle information in the same order. Say you have a new agent who you ask to hold an open house in the afternoon because the showing agent had a family emergency. They agree to the task but already have a buyer's presentation scheduled for earlier that morning. Several obstacles need to be navigated to schedule everything, and not every person will process these obstacles in the same order.

One agent may be more concerned with upsetting you, so they agree before thinking it through. They didn't check to see if their schedule could support the new event but processed their decision on keeping you happy. The result is overpromising on something they can't deliver. Another agent may evaluate how well they can do a certain job before accepting your request. Still others may analyze how much money they can make on the deal before saying yes or no. We all analyze information according to what our personality type deems most important. As a rockstar agent, this is one more thing to recognize when dealing with team members, leads, and clients.

You can avoid any negative effects by asking the right questions. When a buyer chooses House B over House A, don't just write the offer. Instead, ask them: "What about House B made you feel it was the right decision for you?" If they can't articulate a reasonable response, it may be they aren't fully convinced that House B is the right option. It's better you go through this process with them earlier than in the middle of escrow!

Start the Day Early

Many decisions require varying amounts of information to be made well. This can take time and often requires several people or steps to get to the point of making the decision. This is also true when it comes to accomplishing tasks. Oftentimes, there are several people in a chain doing their work before you reach the time to make a decision.

Consider a client who wants a rehab estimate before they decide what price to offer on a home. You ask the contractor, who needs to check with their subcontractor, but the sub is on a job and can't return a call until lunchtime. When the sub gets the request, they need to ask their crews who will be available for a job in a month. Before the crew members can determine that, they need to calculate when the projects they are currently working on will be done. That depends on if the supplies will be available, permits will be approved, and the homeowners they are working for don't want additional work. See how complicated getting what appears to be a "simple" rehab price can be?

This is why you must start your conversations early in the day. Consider your request to be like a volley (think tennis) from you to the next person in the chain. That person will need to volley to someone else, and so on. It's wise to assume someone will forget to volley to the next person, which is why you double-check until you know that they are working on getting you an answer. If you start this early in the day, you give yourself more time during working hours (the only time you should assume people are working) to move information along that chain. Waiting until the end of the day or after work hours often results in catastrophe. You don't get answers, your buying client is anxious, your contractor is frustrated, and the listing agent doesn't know what to tell their client. Use your early morning time for more complicated or nuanced projects that will need more time for back and forth, and save those tasks that don't require multiple steps for later in the day.

➡ KEY POINTS

- One major problem that agents face when communicating is sharing information in the way they think, not in the way the lead or client thinks.
- At its heart, communication is the art of downloading your emotions, thoughts, and expressions into the other person.
- When you can no longer keep up with communication, the first step is to organize how it comes to you. Push your communication to one central chokepoint, where it can be evaluated and delegated.
- The six human needs that motivate all behavior:
  - Certainty
  - Variety
  - Significance
  - Connection
  - Contribution
  - Growth
- The four components of the DiSC profile:
  - Dominance/Decisiveness
  - Influence
  - Stability/Steadiness
  - Conscientiousness/Compliance

- If you tailor your first message to include logic, reason, and rationale but the person receiving it has no context, the nuance of your communication will be completely lost.
- Problems seldom get resolved in the heat of the moment because it takes time for the croc brain-midbrain-neocortex process to work.

CHAPTER TEN

CREATING CULTURE AND HIRING RIGHT

"Culture is simply a shared way of doing something with a passion."

—BRIAN CHESKY

Culture Defined

Your team culture will be wildly influential in the success (or lack thereof) of your business. When you are the only person in your business, you are the culture. When you add new team members, the culture expands, making it difficult to maintain and control. Nevertheless, it's what you must do.

According to Dr. Wayne W. LaMorte from Boston University School of Public Health, "Culture (from the Latin *cultura* [stemming from *colere*, meaning cultivate]) generally refers to patterns of human activity and the symbolic structures that give such activities significance and importance."[26] The patterns your team creates will be a reflection of

---

26 Wayne W. LaMorte, "What Is Culture?", Boston University School of Public Health, May 3, 2016, https://sphweb.bumc.bu.edu/otlt/mph-modules/PH/CulturalAwareness/CulturalAwareness2.html.

you and your business. Leads and clients were drawn to you as a solo agent because of your standards, proficiency, and skills. As you grow your business, clients will still be drawn to you and your culture. If you can't maintain it, your team will devolve, and you'll eventually lose your client base.

I view culture as the "supervisor" that guides everyone's decision making when I'm not there or when they're out at a showing, talking with vendors, etc. I want a team who thinks like me and, more importantly, values what I value. Everything my team does is within the culture that I set.

Culture in a Real Estate Team

Culture is not just your overall values but also the way you solve problems, deal with clients, and emphasize certain parts of the transaction. If you focus on the emotional component of real estate, so should your team. Your reputation, branding, and marketing will all be geared to highlight those strengths. The same goes if you focus more on investors and the financial component to owning real estate, and so on. It's important that you know your focus (as discussed earlier in this book) and how th is perceived by your leads and experienced by your clients. Your leads a l clients will seek out agents who reflect their own values and culture.

Team Values

Below is a table that includes different values and the culture that sur rounds them.

VALUE	FOCUS	MARKETING	BRANDING
Diversity in the clientele you serve	Economics and financial gain	Sharing emotional experiences with clients	High-level service and professionalism
Experts in a specific community	Specific asset class	Having fast response times	Local market knowledge and expertise

High volume (more first-time buyers than other agents)	Experience in the market	Finding off-market or creative opportunities	Removes intimidation for first-time home buyers and excels at holding hands
Luxury real estate	Understanding expectations	Maintaining a family legacy	Portrays your firm as a high-net-worth group that gets results in the luxury space

If you focus on finding great deals for investors, it doesn't make sense to hire agents who can't analyze problems or focus on finding deals. Understanding your values and focus comes first because they are the foundation on which you will build your team, marketing, and branding.

Team Chemistry

Another factor in your business's success will be the chemistry among team members, which (again) is directly related to your personality and leadership style. Bad team chemistry is bad for clients. As the rockstar of your agent band, make sure all your "musicians" are playing in tune. This can work by using the strength of one team member to compensate for the weakness in another. Everyone is good at something, and this synergy is crucial.

Putting the Team Above the Individual

It is human nature to focus on "what's best for me" instead of "what's best for we." In a traditional work environment, this attitude often thrives. A popular Facebook meme was "Boss makes a dollar, I make a dime, that's why I poop on company time," which can infiltrate your culture so that individuals push work onto others to get home early. Pay attention to this! It is only when the team wins that everyone wins. Remind them that if they put the team first, they will have better careers, higher earnings, and a more financially comfortable life.

Creating Efficiency

As detailed earlier in this book, the faster tasks get accomplished and the smoother the process, the more your team will be engaged. Promote those who work efficiently and effectively and mentor or fire those who don't. If one team member is allowed to work slower or without urgency, others may follow suit. Conversely, when your team leaders set the right example, others will work to meet that same level.

Staying Focused on the Team's Goals
An agent who has a different focus than yours will substitute their own goals for those of the team. This is the fastest way to find yourself with an agent who is negotiating for new commission splits, more time off, or lowered expectations. The better job you do of highlighting your team's goals, the more your team will put clients in contract and close deals (i.e., a revenue-generating activity).

Keeping Clients First
When your team operates with the right chemistry, the clients benefit. The reverse is also true. A showing agent who doesn't know the goals of the buyer's agent may say the wrong thing, share inaccurate information, or confuse the client. This means everything takes longer and creates more work for everyone. Administrative assistants who don't know how to correctly schedule agent meetings or properly prepare an agent for a presentation cause the agent to spend more energy cleaning up messes than servicing leads and clients. The bottom line is that a team missing chemistry or operating without a single culture means you can't hit rockstar agent results.

To give your clients an experience that results in glowing testimonials, the following individuals must coordinate and work as a team.

- **Buyer's agents and showing assistants:** Buyer's agents need to communicate with their showing assistants using check-in calls before each tour to highlight how they'd like the showing to go.
- **Listing agents and listing coordinators:** Listing coordinators communicate frequently with sellers, so they know their goals, communication style, and concerns. These need to be shared. Also, avoid mistakes such as when the listing agent knows the home is being sold because grandma died, but the listing coordinator calls to congratulate the sellers on their decision to sell.
- **Agents and administrative assistants:** Assistants help agents be more productive by doing a lot of tasks so the agent can focus on revenue-generating activities, which in turn pay the salary of their assistant. Assistants know how agents prefer to communicate (text,

call, etc.) and what type of information is important to them. This symbiotic relationship is the backbone of your agency.

- **Leadership and their Second-in-Command:** Every manager and sales leader on your team will need a Second-in-Command, which could be an official position but often is not. They may simply rely on the people they trust the most. You can guide these relationships, where chemistry is important, as needed.

Leveraging Work

The point of having a team is to leverage parts of transactions by assigning them to specific people. Your team's efficiency decreases when multiple team members do the same job. When musicians each take a turn in the spotlight, there will always be a point when two musicians are playing at the same time and then one stops playing. The best bands learn how to do this seamlessly to keep the music flowing. As you build systems (e.g., for listings, buyer contracts, events, transaction coordination), there'll be a large degree of inefficiency at first. This is a normal part of the process. As you hone the systems, you'll start to create more clearly defined lines and perfect when one musician passes the spotlight to another. This will leverage work and make your team more efficient.

Promoting Accountability

With a team, there is always the danger of a member thinking, "Someone else will do it." However, if it's not done, it will devastate your team's performance. To avoid this, ascribe clearly defined areas of responsibility and hold leaders accountable for the entire process. When no one is in charge, no one is accountable. When no one is accountable, things will be missed.

Creating Synergy

The role of all band members is to play their part. The goal of the songwriter is to write the music, and the songwriter in your agency is you. If you want synergy in your band, you need to develop it. I do this on the David Greene Team by pairing agents and staff who have complementary skill sets. A few common ones include:

- Analytically minded agents with emotionally aware agents.
- Action-oriented agents with supportive agents.
- Task-oriented agents with agents with strong visions.

- "Rainmakers" (agents who put a lot of people under contract) with highly organized assistants (who manage chaos well).
- Lead-generation experts with conversion specialists.

Marketing Your Culture

Once you determine your values, it's incumbent upon you to market them. It's not important with people who already know you, your standards, and your results—but when looking to generate leads, this is a game changer. Differentiating yourself from other real estate agents and teams will drive new business from leads and clients with your same values. As you consider your marketing, make sure to highlight your values clearly. These examples will guide you so that potential clients will know what they are getting with your team and how it is different from other agencies.

Poor marketing: Your local neighborhood Realtor!
Better marketing: The San Antonio real estate experts

Poor marketing: O'Hara Father and Son Real Estate
Better marketing: The team you need for family-oriented real estate representation

Poor marketing: Top listing Realtors!
Better marketing: Your listing negotiation experts: We fight for every dollar like it's our own.

Poor Marketing: First-time homebuying specialists!
Better Marketing: Anticipating every detail and holding your hand from beginning to end.

Attract What You Want

As the rockstar agent, you will be what attracts team members as well as leads and clients to your business. Both the leads and the talent will be attracted to the same thing: you. The more you showcase your personality, work ethic, and values, the easier it will be to attract the right people to you.

How Culture Works for You

As the leader, you have two main responsibilities: (1) to service clients, and (2) to service team members. Your leadership will be the key to keeping team members happy and wanting to work with you long-term. Satisfied team members increase chemistry/synergy, efficiency, skills, and a host of other positive qualities. As noted throughout this chapter, your character and values will be replicated and amplified by your team in all conversations with leads and clients and among team members. The culture you set will directly influence the success of your business.

Culture Serves as Your Voice

In times of royalty, kings and queens would grant powers to others "in my name," which meant carrying out business in the spirit of the ruler. This was true in my law enforcement days as well: Deputies carried the legal authority of the sheriff. And as the leader of your agency, your staff will carry out business objectives "in your name."

This means they must conduct themselves in a manner consistent with your standards. Consider the team member giving a buyer's presentation. If the agent delivers it haphazardly, appears disinterested by regularly checking their phone, or is unprepared, it sends the message to the lead that your team—and you as the leader—provides poor service. This is true even if it's just one member making that impression.

The last time you received poor service at a restaurant, did you blame your server or the restaurant's management? On social media did you share that the server was having a bad night or that service has gone downhill? When a team member is like that server, it will affect everyone on your team, not just that team member. Now consider the server who provided the poor service. Did they take responsibility, or did they blame having a "bad day" or being distracted? Most people will not hold themselves accountable for actions that have a detrimental effect on the rest of the team. Since you can't expect staff to self-regulate their performance, and even one negative review can significantly impact your reputation, you need something that can act "in your name" to prevent poor performances.

Once again, that is your team culture. When all the agents and staff on your team pride themselves on their work, it develops an unspoken pressure to stay focused and committed. When your team members develop strong relationships with one another, they show up for each other. When your team culture honors excellence, attention to detail, and superior service to your clients, any team member not meeting those standards will be aware of that fact. The pressure they feel guides them to do better work.

Culture Trains Your Team

Your team operating as a collective with the same values, goals, and approaches to business also functions as a guide for new team members. Newer agents learn from more experienced agents on how to solve problems, resolve disputes, and represent their clients. Culture functions as an ongoing form of training. This is why I create the pairings mentioned above. This includes, for example, pairing new showing agents with experienced buyer's agents so the training is firsthand. This tiered training offers more knowledge than you could provide personally, and as your team grows and you take on more management and leadership responsibilities, the entire team helps guide business.

Culture Creates Team Cohesion

Nobody functions well when they feel uncertain. Consider the last time you drove in the fog. How fast did you drive and how confident did you feel in that environment? In the same way, the culture set by the leadership offers new team members certainty and confidence to move faster in their growth. Your culture also allows your team to work together cohesively because everyone knows what is expected of them. When everyone is held to the same standards and same KPIs, there are fewer morale issues. This same setting of culture is used by, for example, college and professional sports teams. They use it because it works.

Culture Makes Clients Feel Your Presence

The most important reason for setting culture is that your clients will feel the same confidence in your rockstar abilities even when working with others on your team. While most clients would prefer to work with you directly, they are willing to work with team members—provided they feel that same confidence.

If you're known for helping clients make money in real estate, then that needs to be the focus of your team too—and that's directly related to the culture of your business. Ditto for being known for guiding first-time homebuyers, and so on. Clients are drawn to you because of what you do and how well you do it. Your team culture keeps up those standards while you continue to grow your business.

Establishing this culture must be part of your training process. If even one agent has values that are different from yours, clients will sense it. The more everyone shares your values, the more your clients will want to work with *your* agency.

Bad Cultural Fits

Along with hiring the right people is recognizing when you didn't. Someone is a wrong fit if they resist following your culture, values, and standards but instead superimpose their own. Firing team members who turn out to be a poor cultural fit is a must.

How to Recognize Poor Fits

Understanding what motivates people is an invaluable skill to develop as the rockstar agent of your business. If you understand why a team member does what they do, it allows you the opportunity to try to correct the issue or to realize the hire is just not the right person for your team. Poor cultural fits include the following.

They Don't Perform Tasks Up to Standards

There is a difference between getting something done and getting something done well. Successful people understand this inherently. Doing something well includes three characteristics: (1) it's done without mistakes, (2) it's done quickly, and (3) it's done with a high quality.

If any of the above three steps are missed, the job isn't done well. For the questionable team member, ask yourself: Do they complete a task without mistakes but take too long? Do they work quickly but make frequent mistakes? Do they not make mistakes, but the work isn't of high quality? Expecting everyone on your team to meet these three metrics for work performance will make it easier for you to see who is underperforming.

They Don't Have the Right Attitude

A bad attitude is most noticeable when surrounded by good ones. If most of your team is excited about hitting the next team goal but one person is not, that outlier sticks out. This makes it easier to identify that person as a poor fit for your business.

Watch closely for a negative outlook because it can spread very quickly through the ranks. Negative information travels faster than positive, so be aware of any team member who complains, criticizes, or spreads negativity, or it can catch on like wildfire. If this happens, you'll spend a lot of energy restoring healthy attitudes and not enough energy on creating revenue and helping clients. It is far more efficient to remove the cause of the problems as early as possible.

They Don't Take Full Responsibility

Most employees will try to fix a mistake they made. However, the right team member must do more than that: They must make changes to ensure the mistake doesn't happen again. An even stronger sense of responsibility is being proactive so problems are avoided. If a team member makes the same type of mistake repeatedly, they are not taking ownership of their mistake.

They Are Focused on "Me," Not "We"

Those who put their own needs ahead of the team are not team material. Teams are not for everyone, and that's okay, but it's not okay not for your business. If you have an agent too focused on their personal goals and not on the team goals, they are a poor cultural fit. The following are red flags of team members who are focused more on their goals than the team goals.

- They ask for more training when they aren't incorporating the personal training already provided, or they are not taking advantage of training videos.
- They look to the team for motivation instead of to themselves.
- They don't plan appropriately. For example, they ask for a 10 p.m. phone call to get help filling out a contract needed the next morning.
- They ask for higher commission splits before proving value to the team.
- They don't use appropriate resources. For example, they go to the team lead instead of the admin assistant, when appropriate.
- They are unwilling to help team members while asking for support.

In a team environment, where everyone shares in the wins and the losses, all staff have to know how to be team players.

The Price You Pay

Retaining staff who are not good cultural fits will hurt you more than you might realize. These folks can, among other things:

- Create a potential mutiny or spread seeds of doubt concerning your ability to lead.
- Spread their poor attitude to clients, and that could destroy the potential for referrals.
- Push work onto other team members or hold up buying or selling processes due to not meeting the three critical characteristics of doing work well.
- Hinder the positive energy of other team members.

One major problem with poor attitude is it's often related to resentment, which forms when someone feels they were treated unfairly or their expectations were not met. You may not have done anything wrong, but the person won't perceive it that way. When someone feels resentment, they feel justified doing negative things, such as treating clients or team members poorly. As the rockstar agent, you must keep a close watch for this.

Vivid Vision

On episode 447 of the *BiggerPockets Real Estate Podcast,* "Vivid Vision," author Cameron Herold described the concept behind his best-selling book of the same name. It's simple: Create a map that is as descriptive as possible of your future company.

Brandon Turner (of BiggerPockets and founder of Open Door Capital) did this when he started his real estate fund. He wrote a "newspaper article" about what his business would look like in the future and included activities such as weekly surfing as a team and all team members growing wealthy together. He then hung this dream news article in his workspace and looked at it every day. He showed his Vivid Vision to all interviewees. Imagine how easy that made hiring for Brandon. It helped him find the right people he wanted and needed and helped them to know where they were going as a team.

Your Vivid Vision

What's your Vivid Vision? What do you want your company to look like five years from now? What about ten years? If you're currently a solo agent, what's your vision for the future? Some will-be rockstar agents will want a "teamerage" model, which is a real estate office that acts more like a brokerage (e.g., high sales numbers, fewer support staff, lower splits), while others will want a team with a few assistants where they still do most of the work themselves. If you don't know what you want your future business to look like, how do you get there? How do you know who to hire?

Creating a Vivid Vision lays the foundation on which to build your culture. Additionally, it helps you find the talent that fits with your culture. When your team understands your vision, goals, and culture, it makes it that much easier to obtain their buy-in from Day One.

Mission Statement

An alternative to Vivid Vision is writing a mission statement, which is a clear, concise statement that sums up the goal of the company. Consider the following mission statements:

- **Tesla:** To accelerate the world's transition to sustainable energy.
- **Google:** To organize the world's information and make it universally accessible and useful.
- **Wix:** Create your own professional web presence exactly the way you want.
- **LinkedIn:** Connect the world's professionals to make them more productive and successful.

These statements make it easy to understand what these companies strive to provide, and therefore, their purpose for being. A mission statement will make it easier not only for your clients but also for your hires to decide if you are the right person for them. Whether you embrace a Vivid Vision or a mission statement, or both, it will help you to attract the right talent and the right clients, grow the right culture, and provide the right amount of direction for your team.

Hiring Right

Hiring is obviously a crucial step. Most agents I've spoken with who have either successfully hired teams or failed in their attempts have said hiring was the most difficult part of building their business. This section offers information to increase your odds of success when hiring, shorten your learning curve, and reduce mistakes as you figure out your hiring practices. I think hiring for a real estate business is particularly difficult, especially compared to other enterprises. That's because:

1. **There are no college degrees or training programs for real estate administrative assistants.** This is the main reason it's difficult to find good talent. A business looking to hire a nurse, engineer, architect, or business manager can find plenty of people with relevant degrees and training. In addition to that, many of the skills in one occupation are easily transferable to another occupation. Real estate sales, however, is such a unique field that it is extremely difficult to find people with prior work experience that translates well. This forces us to dive much deeper into getting to know someone's character, attributes, and talents, and then make an educated bet if they will fit well into our company.

2. **Real estate sales requires being good at many different things.** A good sales agent needs to be a counselor, adviser, negotiator, salesperson, project coordinator, and problem solver, among other things. A good sales agent is, among other traits, patient, organized, and efficient, and understands the urgency described earlier in this book. Finding someone who excels in all these abilities and traits is difficult, which means we must be highly focused to identify and hire the right people.

3. **Not everyone wants to work on a team.** Many people will be drawn to the idea of a real estate team because of its perceived benefits, such as job security and training. However, there are also commission splits and accountability, to say nothing of the odd hours of the real estate industry. Many newer agents like the team idea, but only to benefit from the free training and to gain needed experience. This leads to a high turnover rate, as these agents leave when they think they can finally go it alone, and green agents take their place. To avoid this, don't hire anyone *willing* to join a team. Hire someone who *enjoys* being on a team.

4. **Real estate sales is wildly different from a traditional work environment**. The majority of your applicants will come from the traditional work world, where they were W-2 employees. In those types of jobs, the employer is responsible for the success of the company, so it becomes easy for an employee to show up and clock in every day without doing a whole lot of work.

   Not so in real estate sales. Successful agents generate leads—and a lot of them. They problem-solve. They know that if things don't go well, no one can bail them out or rescue them, and that their success is solely on their own shoulders. This level of responsibility comes with a healthy dose of fear that they may fail, and this fear provides the impetus to keep moving forward. For those joining your team who have never worked in this type of environment, they may struggle with carrying the weight of all this responsibility. Breaking the W-2 mindset is crucial in creating well-rounded and capable salespersons.

5. **Real estate is not like what's on HGTV.** On HGTV, there are no hours of door knocking, cold calling, open houses, or time spent showing houses to "looky-loo" clients. The glamorous side of real estate portrayed on television creates unrealistic expectations for many who get their license and become sales agents. If you combine these wildly inaccurate portrayals with the W-2 mindset that someone else will bring in the leads, it's easy to understand why so many agents are set up for failure before they even begin. You can combat this by being brutally honest with applicants about what they'll be doing; what real estate is really like; and what to expect related to your team's vision, culture, and standards.

6. **It takes time to make real money in real estate sales**. Many new agents find that they can't support themselves in real estate, so they quit or must find a supplemental job. This ramping-up period ends many careers before they even start. Real estate is an industry that moves from famine to feast, but it takes years. Agents start off making nothing, then make just enough to get by, then finally are successful from referrals and incoming leads. Most new agents don't have the marathon mentality they need to get through the initial lean years, so you'll need to sense if an interviewee has the correct expectations before hiring them. You want to avoid a revolving door of hiring and firing/losing team members.

What to Look for in Hiring

From my experience of hiring the right people and hiring many more who did not work out, I've discovered some things that help me make better selections. The following are the traits or experiences I now look for in the hiring process.

People with Great Attitudes

I assure you that once you start interviewing people, you will be tempted to hire someone lacking the right attitude because of some other attractive trait like experience in the field, intelligence, or even a large social media presence or following. Every time I've hired someone based on a trait instead of their attitude, I've regretted it. Keep in mind that when most people interview for a job, they are after the paycheck. Of course, this isn't always the case, but it frequently is. The ideal candidate is interviewing to work on your team and interviewing you at the same time. They already have financial stability but want more opportunities, more freedom, or more earning potential.

When someone is interviewing with you for more than one position, odds are they need employment and will tell you whatever you want to hear to get it. I don't automatically disqualify someone for this reason, but I do look closely at their motivation. I want to hire people with great attitudes all the time, not just when they turn it on to get the job.

People Who Have Done Difficult Work Before

This might be the most important trait for determining if an interviewee will be able to do the job. If real estate is harder than any of their past jobs, odds are against them to succeed. Let me give you an extreme example.

Say you hire a Navy SEAL. You tell them they need to make one hundred phone calls on their first day, and you give them the script to use. To a SEAL, making phone calls will feel effortless. Compare this to someone who, say, rang up customers at a sales counter. The work didn't require much energy or thinking. When you ask them to make one hundred phone calls on their first day, they will be shocked and overwhelmed. What's the difference? Perspective. To those who have done harder things, one hundred calls feels easy. For those who haven't, the job feels difficult. You need to screen for people who hear the job requirements and are excited about them, not scared or don't seem to get it.

People Who Would Be Successful Without You

This is big. In the beginning, I hired people who needed a team environment to be successful because they couldn't make it on their own. They needed to be on a team. In fact, many were drawn to the team model precisely because they saw it as an opportunity to avoid the demanding work of making it on their own. These agents ended up being time and energy suckers. They frequently asked a lot of questions they could have found on their own or sought reassurances they didn't need.

Successful team members have the opposite approach. If they find themselves with a problem, they do everything they can to undo the problem, and only ask me or team leaders as a last resort. I give these team members more responsibility, more resources, and more trust, and they continually grow. One day it hit me: The people I hired who excelled would have excelled without me. It was that simple.

Why would someone join your team if they could make it on their own? Simple. They don't work with you because they *can't do* it on their own; they want to work with you because they can do it faster, easier, with fewer mistakes, and with less energy than if they were on their own. I am a real estate broker, but I don't own a real estate sales brokerage. I own a real estate company within Keller Williams, a national brokerage company. Why? Even though I *could* broker on my own, it's easier to work for someone else who's already figured it out. My advice is to only hire people who would have made it on their own even if they didn't join your team. Your job is to offer them a faster track with more support than they would have without you.

For example, the Keller Williams office supports me through their own staff members. Through them, I have staff I don't pay directly. I use their file coordinator to ensure all documents for each transaction are collected, office broker to help settle legal disputes or avoid legal problems, performance coaches to help new agents be successful and to coach top performers, and a market center administrator to make sure vendors are paid correctly. If you work for a brokerage, make sure that brokerage is working *for you* and be intentional in the ways they support your team.

People Who Put Others First

This is simple but powerful. You will become a successful rockstar agent by putting the success and comfort of your clients before your own. Agents who don't do this don't grow in our industry. The goal is to hire a team that understands that you will perform this way for your clients (who are everyone's bosses), and your team must perform this way for you. Putting the needs of others before our own is foundational to success in this industry.

People Who Take Responsibility

As touched upon above, some staff will take responsibility for completing a task assigned to them, but others will take responsibility for reaching the result behind that task. You need people who get results, not just take orders until they are told what to do next. During an interview, ask them for a list of accomplishments they've done from beginning to end.

People Who Enjoy Serving Others

Our business is demanding. No two clients and no two escrows are ever the same. We don't have the luxury of off hours. We work weekends, evenings, and lunch breaks. We often have to work around others' schedules to get done whatever is required to make the deal work. If an applicant doesn't enjoy working hard for others (and ultimately themselves), they will be miserable in this industry.

Hiring Process

An entire book could be written on this process and still not cover it all. Nevertheless, I want to briefly offer a general outline for your hiring process. Searching for good talent is just like searching for good leads. You start with a broad reach at the top of your funnel and slowly eliminate the weak options until you hopefully are left with a solid prospect. As with potential clients, you want to attract those hires who would be the best fit for your business. Here is the outline of the current system I use for hiring.

1. **Let others know you're looking to hire.** You can advertise in the following ways:
   - **Social media:** Announcing you're looking to hire.
   - **Word of mouth:** Asking for referrals from in-house team members and outside agents you know.
   - **Your SOI:** Asking people you know for referrals.
   - **Online job searches:** Looking on sites like Indeed.com, WizeHire.com, and ZipRecruiter.com.

2. **Advertise what you are looking for.** Your next step is to create a job description and specify how to apply.

3. **Push applicants into a funnel to be processed.** My company uses a single web page, called a squeeze page, as my funnel. A squeeze page collects the applicants' information; this allows us to contact them by email. The squeeze page we create is through a program called ClickFunnels, which gives us a template to collect the information.

4. **Have applicants perform a specific task.** Most applicants will submit resumes, but I don't feel that resumes are effective in our industry because real estate is so different from other businesses. Applicants are welcome to submit their resume, but we also ask everyone to submit a video no longer than five minutes explaining what they feel they can bring to the team. These videos:

   - Set the expectation that we want to know what they can offer our company. What value might they bring to the team? This weeds out those just applying for jobs.
   - Allow us to see how they communicate, which is a big part of real estate sales. For example, we can hear their speech patterns, and I've found that many people speak at the same speed and tempo at which they think.
   - Allow us to see how well they prepared. A large number of "ums" and "uhs" indicate nervousness. In real estate, you can trust that if they are nervous speaking in a video, they'll be nervous speaking with leads and clients.
   - Allow us to see if they can follow the instructions of making a video that is under five minutes long and know how to submit a file that large.

5. **Invite second-round applicants to an online group interview.** For those who have videos we liked, we send a group invitation to an online interview we conduct on Zoom. This is an opportunity for the candidates to interview us and allows them to hear what others are thinking. It's much more efficient to interview one group than to do this individually. Before the group interview, applicants are sent a video that details our team structure as well as our compensation structure. They are instructed to watch it and to bring their questions to the Zoom call. If they have no questions or if they email questions when they were instructed to bring them to the interview, it's a clear indication they don't follow instructions well.

6. **Invite third-round applicants to a second group interview.** Those who impressed us in the group interview are invited to a second group interview. They are sent another video, this one detailing our Sales Funnel, a crucial part of our workflow and sales process. Candidates are then asked questions about the Sales Funnel.

7. **Send fourth-round applicants a personality assessment to be completed.** For those who pass the second group interview, we send a Keller Personality Assessment, which is provided by my brokerage, Keller Williams. The KPA offers us a strong idea of how applicants prefer to be managed, how they respond to stress, what their strengths and weaknesses are, and, most importantly, which positions they would likely fit in within the real estate industry.

8. **Conduct a final interview with relevant staff members present to discuss expectations.** For those who made it to this point, we invite them for a final interview. This is conducted individually with team management from my office and a Keller Williams performance coach. This is an opportunity for everyone to express their expectations of the candidate, should we move forward. We emphasize what would make this a mutually beneficial long-term relationship.

9. **Offer job opportunity.** If everyone approves, we make a formal offer to join the team, compensation is clarified, job expectations are again set, and a start time is decided.

Tools to Streamline

We use several tools to streamline the hiring process.

Loom

Loom is a Google extension that allows me to record myself while I cursor my mouse around my computer screen. For example, I will draw a diagram of our team structure, then record myself explaining the diagram. These are how I make the videos that are sent to the applicants before the group interviews.

KPA

The KPA is available to Keller Williams agents through their market center. We review the results before determining if a leadership/management interview is warranted.

Other Staff
Your staff will be important to this process. In my office, staff members post the job ads, create and manage the squeeze page, email the applicants, arrange the Zoom interviews, send out the KPAs, and schedule the final interviews.

➡ KEY POINTS

- When you add new team members, the culture expands, making it more difficult to maintain and control.
- It is only when the team wins that everyone wins.
- With a team, there is always the danger of a member thinking, "Someone else will do it." However, if it's not done, it will devastate your team's performance.
- As the leader, you have two main responsibilities: (1) to service clients, and (2) to service team members.
- When all the agents and staff on your team pride themselves on their work, it develops an unspoken pressure to stay focused and committed.
- When everyone is held to the same standards and same KPIs, there are fewer morale issues.
- While most clients would prefer to work with you directly, they are willing to work with team members—provided they feel that same confidence.
- When someone feels resentment, they feel justified doing negative things, such as treating clients or team members poorly.
- Creating a Vivid Vision lays the foundation on which to build your culture.
- The ideal candidate is interviewing to work on your team and interviewing you at the same time.

CHAPTER ▶ ELEVEN

TRAINING

As noted in other chapters, training your staff will be a top priority. Training will guide your team members to understand and meet your values, culture, and expectations.

One reason people will want to work for you is because of the training you offer, which you should mention in your interview process. You may find over time that some members will join your team specifically for the training and then decide to leave once they stop gaining value from it. What you want are team members who will grow with your company.

Training is complicated to get right. If you don't provide enough training, your staff may leave, and those who stay won't have enough knowledge to meet your expectations. Your clients will suffer, your business will suffer, and you will suffer. If you provide too much training, your staff may feel overwhelmed and not use all that you offer. And spending more time on training means spending less time on generating leads and high-dollar activities, such as creating new escrows. Again, everyone suffers. The right amount of training requires balance. This chapter focuses on the systems, perspectives, and guidelines to get the training right.

Training Guidelines

The following are the guidelines I developed over time to fix my own training mistakes. My staff uses these with new hires to determine when to train, what to train on, and how much time to spend on training.

Train on Everything (As Needed)

Don't assume your staff knows what needs to be done just because you do. This is a problem for anyone who has achieved any level of success in life: The further along we are, the more we forget what it is like to be inexperienced. For this reason, I advise *not* using your top agents to train new staff. They won't remember what it is like to be new either, so they will often skip crucial, foundational information. Practice extreme ownership in this area. If someone has not had training on something, they shouldn't be expected to know how to do it. This is also a great method to tell if a trainee is not progressing. If they've been shown exactly how to do a task, but they still aren't doing it correctly, you know you may have a problem.

Train in Order of What the New Hire Needs to Know

Not only this, but I also advise training in small, bite-sized chunks of information, then have the trainee either perform the task or answer a series of questions to prove they grasp the concept. Avoid giving information that is several steps ahead, because this will confuse them. Keep your training relevant to the tasks they'll be performing immediately, and train often enough that the trainee is always progressing.

Train, Then Show

After your trainees are taught how to do a task, have them observe the trainer do the same task in real time. This is especially important for tasks that can make agents nervous. These include, among others, training staff on how to call leads from an open house sign-in sheet, how to call listing agents (trainees always worry about doing it the "right" way), how to write an offer, and so on. Hearing how an experienced agent asks questions and gives answers is invaluable because it allows new staff to begin to trust their instincts.

Practice the Training

It's easy to assume that because someone understands a concept, it will translate into effective performance of the task. This isn't true. Don't confuse understanding what to do with the doing of it. Feeding information can feel like training, but it's only half of it. The other half is having the trainee perform the task under supervision. This can help save the trainee in the middle of call so the trainer can offer suggestions in real time. Additionally, it shows how well the trainee is processing information and how they learn best. Most importantly, your trainer sees the ROI on time invested in training. A few tasks that trainees should perform repeatedly under supervision until they feel confident include:

- **Searching prospective homes on the MLS.** Newer agents will likely be unsure about what they should be looking up and where to find the information. Take the time to walk them through where to find the information they'll need, how to check if the home is in an HOA, where the DOM is listed, etc. They should be able to find this information quickly and with confidence before being trusted to perform searches on their own.

- **Calling listing agents to ask questions.** For new listing agents and admins, start with a list of questions that need to be answered. Have the trainer show how to build rapport and establish a good flow of communication. This starts by complimenting the listing and the marketing the agent has done. Trainees listening in on these calls will build their confidence much faster than if left alone.

- **Running comps and creating CMAs for listing appointments.** Creating a CMA is a skill that takes time to build. Have a system for preparing a listing appointment that involves creating a CMA and calling the listing agents of the active and pending properties to get an idea of how much interest and attention the properties are getting. The new administrative assistants must be trained on how to do this to the same standard you expect of yourself.

- **Touring homes with buyer clients.** Don't send your new agents out to tour homes without first doing tours with experienced agents. You have no idea how new agents will represent you in front of clients. Also, they need to be shown how to find and open lock boxes, use the keys to open doors, turn on lights when they enter, answer client questions, make notes to share with the lead agent later, and then reverse these steps when leaving. Train the new agents well so you don't have to worry about them opening a door in front of a client and the seller's dog runs out!

- **Answering incoming phone calls about listings.** This task is less important in a seller's market because the fallout won't be as significant. Even so, if you have a property that is more difficult to sell, it's important that your staff represent your clients' interests well and not miss any potential buyer opportunities. Explain to the new staff that it's not just about answering questions: It's about creating interest. Many buyer's agents need help selling the property to their clients, and this is where the training becomes important. Teach your new agents how to see and explain the strengths and amenities of the listing (e.g., school districts, proximity to hiking trails) to buyer's agents. Selling agents who share this type of information with buyer's agents are more likely to intrigue buyers to look closely at the sellers' homes.
- **Taking "sign call" leads and moving them into the Sales Funnel.** A big mistake new agents make when a buyer calls to ask about a listing is to simply give them the information and hang up. But sign calls are Leads and should be treated as such! Your staff should be able to set themselves apart from the average agent during these conversations and set up an appointment with the Lead while on the call. Train your staff to ask if the Lead is already represented by another Realtor before going all out; if they are not, create the interest in hiring your agency.
- **Inputting listing information into the MLS.** This task must be practiced before it can be done with confidence and accuracy. Don't train with live listings. Instead, create a mock listing or use a property your team has already sold. Your new administrative assistant trainees will need several dry runs to gain competency. Once the trainee understands the steps, have the trainer time how quickly the trainee can do the work, and then check their work for accuracy.
- **Creating forms for client signature (writing offers).** When I was a new agent, it took me two to three hours to write each offer. Why? Because I was entering the same information onto every line on the form. For every offer. After I complained about this to another agent, I found out about cover sheets. It's a tool that allows the same information, such as names, to be autogenerated in the appropriate spots on a contract. My writing time on offers decreased to six minutes. Have the trainer show new hires the offer writing software (zipForm, in many states), and have your trainees practice filling

out forms. Then observe them for accuracy and speed. New agents will usually be intimidated by filling out forms, but using a tool that autogenerates information makes the job much easier.

Following these training guidelines will help you avoid costly and time-consuming mistakes in training new hires. They will also protect your reputation because your staff will be trained properly to meet your standards.

Training Trade-Off

Remember that training means not asking more of your new hires than they can do with accuracy and speed. You need to avoid the following:

1. Giving too much information too quickly. Giving too much information too quickly will oversaturate your trainees and prevent them from being productive.
2. Having agents receive training in exchange for leads rather than just for learning the job. This will hurt your business and not grow theirs. Exchanging training for leads will attract those who will leave you once they receive the training and you'll have to start over with a new candidate.
3. Having trainees generate new revenue instead of learning how to close already generated revenue. You want those you hire to systemize your business to focus on closing team leads, not just learn how to generate their own so they can build a business without you.

The other two things to remember are: (1) to avoid hiring the wrong people (time you spend training agents who leave is time you won't get back), and (2) if your agents don't practice the training, there is no benefit to anyone.

On the David Greene Team, we generally train staff in ways that support our sales leaders. For example, sales leaders are responsible for putting clients in contract and generating the revenue that pays the salaries and commission splits of the junior staff. By ensuring the training will lead directly to revenue generation, you avoid both overtraining and undertraining. Increased revenue generation is the best barometer I've found to maintain the right balance of training.

Training is an investment and needs to be looked at as such. You are investing your team's time and attention. In our business, putting time, attention, and energy into any one thing means we are taking them away from something else. Plain and simple: The time, attention, and energy taken away from lead generation and lead follow-up costs you money. Period. If you own a rental investment property that you bought for less than it's worth, and spending money on rehabbing it would create higher rents, the rehabbing is a worthwhile investment. If you had a property that was already at its top price, you wouldn't spend more than necessary to keep it rent ready. This principle applies to people too.

Some of your staff members will give you an amazing ROI on the time, attention, and energy spent on training them. Others will fail to produce a return. Don't fall into the trap of training staff without an ROI. Value your own time and your team's time. As the rockstar agent, you must know your value and exercise it frequently. I have Keller Williams performance coaches meet with us several times a week to ensure we are getting the absolute most out of ourselves. This is just one way I maintain my value and the value of my lead generators and lead agents.

Investing in the right people will earn you, and them, more money later. Investing in the wrong people or in the wrong training will cost you, and them, money. Time spent training is *not* free time. In our business, time is never free.

Training Tools

In our training and in our day-to-day work, we use the following tools.

CRM

We use the Brivity Platform as our CRM to track our leads and notes, assign automated follow-up plans, manage transactions and agents' individual databases, and more. The CRM guides staff to remember what has been completed and what still needs to be done and by whom. We frequently assign tasks to one another through the CRM, and those tasks remain visible until they are checked off as completed. Find a CRM you like and have your entire team use it—it will be the foundation of your business. Make getting one a priority and build all your systems around it. How we use our CRM is detailed in Chapter Twelve.

Google

Outside of the CRM, we use Google apps for most of our work. This includes:

- **Google Drive.** Google Drive's file sharing allows us to communicate, store information, maintain checklists, and update office protocols.
- **Google Docs.** We use Google Docs for easy access and updates to office procedures; marketing templates and presentations; employee performance reviews; MLS data, including phone numbers; and other administrative info. We even use it for access to training videos.

    For example, to make notes before a scheduled weekly meeting, staff write their questions in a Google Doc for their superior to review ahead of time. This makes for faster meetings and helps the leaders better prepare. Because Google Docs can be edited in real time, information can be answered, changed, and deleted as necessary.
- **Google Sheets.** We use Google Sheets for our Lead Boards. We can easily share templates or review an agent's Lead Board simply by logging into Google Sheets. For example, links can be shared with the showing assistants who are working with the sales leaders, and everyone sees where the work is in process. We use Google Sheets to track expenses and lists of referral partner agents; create dashboards for relevant information; maintain lists to be uploaded into email delivery systems; and import databases from agents' phones into CSV files and then into our team's CRM.

Videos

We use Loom to create videos. For example, I can create a video that allows the viewer to see my computer screen while I explain what I'm doing. These videos are then stored on our Google Drive where they can be accessed by team members, clients, applicants, etc. Videos just for training include, among others, how to:

- Create CMAs in the various MLS systems we use and save a search in an MLS.
- Enter their database into our CRM.
- Deliver a listing presentation or a buyer's presentation.
- Set a client on an automated search/drip campaign.
- Fill out an offer sheet or purchase agreement.

- Analyze an investment property.
- Open a lock box.
- Follow up with a lead.

Training Systems

There are several things you can do to support your training goals and move things along faster. This section shares some of the information that assists in training team members and clarifying responsibilities within the team and business.

Lessons on Training

Having someone watch you as you work can function as a training tool. Consider the two ways of progressing with your team training.

Solo Samantha likes to work alone. She frequently tells other staff members, "It's faster if I just do it myself." Samantha gets her work done quickly and accurately, and she always goes home on time because she values her time away from work. Ultimately, though, this solo attitude comes with a price for your business and for Samantha. When she gets busy in the spring, no one can help her. When she wants to take a vacation, no one can fill in for her, so she must work while sitting on a beach. Eventually, Samantha wants to get out of production and have her own staff. But Samantha never took the time to teach, help, or invest in others.

Team Tanya also loves to work quickly and efficiently, but she sees the bigger picture. She shares an office with newer team members so they can hear her on the phone, complete small tasks for her, and look for ways to assist her. While Tanya's work moves a bit slower than Samantha's because she's also explaining what she did, she is building loyalty with staff by helping them grow. When Tanya needs an open house held, there are plenty of people to do it. When she needs someone to show houses for her, she has several agents trained in exactly how to do it. Tanya is the tortoise to Samantha's hare. She starts off slower, but she finishes faster with teamwork.

Obviously, being a Team Tanya is better for business. Consider that if you do something only by yourself, you will always have to do that task. If you teach someone else to do it, that person will eventually be able to do it for you, and you will be able to move to higher revenue tasks. I used this approach, and while it created a slower start for my business—I could have sold more houses as the proverbial hare—I wouldn't have the tremendous business I have today without it.

My recommendation is to never have your team do anything without someone else observing and learning.

The Road Map

As the ecosystem of my real estate business grew, I created patterns. As people contacted me from various sources, I would warm them up in a conversation and then pass them to various team members for follow-up. Those team members would then use the system we had created to move the Leads down the Sales Funnel, which led to hiring more team members to help the growing list of clients.

To help with this process, I created what I call the road map. It is a general understanding of how we generate leads and move them toward real estate ownership. The road map is shaped like a three-pronged tree. The roots of the road map are my business's lead sources, or where we find leads. The trunk is my inside sales agent, who takes the leads and ensures they are contacted by the appropriate team member. The trunk of the road map then branches off into three main branches related to our three main sources of revenue: loans, sellers, and buyers. Along those branches, assistants and sales leaders, such as loan officers, listing agents, and buyer's agents, turn Leads into Clients and move Clients to Closings.

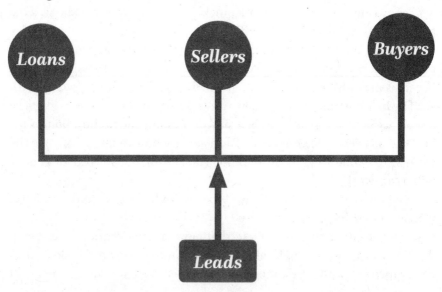

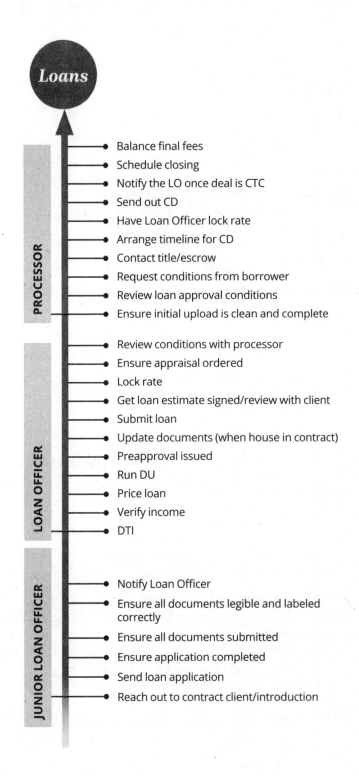

Loans

PROCESSOR

- Balance final fees
- Schedule closing
- Notify the LO once deal is CTC
- Send out CD
- Have Loan Officer lock rate
- Arrange timeline for CD
- Contact title/escrow
- Request conditions from borrower
- Review loan approval conditions
- Ensure initial upload is clean and complete

LOAN OFFICER

- Review conditions with processor
- Ensure appraisal ordered
- Lock rate
- Get loan estimate signed/review with client
- Submit loan
- Update documents (when house in contract)
- Preapproval issued
- Run DU
- Price loan
- Verify income
- DTI

JUNIOR LOAN OFFICER

- Notify Loan Officer
- Ensure all documents legible and labeled correctly
- Ensure all documents submitted
- Ensure application completed
- Send loan application
- Reach out to contract client/introduction

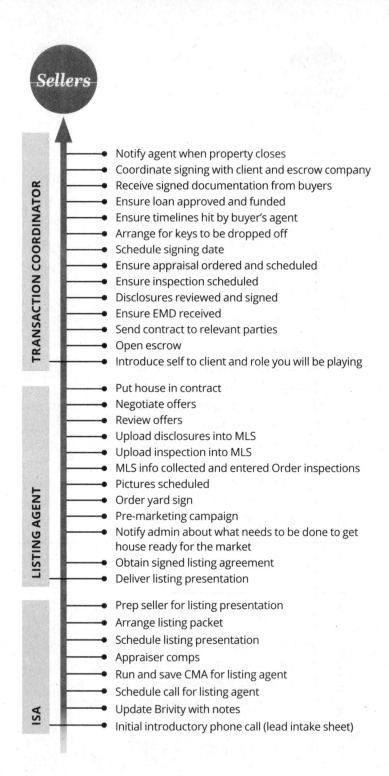

Sellers

TRANSACTION COORDINATOR

- Notify agent when property closes
- Coordinate signing with client and escrow company
- Receive signed documentation from buyers
- Ensure loan approved and funded
- Ensure timelines hit by buyer's agent
- Arrange for keys to be dropped off
- Schedule signing date
- Ensure appraisal ordered and scheduled
- Ensure inspection scheduled
- Disclosures reviewed and signed
- Ensure EMD received
- Send contract to relevant parties
- Open escrow
- Introduce self to client and role you will be playing

LISTING AGENT

- Put house in contract
- Negotiate offers
- Review offers
- Upload disclosures into MLS
- Upload inspection into MLS
- MLS info collected and entered Order inspections
- Pictures scheduled
- Order yard sign
- Pre-marketing campaign
- Notify admin about what needs to be done to get house ready for the market
- Obtain signed listing agreement
- Deliver listing presentation

ISA

- Prep seller for listing presentation
- Arrange listing packet
- Schedule listing presentation
- Appraiser comps
- Run and save CMA for listing agent
- Schedule call for listing agent
- Update Brivity with notes
- Initial introductory phone call (lead intake sheet)

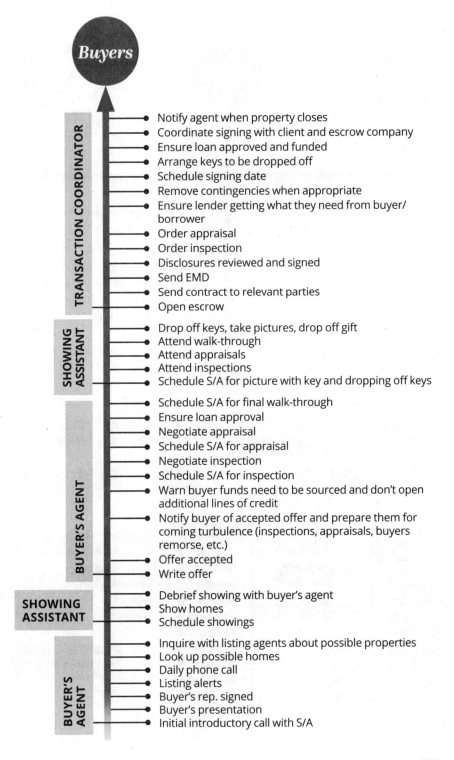

Buyers

TRANSACTION COORDINATOR
- Notify agent when property closes
- Coordinate signing with client and escrow company
- Ensure loan approved and funded
- Arrange keys to be dropped off
- Schedule signing date
- Remove contingencies when appropriate
- Ensure lender getting what they need from buyer/borrower
- Order appraisal
- Order inspection
- Disclosures reviewed and signed
- Send EMD
- Send contract to relevant parties
- Open escrow

SHOWING ASSISTANT
- Drop off keys, take pictures, drop off gift
- Attend walk-through
- Attend appraisals
- Attend inspections
- Schedule S/A for picture with key and dropping off keys

BUYER'S AGENT
- Schedule S/A for final walk-through
- Ensure loan approval
- Negotiate appraisal
- Schedule S/A for appraisal
- Negotiate inspection
- Schedule S/A for inspection
- Warn buyer funds need to be sourced and don't open additional lines of credit
- Notify buyer of accepted offer and prepare them for coming turbulence (inspections, appraisals, buyers remorse, etc.)
- Offer accepted
- Write offer

SHOWING ASSISTANT
- Debrief showing with buyer's agent
- Show homes
- Schedule showings

BUYER'S AGENT
- Inquire with listing agents about possible properties
- Look up possible homes
- Daily phone call
- Listing alerts
- Buyer's rep. signed
- Buyer's presentation
- Initial introductory call with S/A

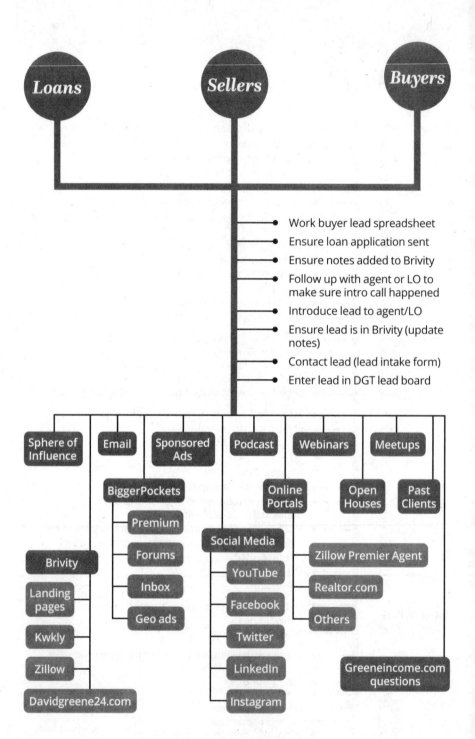

Loans · Sellers · Buyers

- Work buyer lead spreadsheet
- Ensure loan application sent
- Ensure notes added to Brivity
- Follow up with agent or LO to make sure intro call happened
- Introduce lead to agent/LO
- Ensure lead is in Brivity (update notes)
- Contact lead (lead intake form)
- Enter lead in DGT lead board

Sphere of Influence
- Brivity
- Landing pages
- Kwkly
- Zillow
- Davidgreene24.com

Email
- BiggerPockets
  - Premium
  - Forums
  - Inbox
  - Geo ads

Sponsored Ads
- Social Media
  - YouTube
  - Facebook
  - Twitter
  - LinkedIn
  - Instagram

Podcast
- Online Portals
  - Zillow Premier Agent
  - Realtor.com
  - Others
  - Greeneincome.com questions

Webinars
- Open Houses

Meetups
- Past Clients

Not every rockstar business will be structured like this, but every rockstar business needs a road map. I know that many agents prefer not to have so many people involved with clients in transactions. They avoid the team model because, like Samantha, they prefer doing everything themselves. The following is an example of why that's not good for business.

The Restaurant

Let's use the example of a restaurant. You've heard about a restaurant from ads on television, signage as you drive by, and word of mouth. Restaurants have different lead sources, just like the roots in my road map. You arrive at the restaurant and are greeted by a host who gathers basic information such as how many people are in your party and which area of the restaurant you prefer. They also share information on how long a wait is for a table. The host then relays this to the manager, who eventually seats the party, or an experienced host may seat you. It's important that you be greeted when you walk in the door, even if there are no tables available at that moment. The simple act of being greeted keeps you at this restaurant. The role of the host is akin to that of the inside sales agent.

You are brought to your table, given menus, and told who your server will be. You wait patiently until your server arrives to find out what is most important to you. Would you like drinks or appetizers? Do you have any questions about the menu? The server establishes rapport and is your primary source about the menu, your order, and your preferred preparation. The server, in other words, is responsible for your overall experience. While others may assist them, your experience is their responsibility. Your server should direct others (have the bartender make your drink), ensure tasks are completed (did the breadbasket get refilled?) and timely (was the food brought out as soon as it was done?), and stay in touch with you (how is your meal?) during the course of your meal. They delegate, but they remain your primary contact. You don't mind if someone else refills your water glass or brings more bread. In this analogy, the server is the real estate agent.

Real teamwork is throughout. After the waiter takes the order, the bartender makes your drink, a chef or cook prepares your food, a sous chef helps with plating, the server or someone else delivers your food, someone refills your water glass and clears your table for dessert. After you pay and leave, someone cleans and resets your table for the next party. And overseeing all of this is a manager. Like the team in the restaurant, from seating to delivering the check, your team moves the Lead through the Sales Funnel and to Closing.

The server (inside sales agent) will certainly assist in many of these tasks, and in some situations will do the work themselves, but when they are busy with another table, someone else completes tasks. The most important lesson is: No one cares who does the work so long as it's done and up to standards. We just need to know our server is watching out for us.

A few other things to keep in mind:

1. No one remembers if everyone else is great if there is one weak team member.
2. Working as a team means training on timing, culture, and consistency to create the right client experience.
3. Not every restaurant is for every patron. Your business is the same. Your business isn't right for every lead (see earlier in the book about the focus of your agency).
4. Some customers will never be happy, no matter what you do.
5. If the service is not up to standards, it will affect everyone, even the staff who didn't work with the client. Your business's reputation is affected when support staff makes mistakes.
6. Managers hold staff accountable, and every real estate team needs them.
7. The inside sales agent must set the right expectations to move the Lead down the funnel and thus to an agent.
8. You will want to promote your best team members.
9. The strongest agents get referrals.

Teams Within Teams

As your overall team grows, you will notice a pattern of "teams within teams." This happens when a lead agent (on my team we refer to them as sales leaders) gets comfortable with certain administrative assistants or showing assistants. As they gain confidence in this team within a team, the sales leader increases their training. Sales leaders become the primary source of knowledge, and showing assistants and admins become the primary source of support.

Don't resist this and force everyone to use the same agents as trainers. Think about every job you've had—there were always supervisors and team members you preferred over others. This is human nature and why I created the position of sales leader. Every agent on my team is a buyer's agent, but sales leaders are unique in that they:

- Distribute team leads on a regular basis.
- Offer additional accountability and oversight.
- Provide accountability to team leadership for leads they are assigned and the experience of their clients.
- Provide specific team training to mold young talent.
- Recruit agents. They also receive bonuses or small splits of those agents' commission if they train and onboard them.

By creating a sales leader role, you help yourself by:

- Offering a new level of promotion that does not require a salary and/ or a new management position.
- Offering and evaluating leadership skills.
- Adding avenues of training and role models for new staff.

There are, however, possible downsides to this position, which include:

- Building a sense of entitlement in the wrong person or too much separation from the rest of your team.
- Confusing the rest of your team (e.g., Should all showing assistants ask the sales leaders or someone else questions?).
- Promoting dependency on sales leaders that reduce their time for lead generation.
- Creating holes in your overall team approach (e.g., "Why didn't I get that lead? She got the last two.").

Meetings

As discussed in Chapter Eight, I use meetings as powerful training tools. They are scheduled with a Zoom link or at a physical location and are kept to a designated length. The agenda is also shared beforehand.

Team Leadership Meetings

These meetings focus on overall priorities as well as the most pressing problems. They last one hour, whereby we discuss projects, individual team members' performance, KPIs, and creative ideas to grow and improve the business. A Keller Williams performance coach often leads these meetings.

Sales Leader Meetings

These meetings focus on sales leaders' KPIs (discussed in Chapter Eight under "Sticking to the Correct KPIs"), any problems they are facing, and what resources they need from the team to move forward. All sales leaders attend together so they can learn from each other and implement ideas as a team. We often find that sharing this information benefits the rest of the DGT team. A Keller Williams performance coach leads these meetings as needed.

Showing Assistant Meetings

Showing assistants attend weekly trainings led by a member of team leadership or a sales leader. Meeting topics include how to analyze properties, how to negotiate better, how to use the MLS, and how to research specific information, among other topics. The agents not based locally attend remotely, and the local agents attend in person.

Administrator Meetings

Weekly meetings just with administrators cover the projects they are working on, specific areas they would like additional training or clarity on, and suggestions they have to contribute.

Sales Leader, Showing Assistant, and Administrative Assistant Meetings

These daily meetings have only one purpose: to strategize how to move Leads down the Sales Funnel. The meetings center on the team's Lead Board, which is a Google spreadsheet that tracks leads, among other things. The sales leaders focus only on factors in the sheet: (1) Nurtures (to ensure someone stays in contact with the Leads who elected not to move forward), (2) Buyer Leads (to ensure every Lead is contacted daily and moved along the funnel to become a Client), and (3) Active Buyers (to ensure the showing assistants move Clients closer to being in Contract).

Whole Team Meetings

Let me give you an example of a meeting agenda for our whole team meetings. The 60-minute weekly whole team meetings are run by a different team leader every week and involve:

- **Connect time** (10 minutes): Break into groups of three to discuss what each person is working on and if help is needed.
- **Crunch time** (20 minutes): Review team numbers. We review how many houses were put in escrow in the last week, how many total pending properties we have, and the team's current gross sales volume as compared to our yearly goal (see the figures in Chapter Eight). We also review relevant changes to the industry, introduce new hires, and hear about any issues individual team members are facing.
- **Critical thinking** (15 minutes): Preselected team members share preselected information, script practice, market knowledge, areas of success, etc.
- **Celebrate** (10 minutes): Every team member gives a one-sentence shout-out of something that went well or what they are grateful for.
- **Commit** (5 minutes): Every team member states what they are committed to doing for the week.

Team Members Sharing During Meetings

It's easy to assume you have all the information for training, but the foregoing shows that is not correct. Your team members have stories of deals they made, things that worked, and mistakes they made. Your staff will get a valuable education hearing about the experiences of others. The more team members teach, the better it is for you, provided they teach only in their skilled areas. Having different members train hires both helps the new staff and develops the members' leadership skills for future promotions. One clear benefit is that you also have more time to grow your business. I love lead-generating while my staff handles the training and education, and then I can hand new agents leads when they're ready.

Outside Resources

In addition to in-house training, consider the following outside resources to improve your staff's education.

Office Brokerage

As noted earlier in the chapter, if you're a part of a bigger brokerage, take advantage of the resources they offer. Your staff can partake in more trainings, courses, videos, or organized events.

For example, Keller Williams Realty offers courses to train agents and help them build their business. "BOLD" is an intensive coaching and training program that teaches agents how to get clients into contract. "Ignite" is more education-based to teach agents how to build a sustainable business. I recommend both of these options. If you don't work for Keller Williams, ask your broker about what courses are available and then encourage your agents to take them.

Books

In my opinion, there aren't many helpful books specifically for real estate agents (which is why I'm writing this series). Even so, there are books that cover sales, psychology of sales, personal development, self-improvement, and general real estate information. Encourage your team to read as much as possible—and more importantly, to discuss what they are learning with other team members. (See books on BiggerPockets.com/store.)

Podcasts

I'd be remiss if I didn't mention *The Real Estate Investing* podcast produced by BiggerPockets, of course, but there are also other podcasts for real estate agents. I can recommend *Real Estate Rockstars* (with Aaron Amuchastegui, who is also a BiggerPockets author) and *GSD Mode* (with Joshua Smith). The *Tom Ferry Experience Real Estate* podcast and the *Brian Buffini Show* are also excellent. Have your agents listen routinely to hear fantastic ideas about finding leads by listening to others who have done the same.

YouTube

YouTube has an incredible amount of content! Suggest that your agents search for agent trainings, and then have them share the videos with your team members.

Speakers and Outside Trainers

You can bring in speakers—such as title experts, loan officers, home inspectors, and appraisers—to teach on different topics, such as 1031 exchanges, real estate tax benefits, and so on. Encourage your agents to ask as many questions as possible. This will increase their confidence to speak to leads and clients about industry specifics that other agents don't know.

And don't assume only other real estate professionals can train your staff. I also have outside trainers teach on different subjects, such as law, marketing, social media, and even mindset. There is value in other industry experts, particularly those in service and sales. For example, invite people who have built large insurance companies or have even started by selling door-to-door before launching a company. They can teach your staff how to be successful, no matter the field.

➡ KEY POINTS

- Don't assume your staff knows what needs to be done just because you do.
- Train in small, bite-sized chunks of information, then have the trainee either perform the task or answer a series of questions to prove they grasp the concept.
- Training means not asking more of your new hires than they can do with accuracy and speed.
- Training is an investment and needs to be looked at as such.
- Plain and simple: the time, attention, and energy taken away from lead generation and lead follow-up costs you money.
- Don't fall into the trap of training staff without an ROI.
- Time spent training is *not* free time. In our business, time is never free.
- Having someone watch you as you work can function as a training tool.
- As your overall team grows, you will notice a pattern of "teams within teams."
- Your team members have stories of deals they made, things that worked, and mistakes they made. Your staff will get a valuable education hearing about the experiences of others.

CHAPTER TWELVE

MANAGEMENT AND LEADERSHIP

"Extreme ownership. Leaders must own everything in their world. There is no one else to blame."

—JOCKO WILLINK

Management Versus Leadership

Before I get into this chapter, I need to define the difference between management and leadership. For the purposes of this book, "management" refers to supervising staff to make sure people are meeting expectations. This can include clarifying roles and responsibilities, providing training, and doing quality assurance on finished products. It can also include making sure people show up to work on time, ensuring they meet company standards and legal compliance, and reporting mistakes when they occur. "Leadership," on the other hand, refers to those who are responsible for the company's success or failure. I believe every member of a team is an extension of leadership.

Management

Management means making sure all the stuff that needs to happen happens. Being a manager is rarely fun, exciting, or even acknowledged. To be fair, if we could do a fantastic job of our own accord, with no oversight, we wouldn't need managers. But most humans will not do our best without someone managing us.

For example, do we do all we can to save money when it's not our own and we're tasked with buying products for the office? We do when we're beholden to a budget and a manager. The truth is managers and leaders do very different work. Managers ensure staff, systems, and processes are functioning. Leaders, however, determine the direction of the company itself. They both play equally important roles, and one cannot function well without the other.

Leadership

In Jocko Willink and Leif Babin's book *Extreme Ownership*, they state "the most fundamental and important truths at the heart of Extreme Ownership: there are no bad teams, only bad leaders."[27] The point here is simple. A leader is responsible for the results a team achieves, and thus is responsible for the performance of the managers. A real estate leader is responsible for, among other things:

- Creating the vision for the business.
- Getting buy-in from staff, clients, and their SOI.
- Making the "big-picture" decisions by evaluating all options.
- Anticipating problems by making contingency plans.
- Correcting course as needed. That includes following market changes.
- Creating company culture.
- Setting protocols to hire the right people.
- Delegating tasks so they can take higher-level responsibilities.
- Increasing and improving the technology used.
- Making sure the company remains profitable.
- Investing properly in the human resources and the financial resources.

As long as this list is, these are just a few of a leader's responsibilities.

---

27 Jocko Willink and Leif Babin, *Extreme Ownership: How U.S. Navy SEALs Lead and Win* (New York: St. Martin's Press, 2015).

When I'm asked what a leader does, my first answer is: "Everything." As a leader, accept that you are in charge of everything, including what you delegate and to whom.

Why You Need to Delegate

You can't do the higher-dollar activities without delegation, which is why, without a doubt, delegation is the most important concept a leader can learn. If you cannot delegate, you will never have the time or energy to work on the things that will make your company more money and provide more opportunities to others. And that means you must trust those delegated tasks are being done well.

It's from this framework that I'll now dive into the concepts that leaders need to embrace and which priorities to focus on to help your company achieve success.

Everyone Wants to Be Led

One of the first concepts to learn as an effective leader is that everyone wants to be led. Yes, everyone. Even other leaders. Even stubborn people. We find comfort in being directed on what to do and given encouragement to do it. Everyone just needs to know that the person directing them is trustworthy and capable. If you want your staff to follow your lead, they need to trust where you are leading them. If someone loses confidence in you, they'll start to do what is best for them.

Your agents and staff choose to work for you in large part because of their confidence in your ability to lead. Donald Miller, in his book *Building a StoryBrand: Clarify Your Message So Customers Will Listen,* lays out a common story framework: The world is a safe place, something happens to ruin that, and a hero is needed to fix the wrong. But they doubt themselves until they meet a trusted guide who shows them the path, so the hero can rise up to save the day.

Your team sees that you've built a successful business by selling a lot of homes and gaining respect in the real estate community. They look to you for direction and approval. Most leaders worry too much about what they don't know, but your team doesn't know what you don't know. What they follow is what you *do* know. Therefore, you share your knowledge so they can become better agents themselves.

This is how a team takes on the culture of the leader. It's important to remember that those who joined your team *want* to be led by you. Even when you don't see it, your team seeks your approval. And your approval is what drives your team forward.

However, if you lead poorly, or not at all, none of this is possible.

If You Don't Provide Leadership, Someone Else Will

This is one reason it's so important we fulfill our team's desire for leadership. It's our responsibility to provide it and to coach others to be leaders. Within your team, you will see leaders emerge naturally. They will be recognized as such, and other team members will start to go to them for advice. They will help others with open houses and other trainings. If you want your team to learn from your culture and standards, you've got to make sure your natural leaders follow you.

If you don't, team members may quit to work with a different agency. Many of these staff members will seek out someone who cares about them more or is in a better position to help them grow. One big cost of poor leadership is talent leaving and working for someone else.

The Captain Charts the Course

Like the fishing analogy used in Chapter One, there is one ship captain, and that captain charts the course. Crew members are responsible for making sure the ship continues moving in the right direction and that it arrives at its destination. They are crucially important because the journey cannot succeed without them. But their job is to execute the directions of the captain, not to chart their own course or make their own way.

As the leader, you chart how the team moves forward. That includes the lead sources, systems, standards, and scripts that you create. If people don't follow, it's either because they sense you're not leading or don't believe in the direction you have set. As some people are natural leaders, some people are naturally confrontational. They still want to be led, but they make it harder. If this becomes untenable, you might just need to fire them. At the same time, don't assume their actions are simple rebellion. The problem may be with your plan, your communication of it, or the lack of resources to execute it. Creating a leadership group to surround you can help bring clarity when issues arise. Is it you, the plan, or the team member? A wise person always seeks counsel.

What Leadership Provides

This section brings clarity to what a good leader provides by outlining what I offer my agents and expansion partners (discussed in Chapter Thirteen). Making it clear what you offer will let others know if your team is the right fit for them and their goals.

Accountability

The first thing leadership provides is accountability. If you get this one element right, it will likely make your team successful, even if you get everything else wrong. Accountability comes in many different forms; for example, ensuring agents are making lead generation contacts, keeping transaction timelines, and providing customer service. Most of us do better when we're held accountable, and we all slowly start to cut corners if we feel no one is watching us. I've been through several cycles in my own company when the numbers dropped off, and I couldn't figure out why. The following story explains what I discovered and highlights just how important accountability can be in a real estate sales team.

In late 2021, our escrows had dropped from around fifty to thirty contracts at a time. This number continued to plummet to under twenty. At that level, the company was at risk of no longer being profitable. As the leader, it was my job to figure out what had happened and how to fix it. I began by meeting with my sales leaders, and each had a different excuse.

"The lead quality got worse."

"The leads aren't ready to buy."

"The market is too hot."

"The buyers aren't serious enough."

These struck me as odd because nothing had really changed from earlier in the year; if anything, the market had slightly cooled. Our lead sources were the same, the economy overall was slightly better, and we had no significant changes in staff. Because nothing made sense at this level of investigation, I had to dig deeper.

I called our clients who had recently closed as well as a few who were in escrow. I asked about their experience with us and what we could do to improve it. At first, everyone said things were fine and they were happy with their experience. But when I pressed them, they started to give different feedback.

"I wanted more direction from my agent. I felt like I had to look up houses for myself and send them over."

"I was a little unsure what to do, and I would have appreciated some more guidance and direction from my agent."

"I didn't hear much from my agent after our first couple weeks. I mostly spoke to the showing assistant."

It was now obvious that my agents were not as engaged as they needed to be and not communicating enough. I brought this information to the individual sales leaders, which in turn led to several group discussions. I learned that several standards I had set were not being followed. One is that *every* buyer client is contacted *every* day. Another is that showing assistants have clearly defined roles: They can complete administrative tasks and show homes. They are not supposed to be the main contact with the clients because (1) the clients become confused as to who is the agent; (2) the buyer's agents lose touch with what's happening; and (3) the communication is handled by a less-skilled team member.

Agents admitted they had been allowing their showing assistants to communicate with the clients, who felt brushed off by the agent. The agents admitted that when we hit fifty properties in escrow, there were not enough hours in a day to work with every buyer client, so those clients who were more highly motivated got more attention. During this same time, I also cut out on my weekly meetings with each sales leader so they could use that hour to put clients in contract. I then devoted my time to recruiting new agents to help with showing homes, looking up homes on the MLS, calling listing agents, and so on.

It became a disaster. The sales leaders delegated more communication to the showing assistants, many of whom were new and didn't know anything. These conversations, as you can imagine, went horribly. Clients knew they were not receiving good advice or direction, the showing assistants were too afraid to ask for help, and the sales leaders weren't aware any of this was happening. It wasn't until I stepped back in and forced everyone to go back to the standards that I'd created that things began to change for the better.

This was a powerful lesson for me in accountability.

When I stopped meeting regularly with sales leaders, they stopped performing to my standards. This ultimately led to our clients being unhappy, which directly hit our bottom line. Want to avoid this for yourself? Keep a high value on accountability in your business, including on yourself.

Encouragement

In addition to accountability, you must offer encouragement. The real estate sales industry is a brutal one. Your agents will feel kicked around by clients, by listing agents, by office staff, and by their own subconscious when they have a bad month or make a mistake. We face rejection every day in this job. Rejection at open homes, rejection when lead-generating, rejection when a lead chooses another agent, rejection when our offer isn't accepted, and so on. For those receiving a steady diet of rejection, it's important that you offset that with encouragement and positivity. If you don't do it for your team, who will?

You can encourage your agents by pointing out their wins during weekly meetings. You can look for ways to share their achievements on social media or introduce them to others by highlighting the things they are doing well. Whichever way you decide to show encouragement, do it constantly and consistently, especially for those on your team who are most productive.

One area of caution, however: It's common for your underperforming team members to seek encouragement the most. Hold your encouragement until they improve their performance. Let them see that it's performance that gets the reward. If a member remains a drain on your team's energy without showing signs of improvement, they may not be a good fit for your group.

Direction

Leadership includes providing direction—and that means charting the course, as noted earlier in this chapter. Your team members will look to you for leadership and direction: how to do the job, how to make certain decisions, how to conduct themselves, and so on. Everyone will watch you, and the hallmarks of your personality will spread to the team. As a rockstar agent, you provide direction even when you don't realize it.

Be intentional: Offer trainings to provide direction for specific tasks, and conduct weekly meetings to make sure your team hasn't strayed too far from the course you've charted. Everything you do as a leader provides some direction.

Confidence

Confidence comes from a belief that you make smart decisions. I'm confident speaking to large groups about real estate because I believe, no matter what questions are asked, I will give a solid answer. On the other hand, I'm not comfortable talking about fitness, automobiles, or any other category in which I'm inexperienced.

People follow confident people. If you're confident, your team will follow you. To sell a lot of homes through agents (and not by yourself), build up the confidence in your agents. They represent you when they are presenting to clients, and you want that representation to be positive. Your clients will follow your confident team members. Using the restaurant analogy, a diner who has a bad experience with a waiter will blame the restaurant because it is perceived that the restaurant condones the attitude or performance of the waiter. Your team works the same way. Clients are likely to blame you as the rockstar agent when they're unhappy.

You instill confidence in your team members through repetition and practice. Design trainings around commonly asked questions. If someone lacks confidence, see if they have the knowledge required to give confident answers to clients. If you spot a lack of confidence, it can mean bigger problems you had no idea existed!

Knowledge

This final piece is obvious. Your team members will look to you for knowledge about the industry in general and their role in your team specifically. As detailed in Chapter Eleven, the good news is you don't have to provide all that knowledge yourself. Leverage your leaders as trainers and bring in experts.

Your team members will then use their training in interactions with clients. And you'll notice that houses start going into contract and stay there. That's because clients will see your agents as smart and knowledgeable and will be more likely to trust their advice. We need our clients to trust us when they are scared, nervous, anxious, and unsure. Therefore, make sure clients look to your agents as knowledgeable in the same way your agents look to you. Knowledge is a powerful tool to establish and maintain credibility. For these reasons, always liberally share knowledge and training with your team.

Five Pillars of the David Greene Team

When we speak to an expansion team (covered in Chapter Thirteen) or promote a buyer's agent to sales leader, we provide five pillars of support, which in turn supports the agency's capacity to handle clients.

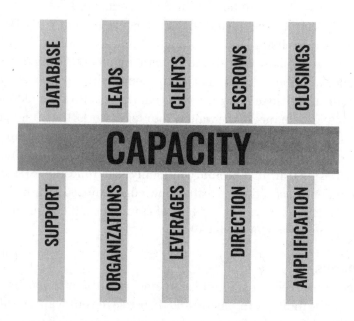

The higher an agent's ability:
- The larger the database of People they can grow and manage;
- The more Leads they can effectively connect and convert;
- The more Clients they can work with;
- The more escrows they can carry and avoid mistakes; and
- The more Closings they can accomplish.

You'll notice that the capacity figure compares to the Sales Funnel in Chapter One: Database and People; Leads and Leads; Clients and Clients; Contracts and Escrows; and Closings and Closings.

In our system, agents move People/Database into Closings using the Sales Funnel, our CRM, leverage, and training. The more capable an agent becomes, the more often Leads turn into Clients. Once an agent is skilled at moving Leads down the funnel, their job is to do it more frequently. We start by measuring conversion ratios and then by increasing the volume while maintaining strong conversion rates.

The five pillars allow our team to focus on building their skills while leaders focus on equipping them to do more volume, and thus make more money and help more people. Our job is to help them increase our volume of clients without losing accuracy or touch. The pillars clarify how we build this capacity.

LEADERSHIP AND MANAGEMENT	TEAM
Support	Moving Leads into Contract; moving Contracts into Closings
Organization	Using the CRM and Lead Boards
Leverage	Utilizing showing agents and lenders, and sharing knowledge
Direction	Adopting the Sales Funnel and a mentality of self-improvement
Amplification	Increasing results through lead generation, referral networks, and teaching agents to lead

Support

The first and foremost leg is Support; the other four pillars refer to the way we provide this support. As a rockstar agent, you want to give your agents everything they need to focus on the two things most important that generate revenue: (1) finding and converting Leads and (2) putting Clients in Contract. I design my support to lighten or replace the load that my agents carry that is not related to these two activities. Support includes:

Training and Coaching

I view the process of getting to closing as being on two sides of a door. On one side is everything that happens before a house is put in contract. This includes lead generation, lead follow-up, delivering presentations, showing homes, writing offers, negotiating, and so on. Training and coaching help agents move Clients into Contracts. Our weekly meetings and outside training set my agents apart and make them more successful than other agents who don't work on my team.

Transaction Coordination

On the other side of the door is what happens after the contract: transaction coordination. Once a Client goes into Contract, agents shouldn't be worrying about the details of getting the transaction to Closing. Concentrating on clients already in contract hurts team sales because (1) it takes agent focus from lead generation, (2) the relief of income on the way makes it easier for agents to lose the urgency of building more revenue, and (3) agents lose sight of the mission to help as many families as possible.

By removing the work involved in closing escrows, we remove the temptation for agents to avoid the more challenging work of sales. Additionally, because agents and transaction coordinators do very different jobs, we improve consistency in the product we deliver and our team's reputation by putting experienced staff in charge of ensuring timelines are met, compliance is followed, and our value remains solid and trustworthy.

Organization

Staying organized is not an easy task in our profession! It's a waste of productivity if an agent spends half their day organizing what needs to be done and the other half doing it. That disrupts dollar-producing activities like lead generation, marketing, and incorporating real estate into daily conversations. Great salespeople flourish when they focus on sales.

What stops this focus? Everything else. Organizational support empowers agents to keep their focus. This is especially valuable for those who excel in sales, as they tend to be the least organized members of a team. DGT provides organizational support through two primary means:

Our CRM

DGT uses the Brivity Platform. Our CRM helps the entire team in the following ways:
- It organizes lead generation by reminding agents who to call or message and when to do so and tracks their notes.
- It allows automatic replies to be sent to incoming leads and to track emails and texts sent from agents to leads or clients.
- It lets agents rank leads from "hot" to "cold."
- It captures information for each contact, including birthdays, addresses, and social media profiles.
- It organizes every file a transaction coordinator has in escrow.

- It assigns tasks by team member—agents, transaction coordinators, showing assistants, etc.—and tracks progress.
- It connects the DGT website with our IDX (see Chapter Three) so agents can see which homes clients looked at, how many times, and when.
- It creates monthly market reports with information pertaining to what a client's home is worth and daily listing alerts with properties that match each client's criteria.
- It allows team members to assign auto plans (see Chapter Three).

Lead Boards

As described in Chapter Three, Lead Boards allow the inside sales agents to track the process of turning Leads into Clients. This is how we ensure leads aren't forgotten and agents know which tasks need to be completed.

Leverage

We provide leverage through three primary sources:

Showing Assistants

Showing assistants reduce buyer's agents' workload by conducting tasks that take a lot of time, including, among other responsibilities, showing homes, looking up information in the MLS, calling listing agents, and reviewing disclosures and reports. Showing assistants allow buyer's agents to keep focused on sales.

In-House Lending Team/Preferred Lender Support

Our in-house lending team makes agents' jobs easier by supporting the information that the agent has already explained to clients. Our lending officers are available after-hours for preapprovals, to talk with clients who have questions, and to call listing agents to let them know that our buyers are approved and can close. Again, our in-house team lets the Realtors focus on sales.

Sharing Knowledge

By having regular team meetings, team members can share knowledge. It's possible to learn from doing and failing on our own, but it's better to learn from others. Everyone's learning curve increases, and mistakes are decreased.

Direction

We offer direction through:

The Sales Funnel

The Sales Funnel is our main tool for providing direction to agents. It clarifies how to turn a Lead into a Client with a Closing and the steps of that process. By training agents in how to use the Sales Funnel, we break down what appears to be an overwhelmingly daunting job into manageable chunks.

Self-Improvement

I emphasize that each member must focus on self-improvement. This is where, again, trainings, exposure to performance psychologists, and guidance from team leaders contribute to the growth of our team members. A dedicated team mentality provides the same direction for the team to move in.

Amplification

The final leg is amplification, which amplifies the results of the team. We do that by providing support in the following ways:

Lead Generation

Our agents receive specific guidance in lead generation strategies. The CRM reminds them of next steps, and we give them complete scripts to use with hot leads and with cold leads who may want to buy or sell with us in the future. Our experienced agents provide new agents training on handling objections, and our leaders provide accountability.

Lead generation is the lifeblood of any business. If you want to see your agents amplify their results, put your efforts here.

Referral Network

We use a referral network comprised of skilled agents throughout the country in the most popular markets. This helps our agents connect our out-of-state clients with competent agents in other markets; in return, those agents pay us referral fees. In addition to saving our agents' time in finding an out-of-state agent themselves, we also increase the likelihood of the agent closing the deal with the client. Referrals are not guaranteed but keeping a list of capable agents in other states is valuable to leads.

Automated 33 Touch

"33 touch" is a phrase that refers to touching (contacting in some way) a person thirty-three times a year. It's a phrase used by Keller Williams for staying top of mind to those in your database for when they need a real estate agent for themselves or someone they know. Brivity, our CRM, provides an auto plan that tells agents who to call, text, or email; when to comment on their own social media; when to mail handwritten notes; and more. It takes the guesswork out of figuring out who to contact and the date of the last contact. Leadership provides accountability to ensure agents are making these contacts.

Teaching Agents to Lead

Clients are drawn to leaders. As discussed earlier, clients hire your agents because they know the market, they know how to negotiate, and they know how to offer advice. Clients want to follow a leader in making a tremendously scary financial decision. If they sense hesitation, insecurity, or uncertainty, those emotions will bleed into them.

Your clients need more than someone with a real estate license. Your clients want to know about neighborhoods, pricing, property taxes in specific areas, how long it may take their house to sell, and how to interpret inspection reports. Plus a lot more.

This is our job, and it's the value we provide. Our experience, knowledge, skills, and confidence are why clients want us to represent them in deals. Train your team leaders to understand this and to always model it. Your agents will follow the team leaders, and the clients will follow your agents.

 **KEY POINTS**

- "Management" refers to supervising staff to make sure people are meeting expectations. This can include clarifying roles and responsibilities, providing training, and doing quality assurance on finished products.
- "Leadership," on the other hand, refers to those who are responsible for the company's success or failure.
- A leader is responsible for the results a team achieves, and thus is responsible for the performance of the managers.

- If you cannot delegate, you will never have the time or energy to work on the things that will make your company more money and provide more opportunities to others.
- Crew members are responsible for making sure the ship continues moving in the right direction and that it arrives at its destination.
- Most of us do better when we're held accountable, and we all slowly start to cut corners if we feel no one is watching us.
- The process of getting to closing is like the hinge separating two sides of a door. On one side is everything that happens before a house is put in contract; on the other is everything after the property is under contract.
- "33 touch" is a phrase that refers to touching (contacting in some way) a person thirty-three times a year.
- Clients hire your agents because they know the market, they know how to negotiate, and they know how to offer advice.
- Your agents will follow the team leaders, and the clients will follow your agents.

CHAPTER THIRTEEN

RUNNING THE BUSINESS

"If you're not working to get your business or investing operation to operate without you, you're thinking too small. Think team and systems."

—ROBERT KIYOSAKI

As you transition from top-producing agent to rockstar agent, you'll go through several difficult transitions. The first, and most important, is exchanging the mindset of an agent for one of chief executive officer. In our industry, your potential won't be found until you become the CEO or you hire someone to lead your business.

According to Betterteam, a CEO's responsibilities include, among others:

- Providing inspiring leadership
- Developing, creating, and implementing vision, policies and strategies, culture, and long-term and short-term goals
- Reporting to the board of directors
- Building partnerships within and outside the organization

- Managing fiscal oversight
- Being the spokesperson[28]

Did you notice what's not in there? Sales. While most successful real estate agents reach their goals by focusing on sales themselves, a successful executive helps others achieve the company goals. *No company goal is more important than sales.*

In my opinion, the reason most top-producing agents never build a team and never become a CEO is because they don't know how to have high sales without doing the work themselves. Learning how to lead is challenging, which is why this chapter focuses on helping you learn the role of CEO and what you need to focus on to do it well. When I was making my leap, nobody told me what I share here.

Shift in Mindset

Becoming a CEO starts with adopting the mindset of a CEO. There are a lot of factors that will be working against you. It was very difficult for me to adapt, and I didn't know why. It took *years* before I understood even some of the reasons why I had such resistance to accepting this new role. My hope is that I can cut that learning curve short for you.

As the CEO, your responsibilities will shift. You will find yourself in charge of the company financials (reading and understanding a profit and loss statement), deciding who to hire, and deciding how to distribute leads. When you begin running your business instead of your transactions, unfamiliar problems will arise that you'll need to fix.

Accepting the fact your responsibilities need to change is crucial. Not only will you set the tone for the rest of your employees to follow (your attitude and approach will affect theirs) but also, while many people on your team are capable of handling sales, you are the only one capable of being the team's leader.

---

28 "CEO Job Description," Betterteam, accessed July 21, 2022, https://www.betterteam.com/ceo-job-description.

Dopamine Withdrawal

In "Is Your Sales Team Addicted to Dopamine?", published in *Forbes*, Lisa Earle McLeod (author of *Selling With Noble Purpose*) highlights the difference between sales teams driven by dopamine and teams driven by serotonin:

> Dopamine is the neurotransmitter that controls your brain's reward and pleasure center. It's associated with chasing a desired object. The quick satisfaction you get from a like on social media or winning the annual sales contest quickly fades. You're left wanting more, and more, and more.
>
> By contrast, our other feel-good brain chemical is serotonin. Unlike dopamine, serotonin is associated with alignment to a larger purpose and long-term accomplishments. To put it bluntly, too much dopamine makes you frantic. Adding serotonin can make you focused.
>
> When leaders prioritize short-term payoff—*Kill the competition and get a dopamine hit*—over longer lasting purpose and impact—*Make a difference to clients and let the serotonin flow*—poor results follow.[29]

McLeod argues that different neurotransmitters influence different behaviors, with dopamine rewarding short-term quick wins and serotonin rewarding long-term strategic wins. Many activities in today's society—checking our phones for text messages, looking for "likes" on social media—produce dopamine. The problem is that as we become accustomed to dopamine hits, it becomes harder to find satisfaction.

How does this affect you as the CEO of your agency? CEOs should focus on big-picture, strategic results, not on immediate performance. CEOs need to follow serotonin-based activities. But if you've spent your career chasing the dopamine reward of getting a listing signed, putting a buyer in contract, or having the top gross commission income (GCI) in your company, your brain will resist the switch to longer-term activities of hiring and training agents, reading profit and loss statements, and tracking net profit over total sales volume.

---

29 Lisa Earle McLeod, "Is Your Sales Team Addicted to Dopamine?", *Forbes*, February 21, 2018, https://www.forbes.com/sites/lisaearlemcleod/2018/02/21/is-your-sales-team-addicted-to-dopamine.

Think about what's driven you to become a top-producing agent. Didn't you like telling everyone you had an upcoming listing? Didn't you feel a huge sense of relief and accomplishment putting buyers in contract? Didn't you tell everyone whenever you had a closing?

Most agents consider it a good day when they close a property, yet that's the result of work that was started at least thirty days earlier. Shouldn't you have celebrated that win back then? Along those same lines, when you put that buyer in contract thirty days ago, wasn't that from work you did at an open house six months prior? And how did you get good at doing open houses anyway? Wasn't that from information you had gained years prior to that? Where'd you gain that information? Was it from that Realtor who helped you when you first started? Why'd they decide to help you, anyway? As you can see, this trail takes you further into the past.

Eventually we are left with the difficult, but inarguable, truth that the success we feel today is the result of the meticulous steps we took in the past. If we want more success in the future, we must make those same meticulous steps today. When we do that, we don't get a dopamine rush. No Realtor was ever excited about putting out open house signs or spending their Sunday standing in someone else's kitchen making sure people signed in. But these are the actions that lead to the closing that makes us feel good.

If you haven't been working a systematic, predictable, repeatable plan, breaking away from chasing dopamine will leave you confused as to what you should be doing. Without a clear plan, we rely on what makes us feel good to determine our actions or the directions to take. More than likely, you've followed activities that led to a dopamine rush rather than the boring but time-proven actions of lead generation or staying current with your database and growing it. As you transition to CEO, you'll need to be aware of this large shift in thinking.

You can't chase dopamine anymore, and it'll be hard to let it go. Getting that listing agreement signed or scheduling that buyer's presentation used to make you feel high. When you stop doing those activities and train your agents to do them, you'll go through a period in which you know you are doing everything correctly, and maybe even seeing progress reflected in the numbers of your company, but you'll feel like something is missing. This pull draws team leaders back into production. There's simply nothing like the chase of the deal, especially when you're good at it!

If you have a particularly close relationship with your agents, you may even feel like a parent who is watching their children make mistakes. You'll want to help them. The problem is: You can't. Not if you want to perform like a CEO. You may find yourself wanting that addictive dopamine hit, but your job as the CEO requires different thinking.

AGENT'S JOB / DOPAMINE THINKING	CEO'S JOB / SEROTONIN THINKING
Get a listing agreement signed	Design an eye-catching listing presentation
Give the listing presentation to as many sellers as possible	Hold agents accountable for delivering listing presentations
Attend sessions for home photos	Ensure the photographer prioritizes your work; have a backup plan
Give buyer's presentations; get exclusive agreements signed	Find a steady stream of leads for your agents to convert
Put buyers in contract	Monitor/improve conversion rates
Handle problems with escrows	Provide the resources to help resolve escrow problems

Learning to live without the dopamine rush that every real estate agent feels will be hard. Your job now is to have a clearheaded approach to make the smart, long-term, and strategic decisions for your company. As the CEO, you're responsible for tracking the metrics that keep your business growing. Give yourself some time and grace to adjust to this new approach, to experience real estate from an unfamiliar perspective, and to develop new skills to succeed at this leadership level.

Learn, Leverage, Lead

As I've grown through the years (from real estate agent to top-producing agent to hiring help and to building a team and my own company), I developed a three-part structure I call Learn, Leverage, Lead. These are the three skill sets you'll need to become a successful CEO. The structure is like a ladder: You have to reach the top of one skill (ladder) and then start over with the next skill (a different ladder), which is often not connected to the skills you just mastered. These skill sets are referred to and demonstrated as "dimensions" in my illustration.

Learning is the first dimension (ladder) of success. Most agents never learn how to be top-producing agents. Mediocrity results in a mediocre quality of life, a mediocre income, and a mediocre relationship with your clients. *SOLD*, the first book in this series, shows how agents can move up the Learn ladder to become top-producing agents.

0%   100%

LEARN

Most agents who work on your team will have spent their careers stuck in Learn. When every employee has a specific list of responsibilities, it makes the job predictable: Learn what needs to be done and do it well. For most people, this is enough, and there is nothing wrong with that. A high income and job fulfillment can come from one well-developed skill. Look at dermatologists, home architects, and rockstar musicians.

However, your job is to move them along, which will help them earn more money for themselves and the company. That path up is simple: Sell more houses by using the Sales Funnel. Agents who conquer the Sales Funnel and its tools will progress quickly. Your top-producing agents will outperform their agent colleagues because they learned the art of selling houses. These agents are active, earn a lot of commissions, and usually lead others on the team. When an agent becomes a top agent, they have two options: (1) continue on this path and try to avoid burnout; or (2) learn to leverage parts of the job to others to get their time back.

Those who choose the first option don't need any additional growth help from you. Those who choose the second option will become the "team within a team" in your organization. You'll support them by hiring and training administrative staff and showing agents for them, assigning junior agents to work with them, and inviting them into upper-echelon meetings. These are the individuals who will become your sales leaders.

When an agent is at the top of the Learn dimension and chooses to move onto Leverage, they will start at zero again.

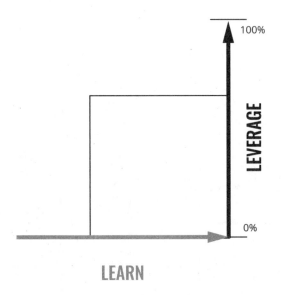

LEARN

The bad news is they'll be starting from scratch; the good news is that they have you. You've mastered leverage, or you wouldn't have your agency. You've made the mistakes, you've paid your dues, you've taken your lumps. The fruit of your education is now ripe. They'll sell more houses, and you'll get a share of their revenue because you helped them up the Leverage ladder and allowed everyone to work more efficiently.

When an agent is learning how to leverage the power of others, they quickly understand the importance of models and systems. When we are dependent on others to get more work done in the same amount of time, these become crucial. It's at this stage, when an agent is climbing the leverage dimension, that you'll see their real growth. And they'll have a new appreciation of the process and models you created for them. Your relationship with these agents will likely get stronger, closer, and deeper. It's a fulfilling season in your CEO career in real estate sales.

Now, some of your agents will be more successful building their teams than others. Some may remain at the Leverage stage for the remainder of their careers. Those who do get to the top of the Leverage ladder will become the leaders in your company.

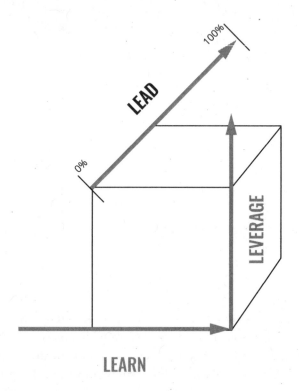

LEARN

These leaders will be your most talented, dedicated, and valuable assets. These are the people you want as examples to show what is possible in this career. Your priority is to take care of these leaders and to teach them to work with character and a commitment to the betterment of others. They will be the bedrock of your success, and, if you want it, the key to earning passive income for yourself.

Shift in Responsibilities

As described earlier in this chapter, letting go of old habits and patterns to form new ones takes time and is challenging. When I switched from asking myself the simpler, task-based question, "What is my job today?" to the more complicated, results-based question, "What outcome am I responsible for?", the shift happened. The difference was that I made myself responsible for a result, not a task. This change led to my growth, and my growth led to more success. Getting your team to ask this more complicated question will lead to more success for them and the company.

TASKED-BASED AGENT QUESTIONS	RESULTS-BASED AGENT QUESTIONS
What do I have to do today?	How can I help this company succeed?
What do I need to do to get a listing ready for the market?	What can I do to make the seller feel comfortable?
What are the boxes I need to fill out in a contract?	How do I convince my client to write an offer strong enough to get the property?
How do I set up the home inspection?	How do I ensure the home inspector always prioritizes my requests?
How do I look up homes in the MLS?	How do I identify the properties my client would like and eliminate the others?
How do I get my broker to answer my 10 p.m. text?	How do I ensure my questions are answered before there's an emergency?
Why isn't there clarity in this area?	How do I bring clarity in this area?

Shift in Skill Set

Being the CEO means operating your business as opposed to being an employee in it. New skills include, for example, monitoring the money flow into and out of the company. At a certain point, you will need to hire people to assist you with this too. This typically starts with hiring a bookkeeper, then a controller, and culminates in creating and filling the position of chief financial officer. I've currently hired a bookkeeper and have my COO meet with them weekly to review expenses and revenue.

If/when you want to earn passive income from your business, you'll also hire a chief executive officer. At that point, someone else will have the responsibilities of the day-to-day business while you retire or move on to other passions.

Profit and Loss Statements

A profit and loss (P&L) statement is a document that tracks the income coming into and flowing out of your company. Learning to read a profit and loss statement is a fundamental skill for anyone who has an executive leadership role. Most financial issues can be found in a review of the P&L. Many growth opportunities will reveal themselves through this review as well.

Creating P&L Statements

Hiring or outsourcing a bookkeeper to produce your P&L statements is an easy way to buy yourself time. Just like most agents delegate to a transaction coordinator for specific elements of the job, most executives delegate the financials to a bookkeeper. Experienced bookkeepers have systems in place and know the software to do the job. I do not recommend that you create their bookkeeping system, especially when you have more important income-producing responsibilities.

In addition to saving you valuable time, your bookkeeper can explain the process of keeping books. Everything I know about bookkeeping is from questions I asked my bookkeeper as we reviewed my P&L statements. My understanding of costs of goods sold, tax-deductible items, and the highest profit-producing activities came from working with an experienced bookkeeper.

You will share the receipts of items you buy (think software) or spend money on (think client dinners) with your bookkeeper. This can be done through Google Drive, Dropbox, email, or any agreed-upon method. For example, some apps allow you to take a picture of a receipt and automatically send it from your phone to your bookkeeper's software. The clearer you label your company's expenses, the easier your bookkeeper can document them on the P&L statement.

Income works the same way. Because there is typically less variety in how income is received than how money is spent, the process is simpler. We provide the bookkeeper with sheets on which commissions are split up among the agents, brokers, and other parties; these sheets are first reviewed by an admin assistant before the bookkeeper gets them. The bookkeeper then tracks on the P&L how much money came into the company and ensures it was divided up correctly.

I also give my bookkeeper "read only" access to the company's bank account where checks are deposited and expenses are withdrawn. Each month, the bookkeeper reconciles this account and ensures every check made it into the bank and every expense has a receipt associated with it.

Understanding a P&L Statement

The following is an example of a business P&L statement.

10:51 AM | 04/05/22 | Accrual Basis

Real Estate (Sample)
Profit & Loss | All Transactions | December 31, 2021

Ordinary Income/Expense	
Income	
BPO Services	150,231.00
Commission Income	1,041,894.56
Marketing Service Agreement Inc.	34,821.00
Total Income	**1,226,946.56**
Cost of Goods Sold	
Commissions Paid	851,714.69
Total COGS	**851,714.69**
Gross Profit	**375,231.87**
Expense	
Advertising and Promotion	1,901.17
Automobile Expense	12,420.00
Bank & Interest Charges	1,642.84
Business Licenses and Permits	5,576.00
Computer and Internet Expenses	520.57
Continuing Eduction	1,308.69
Dues and Subscriptions	27,933.26
Insurance Expense	
E&O insurance	6,443.76
Insurance Expense—Other	965.00
Total Insurance Expense	**7,408.76**
Meals and Entertainment	2,262.45
Office Supplies	611.35
Postage	4,225.59
Rent Expense	39,130.00
Staging Expense	4,550.00
Taxes—States	9,607.05
Transaction Coordination	29,600.00
Total Expense	**153,800.67**
Net Ordinary Income	**221,431.20**
Net Income	**221,431.20**

According to Tom Wheelwright in *Tax-Free Wealth*, there are three primary factors to consider when reviewing a P&L statement:

1. **Income is meant to create cash.** Receivables do not create value until collected, so someone who appears to be a great customer can turn out to be a lousy customer if they take your up your time and resources but don't pay on time.

2. **Expenses should not be more than income.** Review your expenses to see if any expense costs more than the income it brought in. If it does, get rid of the expense.

3. **There should be no personal expenses on your P&L.** They are not tax-deductible from your business, and they do not create income.[30]

Now, let's look at the first two factors in detail. (The third is self-explanatory.)

If the purpose of income is to create cash, you want a business where the *income* you make is *cash* at the end of the day. While income and cash sound synonymous, they are not. Income is all the money that comes into your business. Cash is the money that's left after expenses have been deducted. Thus, cash means profit. This puts an emphasis on the money that's left over. As a single agent, you likely were always aware of your gross commission income (GCI), but that was your income, not your profit. Reviewing a P&L statement will focus your attention on profit, not income.

If the aim is to keep expenses relevant and low, it's your responsibility as the business owner to ensure that these expenses are both necessary and *create more income* for the company. If an expense is not creating more income, eliminate it or use it differently. The following table includes examples of expenses that may need to be addressed with your leaders.

30 Tom Wheelwright, *Tax-Free Wealth: How to Build Massive Wealth by Permanently Lowering Your Taxes* (Scottsdale, Arizona: RDA Press, 2015).

EXPENSE	CEO QUERY
Gifts for clients at closing	Are agents following up after gifts are delivered to ask for referrals? If no referrals are received, the gifts have no ROI.
CRM software	Are agents using it to increase their productivity? Not using it at all or using it improperly means lost income.
SEO ads	What are the conversion rates on Leads from SEO ads who moved down the Sales Funnel? If agents are only breaking even on ads, or worse, losing money, move to organic (and free) lead generation.
Online leads	What are the conversion rates on these types of ads? Agents should not be spending time if the conversion rate is low.
Boosted social media posts for listings	How many additional leads came out of these paid ads?
Software subscriptions	Is all software improving efficiency?
Office supplies	Are supplies helping your team hit their goals?
Agent commission splits	Is the commission split structure within set margins?

Monthly P&L Review

I recommend reviewing your P&L statement with your financial staff no less than every month. You'll recognize if things are starting to fall apart and can stop it before it gets too bad. For example, you may identify unlabeled expenses before the next statement.

I look at three particular items with the bookkeeper: gross sales, net profit, and profit percentage. After we review these numbers, we then look at the P&L line by line, especially for (1) expenses not on last month's P&L; (2) expenses that are significantly higher than on last month's P&L; and (3) income that is significantly different than on last month's P&L.

These changes may require some detective work. For example, if the income from listings is lower than a normal month, ask your executive team why that may be. It could be because management isn't ensuring Realtors are meeting lead generation expectations, your top-producing agents became unfocused, or there is a shift in the market.

Every problem in your business's finances will show up in the profit and loss statement. Consider the P&L your map for deciphering, for example, if less revenue is making its way into the bank account. Or if expenses plummeted or skyrocketed. When changes occur, it's time to put on your detective hat to find out why. This will eventually lead to discovering where money is being lost, where sales are being dropped, or why conversion ratios are slipping.

Profit Margins

Wendy Papasan is Keller Williams's top-producing agent as of the writing of this book. She *knows* real estate. Her husband, Jay, cowrote *The Millionaire Real Estate Agent* with Dave Jenks and Keller Williams's cofounder Gary Keller. When it comes to profit margins,Wendy provided me with the following advice directly:

> I think a lot of people get confused by profit margin and net income. MREA [*Millionaire Real Estate Agent*] was always about net income, not profit margin. I operate at a 32% net income and that factors in my salary, the few deals I do, and my profit. Most teams I know operate around this level. Those that are higher usually have a rainmaker who is doing a lot of the sales themselves.

Wendy advises running at a net income of 32 percent or higher *after* your salary is deducted from your profit margin. There are three compensation models that you can use to achieve this percentage.

One compensation model is hourly pay, which is the easiest to track and has the potential to be the most profitable—but it's also the riskiest model for the team. The commission compensation model can be more difficult to track but can create incentives and be less risky to the team— but riskier for team members. Then there is the hybrid compensation model that combines these two models and can be custom built for your team's unique situation.

Hourly Pay Compensation Model

Many of your employees will be paid under this model. This is most appropriate for those who want to work specific hours, or during a specific time frame, or in a specific location. Hourly employees who are productive will save you money. At volume, it costs less to run a business on this model than on the commission model. This is why many companies pay hourly or have salaried employees.

Hourly pay becomes an expensive model if business slows down. If you don't have work for your employees, you'll run out of revenue to pay for work but have no work to do. You are obligated to pay hourly employees even when deals are not closing. This why the hourly pay compensation model is the riskiest for your team.

It's also expensive if an employee is unproductive. This is why your leaders or management team must monitor that the staff working under this model do their jobs and remain productive.

Commission Compensation Model

The commission model decreases your company's risk because staff are paid only when homes are sold and revenue comes in. While this is the least risky for your agency, it can also become the most expensive. When you have a higher number of homes selling, you'll pay out more on a commission-based model than on an hourly pay model. This is the trade-off. If you reduce risk by using a commission model, you lose profit when volume increases. I discuss commission splits later in the chapter.

Hybrid Compensation Model

This model is when you combine the stability of hourly pay with the upside of commission income. However, this model comes at the expense of losing the higher end of each. Teams using this structure pay their agents, administrators, and so on a monthly stipend, which is less than an hourly amount, but they have the opportunity to earn additional income through bonus or commission structures.

I used this hybrid model for several years with Krista, my first hire. Krista was paid an hourly wage and given a referral fee of 25 percent of the commission for every client she brought into the team. She also earned bonuses when she communicated with home inspectors, loan officers, repair people, vendors, and so on. This allowed her to earn potential bonuses during work hours while getting paid her salary.

Many agents use a compensation model for outside sales agents and inside sales agents; they also use it for showing assistants seeking a stable salary.

Commission Splits

For agents who work on commission splits, how do you determine that percentage? After speaking with many rockstar agents about how they do it, I can offer you advice on what to consider:

- Don't pay agents too much commission or they may lose interest in working hard.
- Don't pay agents too little commission or they may leave for an agency that offers more lucrative splits.
- Don't make the commissions to the agents too high or you won't have enough income left over to pay for support (from staff to software).
- Don't make your own commission too low or you'll lose motivation because you won't be making enough profit to justify your efforts.
- If you start agents at a higher commission, you won't be able to reward their progress with a raise.
- If you are compensating your agents with training, they should expect a lower commission in exchange. Compensate agents with money or with training, not with both. You don't want to train for free, and you don't want to train agents if they aren't bringing in revenue.
- If you pay too much in salary to new agents, they may lose motivation to earn commission, but if you only pay commission, they may quit when they can't make enough money to live on.

As you see, getting the right commission structure is like walking a blade's edge. It's hard to get right and easy to fall off. Prepare yourself that you may start off with one commission structure and adapt it over time. The details may change, but the principles will not. As you tweak your compensation models, remember that the point is to maximize company profit margins, team motivation, and your motivation.

Securing the agency's bottom line first is smart because you need your company to succeed. By maximizing profit, you are forced to keep your team members motivated and productive. The same is true of yourself. A thriving company has a thriving leader. If the leader loses motivation to keep things moving forward, the company will soon cease to exist.

Paying Buyer's Agents

Buyer's agents make the highest impact because they are the primary sources of income for your company; they bring in significant revenue from their SOI and by closing on a high percentage of leads. Buyer's agents also carry a significant amount of emotional stress by shouldering client complaints and a fluctuating income.

The phrase "buyer's agent" typically refers to agents who primarily help buyers, but the buyer's agents on my team also do listings after they've been trained to do so. These agents typically generate income for the team in two ways: (1) by closing buyer leads provided by the team; and/or (2) by closing their own leads and providing a commission split to the team.

Some agencies start at a 50/50 split with their buyer's agents. Some increase the split when buying agents close more deals or increase their sales volume. I'm not a fan of increasing the commission split throughout the year, primarily because of the accounting headache it creates and the potential for other team members to guilt you into the same higher split (even if they aren't performing).

Other agencies pay a split that's lower than 50 percent when the team generated the lead, because it is the team that pays for the lead, the software, the rent, the salaries of the support team and showing assistants, and more. At DGT, we pay 25 percent of the commission to the buyer's agent if it's a team-generated lead. (We pay the showing assistant out of the split ourselves; the buyer's agent doesn't pay.) When a DGT buyer's agent closes twenty-four deals in a year, they are eligible to receive team leads at a 50 percent split.

However, I prefer to compensate high performers in ways other than splits. One way is by providing logistical support—for example, by hiring showing assistants to take over more of the buyer agent's duties or by assigning an admin to schedule their showings, manage their lead flow, and help with their escrows. In general, as agents bring more properties into escrow, they want to leverage other people (primarily administrators) to do a greater portion of their job that isn't sales. Your first response should always be to leverage their work so buyer agents have more time to generate leads or to put more buyers in contract.

You can also compensate them in the following ways:

- Provide listing leads in addition to buyer leads
- Provide a high number of leads through lead generation; high-quality leads who are easier to close (e.g., someone from your SOI); and higher price point leads

- Provide leadership meetings or special VIP top-producing agent sessions
- Provide specific training sessions
- Provide a paid-for vacation
- Pay quarterly bonuses or a yearly bonus

Don't assume the only way to compensate a salesperson is with a higher commission split. That may be the first thing they ask for, but it isn't your only option.

Paying Showing Assistants

The showing assistant position is relatively new to the world of real estate. Because teams themselves are relatively new, there is a lot of variation in how showing assistants are paid. Some agencies pay them a salary and expect they will do showings all week. Others, like mine, pay a portion of the commission and offer the benefits of training, mentorship, and guidance.

My first compensation model for showing agents was a tiered system. They started at tier zero and were compensated 5 percent of the commission. They were responsible for entering client info into the CRM, scheduling showings, showing homes, and other tasks. When a showing agent showed proficiency, they were moved to tier one, where they earned 10 percent of the commission but had additional job responsibilities assigned to them. This split increased by 5 percent at each new tier, along with responsibilities, until they reached 25 percent of the commission.

The idea was for showing agents to perform at the buyer's agent's level by the time they reached the 25 percent level, thus relieving buyer's agents of most tasks outside of closings. There was one problem with my plan: None of my showing agents made it to the 25 percent level. By highlighting so clearly the progression from 5 percent to 25 percent, I made it easy for them to pressure my management team for percentage increases. The plan had been to have them take on more responsibility primarily so they could learn.

What I found instead was that showing agents would work with two clients, claim they were proficient, and then ask for a higher percentage. When asked to explain how they were proficient, it led to hurt feelings and lost relationship capital. I made the adjustment that all showing agents would be compensated at 10 percent of the commission, and if they felt that they deserved a higher percentage or it wasn't worth their time, they were allowed to turn down the client.

Showing agents who demonstrate excellence now receive higher percentages independently. This has removed showing agent pressure from management and has given us the flexibility to pay handsomely when showing agents earn it.

To avoid morale issues, it is incredibly important for my team to highlight to showing agents that they are compensated in mentorship and career building, with the *addition* of a 10 percent commission. Making this clear sets expectations at the correct level. We want our showing assistants to grow into buyer's agents. We thus need to provide hands-on training in ways that few to no other agencies do. This is one reason why showing agents join—and stay—with the DGT team.

Paying Inside Sales Agent and Outside Sales Agent

The hybrid model is often used to compensate inside sales agents and outside sales agents. They receive a stipend of perhaps a few thousand dollars a month and then earn money through performance-based bonuses. These bonuses are paid at $100 to $200 for appointments they set.

Inside sales agents and outside sales agents set up your seller and buyer's agents for success and increase revenue. They normally focus on the early section of the Sales Funnel: turning People into Leads and then into Clients by setting the initial presentation appointment for the salesperson to seal the deal. We compensate based ón performance, not hours, because at the end of the day, everyone has to bring money into the company.

The ideal situation is to have inside sales agents and outside sales agents work on the commission model, but many hires won't accept a pure commission offer, which is why they are paid a stipend. Many agencies also pay their inside sales agents and outside sales agents a 10 percent split of the commission for listings they bring into the team.

Organization Chart

I discuss my org chart in detail in *SKILL*, so I'll try not to repeat myself here. Once you have a firm understanding of how your team structure should operate, you will be able to (1) streamline processes; and (2) expand your system into different marketplaces.

For example, having positions with clearly defined roles and responsibilities will help with:

- Advertising for hire.
- Managing your employees and team members.
- Pairing up people.
- Creating standard operating procedures.
- Providing a framework for promotional opportunities and growth.
- Delegating work.

Team building is a process. You don't jump from top-producing agent to rockstar agent with an agency and managing one hundred people overnight. The following offers first milestones.

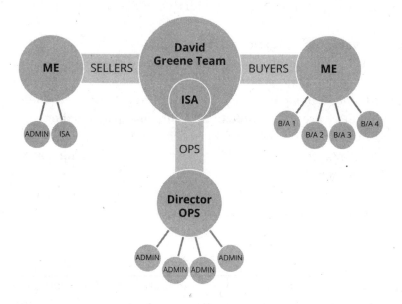

As I point out in *SKILL*, I remain the primary salesperson, and I control the quality of the client experience; avoid mistakes being made; and stay in close touch with my team, who see me working and are learning from the way I do things. I suggest that rockstar agents try this model because it allows you to learn how to manage a team without risking massive failure for your clients and reputation.

As you gain traction, your leadership and management skills will improve. At that point, you can step aside from working with clients and into developing staff, systems, and resources. This will give you the opportunity to run next to the boulder rolling downhill at top speed. You can scale your business to hit big numbers, make big money, and make big moves.

To zoom in further, let's reconsider the hierarchy from an image in Chapter Three. The "Me" could easily be your lead agent who supervises buyer's agents, or the second-tier buyer's agents who supervise the showing agents. This makes management and quality control easier.

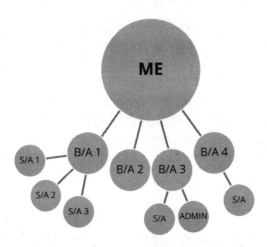

Expansion Teams

After your organization is structured and well managed, you now have the possibility for expansion. Exciting times! This is when you can start looking for other leaders who share your morals, values, principles, drive, and skill sets.

You'll have to once again expand your thinking. As a top-producing agent, you focused on helping clients to buy and sell homes. As a rockstar agent, you focused on systems and lead generation. As an expansion entrepreneur, you will focus on identifying, leading, and building other rockstar agents. Expansion is the shift from systems development to human development.

Expansion Agreement

In the same way you have a team agreement with every agent, you will need an expansion agreement for every expansion partner. This expansion agreement will include the information in your team agreement (i.e., the expansion partner will agree to the same team terms for their team). It will also include the terms of your partnership. Most important is that you must empower your expansion partner for growth and your partner must trust you to do so. The goal is for the expansion partner to work through the same progression as you did, but faster and with fewer mistakes, and for you to expand your organization, influence, and income levels far higher than possible with one agency.

The following list offers a good place to start in your negotiations with another agency.

- You are a 50/50 owner of the expansion partner's business.
- All revenue and expenses are shared 50/50.
- Sales income (e.g., commissions, referral fees) is placed in a shared business account.
- Company expenses are withdrawn from said account.
- An agreed-upon reserve is kept in the account (i.e., salaries, rent, and other expenses for three to six months).
- Monthly revenue above the reserve amount is withdrawn and dispersed 50/50.
- You act like a CEO.
- Your expansion partner acts like a COO.

THE CEO PROVIDES	THE COO PROVIDES
Systems	Commitment to switch to your systems
Guidance	Their team's ability to learn new systems and processes
Coaching	A partner and team with open minds, positive attitudes, and coachable spirits
Insight	Willingness to see things from your perspective
Executive decision making	Full honesty for you to make appropriate business decisions
Resources	Using the resources to produce a profit
Direction	Assurances to stick to the plan you create for the expansion team
Leadership	Support, encouragement, and ROI on your time
Support	Valuing of resources
Branding	Upholding your name and integrity of your brand

Your expansion partner handles their own listings with the help of an admin. They can start to build their agency by working with buyer's agents and using showing assistants. As the showing assistants show their growth, they are promoted to buyer's agents and given showing assistants of their own. The best buyer's agents become sales leaders and teams are built under them.

As the levels of agents increase, the expansion partner takes on executive-level responsibilities. This is the same model that you followed. To repeat, with your guidance, resources, and direction, your expansion partner should follow your growth but at a much faster pace and with a higher volume while escaping your mistakes. This is why they are willing to split their commissions 50/50. When correctly executed, your expansion partner will have higher-dollar activities and can again expand the number of agents on their team.

Leadership Structure

When incorrectly executed, your expansion partner works harder, makes less money, and feels more frustration. At a certain point (everyone has their own limit), they may end your agreement and go back to working for themselves. This will feel more profitable than a team model when the team model is not working. With such high stakes, it's incredibly important that you choose the right partner and provide the level of support they need until they can hit cruising altitude. It's at cruising altitude where they can focus on building their staff instead of working with the clients.

In your original organization as CEO, you were above the sales leaders in the org chart. At this point, though, your job is to lead your expansion partner's team. (And you'll do this until you decide to hire someone else and make yourself director of expansion.)

You have two options for replacing yourself: (1) You can promote your top leader, or (2) you can hire someone from the outside. Finding someone from the outside will be hard because there aren't too many people with the experience of running real estate teams. Even fewer do so successfully. With this being the case, you will have to wait until someone on your current team can develop the leadership skills necessary. This can take years to develop.

A word of warning here: Because developing leaders is time-consuming and costly, you will often rely on the same proven, dependable talent in your organization. Be sure to take care of these people! Without them, your whole structure will fail.

Accountability

The best way to keep leaders accountable is to establish and maintain regular meetings, as discussed earlier in this book. This keeps focus where it needs to be. This is no different with your expansion partner. Your director of expansion (you, if you don't have one) should conduct weekly meetings with your expansion partner to cover:

- Leads generated.
- Leads converted into Clients.
- Agents brought onto the team.
- Agent-produced leads/escrows.
- Total homes in contract.
- Percentage toward yearly goal (to determine if there are any issues).

Your expansion partner will also meet monthly with their individual sales leaders, if they have any. If they don't, they'll meet with their lead buyer's agents to cover:

- Leads generated, and where they are in the process.
- Leads converted into Clients.
- Self-produced leads/escrows.
- Total homes in contract.
- Percentage toward yearly goal.

Consistent Experience

As with any brand, the goal is to provide a consistent experience the consumer can trust. We don't go to McDonald's for a burger because it's the best burger; we do it because we know what to expect, and there is value in predictability and consistency. As the rockstar agent and brand developer, it's your responsibility to ensure a consistent experience for all clients drawn to your branding and reputation.

This isn't easy! The bigger you get, the more difficult it becomes to ensure quality control. It is why we first hesitate to turn our clients over to our agents. We simply don't believe they will do the same level of work because they don't care as much as we do.

And sometimes this is true. The difference between a successful business and an unsuccessful one is in the planning. As your team grows, every leader and high producer must demand the same excellence from those beneath them. As you lead the leaders, encourage them to push that level of urgency throughout your org chart.

Providing a consistent experience to every client requires consistent accountability in your company.

➤ KEY POINTS

- As you transition from top-producing agent to rockstar agent, you'll go through several difficult transitions. The first, and most important, is exchanging the mindset of an agent for one of chief executive officer.
- If you haven't been working a systematic, predictable, repeatable plan, breaking away from chasing dopamine will leave you confused as to what you should be doing.
- Leaders will be your most talented, dedicated, and valuable assets.
- Learning to read a profit and loss statement is a fundamental skill for anyone who has an executive leadership role; reviewing a P&L statement will focus your attention on profit, not income.
- Hourly employees who are productive will save you money, but hourly pay becomes an expensive model if business slows down.
- While commission-based pay is the least risky for your agency, it can also become the most expensive.
- The hybrid model is when you combine the stability of hourly pay with the upside of commission income.
- After your organization is structured and well managed, you now have the possibility for expansion.
- In the same way you have a team agreement with every agent, you will need an expansion agreement for every expansion partner.
- Because developing leaders is time-consuming and costly, you will often rely on the same proven, dependable talent in your organization. Be sure to take care of these people! Without them, your whole structure will fail.

CHAPTER ► FOURTEEN
TYING IT TOGETHER

"No one succeeds alone and no one fails alone. Pay attention to the people around you."

—GARY KELLER

I wrote *SOLD*, *SKILL*, and now *SCALE* for agents, and they each focus on a specific aspect of the real estate business.

SOLD focuses on learning how to be an agent and make money. The first step in this process is making our way from knowing nothing to learning as much as we can.

0%   100%
LEARN

The second book, *SKILL*, teaches you how to be so successful that you can no longer do it on your own and must learn leverage. This success leaves you with no choice but to create systems and build a team, or else you will lose clients and revenue opportunities. One Keller Williams motto is "Success through others." It is the belief that to give every client the best experience possible, we must use the power of leverage. It's a skill you must learn to be successful at this stage.

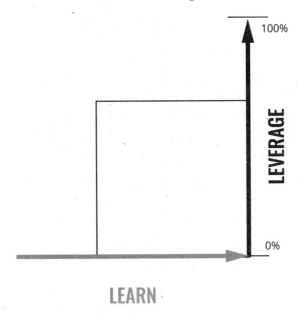

This book, *SCALE*, as you now know, is about stopping doing the jc and starting to build a business. You must learn how to be an executiv and create opportunities for others. A team forms through a mitosis-lik process. You "split" into two when you hire an admin, and they handl support while you do sales. You split again when a buyer's agent come: on board to handle your buyers. There is another split when showing assistants how to take over showing duties. With each task that you "split off," you win back time and energy to bring in more clients. The further you get from servicing these clients yourself, the more you must develop your leveraging and leadership skills. And if you want to own a passive business that can scale or allow you to retire, you'll need both of these skills.

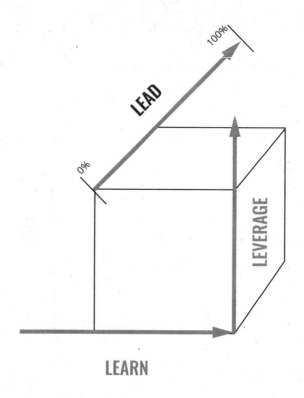

Finding the Missing Pieces

One thing I wish I had been told was that how I built my team will not be the same as how someone else built their team. The reason there isn't one blueprint is because no two agents are alike. You must build your team around *you*, and no one can do it for you.

Let's go back to the analogy in Chapter Two with the New England Patriots franchise. Championship teams are built around one or two players who provide most of the value. Every team that wins a championship does so with standout, top-tier talent, but that's not enough. In addition to talent, the team needs chemistry. And the top talent must be supported with team players who make up for the top talent's weaknesses.

Many agents will not become rockstars, not because they don't have the talent, but because they don't believe *they* are the talent. I suffered from this impostor syndrome myself. When I first began to grow my team, I hired people who were good at the same things as me. I started to make traction only when I hired people to shore up my weaknesses. This realization and adjustment made all the difference in my success.

It was a long time coming, though, because I was afraid to acknowledge I was really, really good at some things but needed others to cover for my weaknesses. Bringing in support staff to fill in the holes I had is what the company needed. It forced me to take center stage, grab that mic, and let the crowd see what I was made of. I faced overwhelming fears of failure and being exposed as an impostor. It wasn't until I accepted that I was able to carry the band and started hiring people to do the things I didn't enjoy or didn't do well that my success took off.

Are you feeling similar emotions while reading this? Are you asking yourself if you really have what it takes to be a rockstar agent? Do you feel greedy or arrogant to even consider owning a business where you don't do all the work? Is it intimidating to think about a seven-figure salary with room for growth? You're not alone if you feel this way, but these thoughts are not your friend. Here's the uncomfortable truth about our industry:

- There are not enough mentors to help new agents, so many new agents fail, quit, or give up.
- New agents want constructive, useful, productive advice, and only an experienced agent can provide this.
- Brokers cannot provide the direction agents need.
- Solo agents have no incentive to provide direction to new agents.
- Most so-called guru real estate agents are more interested in preying on new agents, not helping them.
- Experienced agents want their time back, and new agents want to learn. Only a team setting can solve both problems.
- Your clients don't need you, per se; they need someone with your standards.

To be a rockstar agent, lead a team, and provide the team experience and direction so rare in our industry, you must face your fear of success. Our industry needs more rockstar agents to create these opportunities and overcome the terrible reputation we face as real estate professionals.

Your Weaknesses

When it comes to your weaknesses, there are two basic schools of thought. The first is you double down on your strengths and hire someone who can overcome your weaknesses. This allows you to put energy into improving your strengths.

For example, if you are not comfortable with organization, you can hire someone who is organized, and you can put your effort into sales or creating a vision. This approach creates specialists within a team, so it tends to work best in larger companies. But focusing only on your strengths prevents you from improving your weaknesses.

The other school of thought is you should improve your weaknesses to become a well-rounded individual. This approach tends to work better in smaller business. When you don't have high volume, you can't afford full-time employees doing one set of tasks. But when you focus on improving your weaknesses, you do so at the expense of developing your strengths.

The size of your business will determine which is the better approach for you. I decided the best solution for me was to combine both approaches.

I initially improved my weaknesses before leveraging them because I had to learn enough to teach those things to someone else. If you don't know how to teach to leverage, it will be difficult for you to move on to higher-level tasks.

To illustrate an example of which skills you are better off improving and which you are better off leveraging out, consider a basketball player who is a terrific shooter but a poor ball handler. This player scores a lot of points, which makes them an asset to the team. As a poor ball handler, however, the player can't get open to shoot. Without getting open, their ability to shoot is irrelevant. In this case, the player should improve their ball handling so they can capitalize on their strengths. This is different than improving a weakness purely for the purpose of improving a weakness.

Let's bring this back to the real estate business where you're not good with organization but are strong in sales. Trying to make yourself a rockstar organizer doesn't make much sense when you can bring more value through sales. However, if your lack of organization is causing you to *lose* sales, you've got a problem. In this scenario, you need to improve your organizational skills enough so that they aren't hindering your sales ability.

My caveat is that if your weakness is not a hindrance to your strengths, look for a way to just leverage your weakness.

Your Strengths

Your successes will come from amplifying your strengths. As your business grows, you'll find yourself and your team members focusing more on the areas you're good at. With more people in your organization, you can diversify the workload and capitalize on everyone's strengths.

At DGT, we identify the strengths of our team members so we can put them where those strengths are used best. For instance, if a team member excels at putting buyers in contract, we support them with admin help, showing assistants, and team lead generation. Do you know what your strengths are as a leader? One of my strengths is my ability to see what is happening in the market and to make adjustments quickly. This helped me build my portfolio of homes in areas of the country where demand would be growing.

Because this is a strength of mine, I do my best to equip my sales team to handle our clients so my focus can remain on observing the market and making adjustments to keep us profitable. Knowing this about myself, I hire salespeople with similar personalities to mine so that our clients can communicate with them, and they don't need me.

As I detailed in Chapter Two, I'm not organized, and I'm not good at remembering details or following up after conversations. Recognizing this, I have my administrative assistant follow up with *me* so I don't forget important responsibilities. When I refused to accept these as weaknesses, I frequently made promises I failed to deliver on. This is a cardinal sin in real estate sales. Now, my admin uses my Google calendar to keep up with me. My weakness is counterbalanced by the strength of my administrative assistant. In truth, my weakness eventually led to an entire system being created for quality control: Our admins and showing assistants now look at all agents' Google calendars to make sure things are done as promised.

The same will happen for you when you accept both your weaknesses and your strengths. Are you better at directing others what to do than doing it yourself? Are you talented at research but uncomfortable in live conversation? Do you love meeting new people and collecting their contact information but never remember to put it in the CRM? Hiring someone to make up for these weaknesses will allow you to emphasize your natural strengths.

Your business won't grow until you develop, improve, and trust your strengths. The more time you spend doing what you're good at, the better results you'll get. And spending more time on what you enjoy will help preserve your energy. We all know the feeling when we do the parts of the job we love. Nothing can stop us. We tend to skip right to that part and ignore all the other things anyway. What would it be like if your entire day was filled with that feeling? If you're not sure what your strengths are, start by asking: When do I feel most confident? What makes me excited? Then ask those closest to you what they think you are best at. It's quite common for others to see us more clearly than we see ourselves. Finally, ask yourself what would be most valuable to your business. (Hint: Lead generation and hiring right are definitely valuable.)

When I give personal training to my agents, we work on developing their individual strengths. Those who analyze deals well may get training on how to clearly communicate their findings with clients. Those who have sparkling personalities may get training on networking. Those who do well with open houses may get training on improving their follow-up and conversion ratios. My advice to you is to recognize your own strengths, work to amplify them, and then do the same for those on the team you're building.

Growth

As a team leader, you will constantly have your limits challenged. But the more limits you break through, the more money you can make, and the greater success you can achieve. Your success is directly proportional to your willingness to grow your strengths and accept your weaknesses.

Along with breaking through their limitations, leaders also carry the weight of their team on their shoulders. The question is: How many of us willingly look to add weight to our shoulders and make work even more complicated? Yet as the rockstar agent, any weight that your team members don't carry will make its way to you. You have your own responsibilities, plus the weight of those on your team who cannot, or will not, solve the problems they encounter. This comes with the territory of leading a team: Success comes from leadership, not from luck. Elon Musk, owner of Tesla and SpaceX, made this clear when he said: "You get paid in direct proportion to the difficulty of problems you solve."

Those who embrace this philosophy do better in both life and work. Those who look to make money or have success but avoid difficult problems end up disappointed, jaded, and resentful in both. Every client has a puzzle that we need to help them solve. If we solve their buying and/or selling puzzle, we earn a paycheck. If we don't, we won't. The more of these problems we solve, and the greater their complexity, the more we earn.

That's why hiring the right team is vital, but hiring is hard. It's a problem to be solved, and there is no way around it. Finding people who are a good fit takes time and experience. Only leaders who learn to solve this problem can make good money and outperform their competition. The "doing it myself is faster" method is the easy route, and it will keep you from being a top-producing or rockstar agent. What's wiser but harder is hiring showing assistants and buyer's agents to close more deals. What's wiser but harder is hiring admin assistants to set up your listings. What's wiser but harder is hiring agents who are willing to give up a chunk of their commission in exchange for training. All of this is harder than doing it yourself. But solving your hiring problems leads to a far, far more profitable business than doing everything yourself.

Don't take the weight off your shoulders and put it on anyone else's. It's easy to think you've won if you do this. But you're only building up someone else's capabilities, not your own, and it won't force your own continued growth as a rockstar agent. It is your growth that builds your agency and leads to more money. The more people you have around you, the more problems you'll need to solve, but with that comes success.

NBA player Blake Griffin said it simplest: "You have to fall in love with the process of becoming great." As a leader, you will continually be challenged and have your limitations tested. How miserable would life be if you hated this process?

None of us can control when life will pull the rug out from under us or add weight to our shoulders. We just know that, at some point, it will. With this being the nature of life, why not fall in love with the process of change and becoming great? Why not welcome and embrace the weight?

When asked to contribute a quote about greatness for this book, mixed martial arts and UFC championship challenger Michael Chandler shared: "For a guy like me who grew up with a limited mindset, it's imperative that I actively seek out ways to find exponential growth as a human everyday [sic]. Expanding my mind to the possibilities of what I can accomplish has been a large part of any success I have found in life." To be successful, Chandler had to challenge his original mindset. For someone who risks life and limb climbing into a cage for a living, it's not hard to see why he would value growth.

Those who embrace becoming great often find themselves addicted to the process. For example, Elon Musk helped create PayPal and sold it for *a lot* of money. Did he retire? No. He developed energy-efficient electric vehicles and made spacecraft being used by NASA. His advances came from his willingness to embrace new challenges.

I offer this perspective because as you advance through Learn, Leverage, and Lead, you will no doubt find yourself challenged. If you don't learn to fall in love with challenges and become addicted to growth, you won't grow your team. There is great joy in seeing yourself with more success than you ever thought possible!

Barrel of Monkeys

My final piece of advice involves who you surround yourself with. When we surround ourselves only with people who look up to us, it may feel good, but it can be bad for our ego and can lead to "big fish in a little pond" syndrome. Conversely, when we surround ourselves only with people who we think are doing better than us, we may feel inadequate, and it can be deeply discouraging.

The solution for the first situation is to never forget how far you still have to climb. For the second, don't forget to gauge how far you've come.

My approach in business is to always have one hand reaching up for help from those above me and one hand reaching down to pull up others who are behind. Through this connection, the information passes from those who are above to those who are below, and the admiration from those below provides the confidence to keep reaching up.

When I was a kid, I played with the Barrel of Monkeys toy. The point was to join each monkey to another monkey by one arm, thus creating one long chain supported by the top monkey. I keep this image in mind as I pursue my own growth. Agents like Ryan Serhant have mastered elements of real estate sales I have not even come close to. Businesspeople like Gary Keller have created systems and models I could never have imagined on my own. Authors like Jay Papasan have written books more succinctly, clearly, and articulately than I ever could. These people are my models for inspiration and direction, and I'm always learning from their examples as they freely share information.

I know that there is an audience from my BiggerPockets podcast who look to me for my advice. Knowing this keeps my confidence level high and renews my commitment to excellence, stretching my limits, and studying our industry. The leaders on my team do the same.

The Path

I encourage you to find your own Barrel of Monkeys. Who might mentor you? Who in your office can you mentor? We tend to look above first, seeking the mentor who will take us to the next level, but we learn even more when we teach someone else.

When mentoring, you learn what you don't know because the holes in your knowledge become apparent. As a real estate agent, maybe you learn in the mentoring process that you need better systems or documented information to share your knowledge. This understanding is a great gift. You learn where you need improvements. As you learn more, you see your mentee grow. This leads to the opportunity to leverage. This will improve the service you give your clients and the number of homes you sell, and it will decrease the time you spend accomplishing the same tasks. Giving back through mentorship helps make you great.

As you take on more mentorship, you'll no doubt realize at some point that they need resources you don't have. You won't know what's missing until someone asks about something. This is often the precursor that drives agents to seek out more successful people for help. You'll need your own mentor when those beneath you are looking for things you can't give.

You unlock more of your potential when you are simultaneously mentoring and being mentored. This is the rhythm of life. We come into the world knowing nothing, dependent on someone to teach us. Those who help us in those most vulnerable times are people we appreciate for the rest of our lives. Loyalty is created by those reaching out to us, and we become loyal to the mentors we reach out to.

In a quote for this book, UFC champion Aljamain Sterling wrote: "Anything you start requires being some kind of a student in order to succeed. Your desire to learn, or lack of, can be your best friend or worst enemy."

You can start your journey to being a rockstar agent by looking for someone to mentor and looking for someone to mentor you. Become involved in the success of others. See the inner leader inside you start to rise to the surface. As your leadership skills grow, so will your confidence and success. As you bring people into your business, sharing in their success benefits everyone.

This is how teams are built and how you turn a job into a business that allows you to scale to a size you can only dream of. I encourage you to take action today. So I ask you, are you ready to move from playing local gigs at dive bars to being the rockstar your potential demands? Your market, your clients, and the huge community of agents craving leadership are waiting!

Become a **BiggerPockets** **Featured Agent—TODAY**

The best way to fuel your pipeline with high-intent leads

- Stand out in the largest network of real estate investors

- Instantly match with buyers interested in your market

- Save time and sell more with better leads

"...BiggerPockets is our best performing lead source. The clients that reach out through BiggerPockets are already well educated in the buying process and many are already preapproved and ready to go."

—Jonathan Bombaci of Boston

"The program is fantastic. I've received so many qualified leads that I'm expanding my team to handle the increase in volume."

—Peter Stewart of Indianapolis

How It Works

❶ Pick your top markets

❷ Get featured when investors search for agents in your markets

❸ Receive instant text alerts when investors want to connect

Get started now
at **www.biggerpockets.com/ featured-agent/skill** or scan the QR code!

More from
BiggerPockets Publishing

SOLD: Every Real Estate Agent's Guide to Building a Profitable Business

Most agents lack the necessary mentorship, guidance, and training to succeed in the competitive and independent world of real estate. *SOLD* provides a much-needed look at how successful real estate agents build their business, close deals, and generate commissions. Best-selling author and expert real estate agent David Greene shares everything he wishes someone had shared with him—including the exact processes he used to become rookie of the year and top agent in his office.

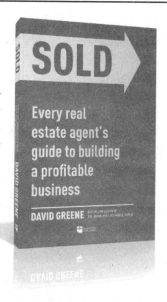

SKILL: A Top-Producing Agent's Guide to Earning Unlimited Income

Nobody gets their real estate license to be mediocre—so what do you do if your business has stagnated? If 80 percent of sales go through the top 20 percent of real estate agents, making it into the top tier is what matters most in the competitive landscape of real estate sales. Once you beat your competition, you can run a thriving, fun, and lucrative business with more leads and clients than you know what to do with. In *SKILL*, you'll step up your game with the same framework that top-producing Realtor David Greene shares with his very own award-winning team.

If you enjoyed this book, we hope you'll take a moment to check out some of the other great material BiggerPockets offers. Whether you crave freedom or stability, a backup plan, or passive income, BiggerPockets empowers you to live life on your own terms through real estate investing. Find the information, inspiration, and tools you need to dive right into the world of real estate investing with confidence.

Sign up today—it's free! Visit www.BiggerPockets.com
Find our books at www.BiggerPockets.com/store

Long-Distance Real Estate Investing

Don't let your location dictate your financial freedom: Live where you want, and invest anywhere it makes sense! The rules, technology, and markets have changed: No longer are you forced to invest only in your backyard. In *Long-Distance Real Estate Investing*, learn an in-depth strategy to build profitable rental portfolios through buying, managing, and flipping out-of-state properties from real estate investor and agent David Greene.

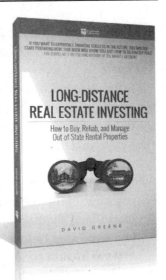

Buy, Rehab, Rent, Refinance, Repeat

Invest in real estate and never run out of money! In *Buy, Rehab, Rent, Refinance, Repeat*, you'll discover the incredible strategy known as BRRRR—a long-hidden secret of the ultra-rich and those with decades of experience. Author and investor David Greene holds nothing back, sharing the exact systems and processes he used to scale his business from buying two houses per year to buying two houses per *month* using the BRRRR strategy.

More from
BiggerPockets Publishing

6 Steps to 7 Figures: A Real Estate Professional's Guide to Building Wealth

It's difficult to build a real estate business, and it's even more difficult not to lose yourself in the daily grind. *6 Steps to 7 Figures* contains all the tactics that the best real estate agents use to promote their businesses, become financially free, and pursue the lives of their dreams. Pat Hiban is one of the only residential real estate agents to hold the title Billion-Dollar.Agent, and he compiled two decades of invaluable experience into this manual. A combination of motivational success strategies and practical tips for flourishing in real estate, this expanded and revised edition also contains two new chapters on what the author learned from giving up the workaholic lifestyle.

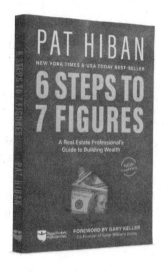

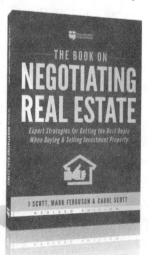

The Book on Negotiating Real Estate

When the real estate market gets hot, it's the investors who know the ins-and-outs of negotiating who will get the deal. J Scott, Mark Ferguson, and Carol Scott combine real-world experience and the science of negotiation in order to cover all aspects of the negotiation process and maximize your chances of reaching a profitable deal.

If you enjoyed this book, we hope you'll take a moment to check out some of the other great material BiggerPockets offers. Whether you crave freedom or stability, a backup plan, or passive income, BiggerPockets empowers you to live life on your own terms through real estate investing. Find the information, inspiration, and tools you need to dive right into the world of real estate investing with confidence.

Sign up today—it's free! Visit www.BiggerPockets.com
Find our books at www.BiggerPockets.com/store

The Intention Journal

Some people can achieve great wealth, rock-solid relationships, age-defying health, and remarkable happiness—and so many others struggle, fail, and give up on their dreams, goals, and ambitions. Could it simply be that those who find success are more intentional about it? Once you build intentionality into your daily routine, you can achieve the incredible success that sometimes seems out of reach. Backed by the latest research in psychology, this daily planner offers an effective framework to set, review, and accomplish your goals.

The Book on Tax Strategies for the Savvy Real Estate Investor

Taxes! Boring and irritating, right? Perhaps. But if you want to succeed in real estate, your tax strategy will play a huge role in how fast you grow. A great tax strategy can save you thousands of dollars a year. A bad strategy could land you in legal trouble. With *The Book on Tax Strategies for the Savvy Real Estate Investor*, you'll find ways to deduct more, invest smarter, and pay far less to the IRS!

CONNECT WITH BIGGERPOCKETS

Live Life on Your Terms Through Real Estate Investing!

Facebook
/BiggerPockets

Instagram
@BiggerPockets

Twitter
@BiggerPockets

LinkedIn
/company/Bigger
Pockets

Website
BiggerPockets.com